WND BOOKS
COLLECTOR'S EDITION

To Bob and Linda

WHEN HELL WAS IN SESSION

WHEN HELL WAS IN SESSION

ADMIRAL
JEREMIAH A. DENTON

WND Books

WHEN HELL WAS IN SESSION
WND Books

Published by WorldNetDaily
Los Angeles, CA

Library of Congress Cataloging-in-Publication Data
Denton, Jeremiah A.
When hell was in session.
I. Vietnamese Conflict, 1961-1975-Prisoner and prisons, North Vietnamese.
2. Vietnamese Conflict, 1961-1975-Personal narratives, American.
3. Denton, Jeremiah A.
Brandt, Ed, joint author. II. Title.
DS559.4.D46 959.704'37 76—18981
ISBN0-935280-00-6
1098765

Jacket design by Linda Daly

WND Books are distributed to the trade by:
Midpoint Trade Books, 27 West 20th Street, Suite 1102, New York, NY 10011

WND Books are available at special discounts for bulk purchases. WND Books, Inc.
also publishes books in electronic formats. For more information call (310) 961-4170
or visit www.wndbooks.com.

ISBN 13-Digit: 9781935071150
ISBN 10-Digit: 1935071157
E-Book ISBN 13-Digit: 9781935071693
E-Book ISBN 10-Digit: 1935071696
Library of Congress Control Number: 2009938245

WND Books

Printed in the United States of America
10 9 8 7 6

To those who strive to make
this one nation under God,
who are willing to sacrifice to protect her,
who thank God for such great beauty
as she has developed,
and who patiently tolerate her imperfections.

TABLE OF CONTENTS

BIOGRAPHY

A graduate of the United States Naval Academy, Jeremiah A. Denton served on ships, in many types of aircraft, and as a staff officer during his Navy career. He also served as test pilot, flight instructor, squadron leader, and student at the Armed Forces Staff College and Naval War College, where he received the President's Award for the most outstanding master's thesis.

In June of 1965 he began flying combat missions in Vietnam. On July 18, he was shot down during an attack on enemy installations near Thanh Hoa, and spent the next seven and a half years in several North Vietnamese prisoner of war camps.

Promoted to the rank of Captain while imprisoned, Senator Denton provided the first direct evidence of torture by the North Vietnamese. He did so by blinking in Morse Code the word "torture" during a televised interview.

Upon his release in 1973, Senator Denton demonstrated that long imprisonment had not broken his spirit. Upon landing in the Philippines, he made the following statement:

> "We are honored to have had the opportunity to serve our
> country under difficult circumstances. We are profoundly

grateful to our Commander-in-Chief and to our nation for
this day.

"God bless America."

Since his retirement from active service at the rank of Rear Admiral,
Jerry Denton has been active in public affairs. He has especially emphasized
the connection between family strength and national morality and the defense of civilization. In 1980, he was elected to the United States Senate from
Alabama, where he serves on the Judiciary Committee, the Committee on
Labor and Human Resources, and the Armed Services Committee. These
committee assignments enable him to pursue the interconnection between
moral strength and the security and well-being of our society. In December
of 1981, he became Chairman of the Board of United Families of America, a
national, grass-roots lobbying group specializing in family issues.

x

PREFACE

Most of the prisoners of war held by North Vietnam were kept in camps or prisons in and around Hanoi, the best known of which was Hoa Lo Prison, a huge, French-built complex near the center of Hanoi. It was named the Hanoi Hilton by the American prisoners.

There were also the Zoo, Alcatraz, the Plantation, and the Powerplant in or near Hanoi. The Briarpatch, Camp Faith, and Son Tay (also known as Camp Hope) were within about thirty-five miles of Hanoi. The Dogpatch was ninety-five miles north of Hanoi near the Chinese border. There were other camps that were phased in and out at various times.

The Hanoi Hilton was divided into sections and named by the prisoners: New Guy Village, Heartbreak Hotel, Little Vegas (which included the Stardust, Desert Inn, Thunderbird, and Riviera), and, near the end of the imprisonment, Camp Unity. And even these units were subdivided and given names.

Eventually, more than seven hundred prisoners, most of them Air Force and Navy officers, were kept in these camps and prisons. Navy Lieutenant Everett Alvarez, Jr., held the tenure record for a U.S. prisoner. He was shot down in August 1964 and was released in February 1973.

Of course, there were hundreds of prisoners held in camps in South Vietnam, Laos, and Cambodia, living off the jungle in many cases, some confined in bamboo cages, suffering from hunger and disease. Many of them died. Most of the survivors were brought north up the Ho Chi Minh Trail in 1968-69 and 1971 and kept in camps within a thirty-mile radius of Hanoi until the releases began in February 1973.

After the releases, North Vietnam returned the bodies of twenty-three prisoners who had died in captivity. They also notified the United States that they had a twenty-fourth body, but they refused to surrender it, saying the peace agreement stated they had to return only the bodies of men who had died in captivity. Perhaps the twenty-fourth was an airman who had died in the wreckage of his plane; perhaps he was killed by villagers. The North Vietnamese would not say, and the body remains in North Vietnam, unidentified, one of 834 men listed as missing in action.

Communications among the prisoners of war were recognized early by the North Vietnamese as being a vital support to prisoner resistance and morale. Thus, they struck at the communications system constantly.

There were two major codes in use in the prison camps, the Morse code and the tap code. Morse was used early in the imprisonment period, but the tap code eventually became the standard method of communicating.

The Morse code, of course, was well known by most of the prisoners; its modes of transmission varied depending on the circumstances. For instance, a prisoner might tap once on the wall for a dot and thump with his fist for a dash. Or he could give a short whistle for a dot, a longer whistle for a dash. Whistles could also vary in tone: a low whistle for a dot, a higher one for a dash. The same method would be used by scraping with a nail or a broom, or even a fingernail; prisoner hearing became quite acute, and many could detect slight sounds from distant cells.

The tap code actually became the staple form of communication because it was simple and could be sent in a wider variety of situations than the Morse code, which was somewhat faster to send. Getting the tap code to a new prisoner was a top-priority matter.

The tap code is based on the following chart:

1	2	3w	4	5	
1	A	B	C	D	E
2	F	G	H	I	J (K)
3	L	M	N	O	P
4	Q	R	S	T	U
5	V	W	X	Y	Z

Thus, A is 1-1, B is 1-2, H is 2-3, R is 4-2. (The letter K was dropped in order to make the 5-by-5 chart possible. If the letter was needed, it was sent as 2-6.) The numbers could be tapped, waved, scraped, swept, or whatever. The prisoners standardized numerous abbreviations, and with practice, they could send messages quite rapidly.

The tap code was sent with and without encryption. If encryption was needed, the chart could be moved around. For instance, the chart could be moved "up two" so that C would read as A, D as B, E as C. Words were also sent in reverse (TAE for EAT) or even in pig Latin.

A third code, the vocal tap code, was one that I invented at Alcatraz; it later spread to other camps, where it was widely used. It employed coughs, sniffs, hacks, and sneezes in place of the usual taps, whistles, and so on. Since so many of the prisoners had respiratory problems, this code was difficult for the Vietnamese to detect.

In the vocal tap code, one cough or sniff was the number one. Two coughs or sniffs were the number two. Clearing the throat was the number three. A hack was four, and a spit or sneeze was five.

Several codes were also devised for written messages in case they were discovered by the North Vietnamese.

CHAPTER ONE

Robert S. McNamara, United States Secretary of Defense, looked slightly uncomfortable in the set of Mickey Mouse earphones clamped around his head. He could hear the deck handlers talking as they readied the aircraft for takeoff, though the muffin-shaped phones weren't quite thick enough to keep out all the jet noise.

Mr. McNamara, in the middle of one of his inspection and fact-finding tours of Vietnam, braced himself against the thirty-five-knot wind blowing across the deck of the carrier *Independence* and watched from off the right wing tip as I taxied my A6 Intruder toward the catapult and issued a salute from under the Plexiglas canopy. Only later would I realize the fateful implications inherent in the U.S. Secretary of Defense seeing me off to work.

- - - - -

The launch, the only one to go off the *Independence* that day, had been delayed a few minutes to give McNamara, who had just arrived on board, time to get out to the flight deck. We had already started our engines when the secretary, dressed in civilian clothes, emerged from the carrier's island into the searing heat, noise, and wind, and walked briskly across the flight deck to the aft No. 3 catapult.

The weather on July 18, 1965, at Yankee Station in the Gulf of Tonkin was cloudless and hot, the sun so bright that I had to bend my head and cup my hands over the fire warning light in the cockpit of my plane to see if it was testing properly.

McNamara's expensive, conservative business suit was flapping wildly in the wind as my A6, with eighteen Mark-82 five-hundred-pound bombs tucked in racks under the wings, taxied onto the catapult and suddenly shot out over the bow of the 78,000-ton *Independence*.

I climbed to about four thousand feet and circled the carrier while the rest of the flight, a mixture of A6's, A4's, and F4's, twenty-eight planes in all, joined up with me. The planes eventually formed up in a flight of V's. As flight leader, I led the first V. It was my twelfth combat flight and twelfth assignment as flight leader, an assignment, I had learned, that was to be followed in just two days by a long-awaited event.

Three days previously, on July 15, a letter marked Official Business and addressed to Mrs. Jane Denton had arrived at my home, 3125 Watergate Lane, Virginia Beach, Virginia. Inside was a printed invitation from the commanding officer of Attack Squadron Seventy-five, requesting the pleasure of Mrs. Denton's company for a change-of-command ceremony "on the twentieth of July at 9:00 o'clock on the forecastle of the United States Ship *Independence*." I was to relieve my friend and classmate, Commander Swoose Snead, as commanding officer of Attack Squadron Seventy-five. Jane, with seven children to care for six thousand miles away, respectfully sent her regrets.

But there was no thought at the moment for the impending reassignment. My mind was on leading the flight into the best-defended area in North Vietnam, the complex surrounding the Thanh Hoa Bridge about seventy-five miles south of Hanoi. Our forces had hit the complex regularly in the previous two weeks, and on one Air Force strike, five planes had gone down.

I was usually a little squeamish while preparing for an Alpha strike—a raid against a prime, heavily defended target. There was that butterfly feeling an athlete gets before the big game, but once I plunged into the planning for the raid the feeling disappeared.

During the preflight briefing for the Thanh Hoa strike, I did not have to warn my group about the two large mounds of earth bristling with antiaircraft guns on either side of the bridge. They knew how formidable the positions were. Because of heavy previous strikes, however, I told them that the North Vietnamese were probably low on ammunition for their heavier-caliber guns. Some smiled, thinking that I was whistling past the graveyard. I conceded that we could expect substantial resistance from the light to medium guns on the mounds and along the Ma River.

The A6 Intruder, then an advanced attack aircraft in development since 1956 by the Grumman Corporation, had only become operational in 1963, and while it was the most useful tactical aircraft then available, its electronic navigation system was not working reliably when the plane was ship-based, leaving my bombardier-navigator and friend, Lieutenant (j.g.) Bill Tschudy, with some unwelcome time on his hands. Tschudy, crouched in his seat to my right and slightly below me, would use the radar for what it was worth, would set up the armament panel just before our dive, and would call out the altitudes during the dive-bombing run. He would also take pictures of the target area for damage assessment and flak concentrations. But I would do the navigating and release the bombs.

From about 28,000 feet, the Gulf of Tonkin was a gorgeous Mediterranean blue stretching below us on the two-hundred-mile flight to the mainland. At a true air speed of about 480 knots, the distance was covered quickly, and before long the flat, sandy coastline of North Vietnam passed beneath our wings.

We crossed the coast at a slight angle on a path that would appear to bypass the intended target, and began lowering to attack altitude. The movement would confuse the enemy as to the target and would bring the flight around on a great circle and into the target from the landward side so that it would be pointed toward the sea at the completion of the bombing run.

There was little time for sightseeing, but when I glanced down occasionally I could see the small, square rice fields, marshy from the flood season. It was a beautiful, pastoral Sunday scene. Nice day for a drive, I thought.

It was only eight and a half miles from the coastline to our target. Ten large warehouses clustered on the south bank of the Ma River about a mile east of the Thanh Hoa Bridge. The warehouses were a staging area for military equipment, which was barged there and stored before being moved south into the war zone. The system compensated, to a degree, for the railroad bridge, which bombing had made unusable.

Eight and a half miles is no distance at all for a twin-engine jet, and even with the circling maneuver, in moments the flight was forming itself into a line for the bombing run. Some of the F4's began to drop below and slightly behind the main flight to attack troublesome flak emplacements.

We were about to take the biggest roller-coaster ride in the world, and I called out over the intercom: "Rainbow Flight from Rainbow Leader, target at ten o'clock...Rainbow Leader rolling in...."

As predicted, the medium flak was heavy, but I hardly noticed the tracers and the black puffs as we screamed through them toward the 6,000-foot release point. Tschudy called out the rapidly decreasing altitude over the intercom at thousand-foot intervals, and I was concentrating on maintaining the proper dive angle while lining up on the target a large, square warehouse in the middle of the cluster.

The tension can be almost unbearable at this point. Dive bombing demands total concentration, and mine was total as I pressed the button to release the bombs. At that instant, there was a jolting motion, as though the plane's left wheel had run over a curb while taxiing. It was my impression that a bomb had gone off upon release. I glanced in the rearview mirror. Dark fluid was streaming aft. And there was a whining sound in my ears as the radio went dead. Even more ominously, the speed brakes weren't working. I had to pull the plunging, overspeeding airplane out of its dive gently, at a somewhat lower altitude than the planned 3,500 feet, to minimize the risk of pulling the wings off.

A second or two after the hit, I flicked a hydraulic switch, hoping to isolate the leaks from the flight control system. It may have been a lifesaving move. It gave me some control through the pull-up, and I heaved a tremendous sigh of relief when the plane responded. Maybe we could get out of this yet.

Since the radio and intercom system had failed, I couldn't transmit my problems to the other pilots or to Tschudy, who remained crouched in his cockpit, completely unaware of the dangers we faced. As the nose passed through the horizon and the plane began a gradual climb, I tried to turn to the left and go into a steep climb. But at that point, there was another ominous development. My seat jerked to the right and the controls failed completely. The aircraft apparently had received another hit as it wallowed, unprotected by evasive turns, in a sky full of fire.

It rolled slowly to the right, and I slammed my left foot hard on the rudder to try to keep the plane level. In doing so, I snapped a tendon in my thigh. As part of the tendon recoiled, and curled up into my abdomen, the leg became useless.

The engines had not responded when I had thrust the throttle forward during pull-out, and now the uncontrollable roll told me there were no options left. As the plane rolled to my side again, I looked out of the cockpit. The ground seemed very close. My heart pounded. It was over. I was very frightened, and near panic.

I knew the $5 million dollar airplane was gone, and maybe Tschudy and myself as well.

It was now a life-or-death matter that we get out quickly. The A6 training manual requires ejection immediately upon control failure from loss of hydraulic fluid, and we were already well past the "immediate" stage. Ejection from an aircraft can be dangerous; ejection from a rolling aircraft is very dangerous. If the passengers go out while the airplane is rolling, the parachutes might tangle and become useless or impaired.

Tschudy was still unaware of the seriousness of the problem. I hit him on the shoulder, pointed upward, and as the plane slowly rolled into a level position, reached for the ejection bar and made pulling gestures. Tschudy, startled, hesitated. Bombardier-navigators don't like to go out before their pilots; the pilot might change his mind. Tschudy deferred to me. I gave him a dirty look from under my oxygen mask and yanked down on the ejection bar. Tschudy, after a respectful but brief interval, came out behind me into the hot and cloudless sky.

Like Alice in Wonderland, we were falling from one world into another.

- - - - -

The swift-moving, muddy Ma River stretched out below me as I oscillated wildly in a 180-degree arc beneath the parachute. I grabbed at the straps in an effort to control the swing and looked down from 4,000 feet. From that height, I got an excellent view of the entire scene. An American airplane was buzzing down the river like an angry bee. As guns on the bank opened up with a tremendous roar, it pulled up into a wide, graceful circle and started back.

As I was to learn years later, Commander Bill Bowers in his A4 had just pulled out of his bombing run when he heard someone shout "two parachutes" over the radio, and looked up in time to see Tschudy and me drifting toward the river. Bowers heard Commander Bill Sallada give the

Mayday call in order to get a rescue try started, then circled his own plane back toward the river to see what he could do to help.

As I continued to drift down toward the river, I was assaulted by the deafening roar of the North Vietnamese guns, which were firing at the circling U.S. planes. Insulated as I had been by the airplane's cockpit and the sweet hum of my jet engines, I found the din disconcerting. Nonetheless, I began to devise an escape plan. It was my intention to steer for one of the flooded fields on the other side of the river and hide until dark, then move to an area suitable for a helicopter landing. Unhappily, a wind current flowing above the river caught me up and prevented me from crossing. I saw that there was no way I could stay out of the Ma and away from the scores of soldiers now converging on the bank.

But there were alternatives, and I measured them carefully as I descended. A strong underwater swimmer, I would steer for the center of the river, slip my gear, and while the soldiers chased down and then searched under my chute, I would swim downstream under water and come ashore. There I would hide in a marshy area and remain below the surface of the water, breathing through a hollow reed until darkness. I realize it sounds like the stuff of movies, evoking images of bandy-legged little men dressed in khaki poking among the weeds with their bayonets. Surprisingly, though, it had worked for others, and I was confident I could get to some place where I could be picked up. There was no overestimating the rescue capabilities of the helicopter people.

The descent was agonizingly slow as I swung gently in the hot sun, studying the scene below, and for a couple of minutes I could do nothing but think about escape. Dozens of soldiers stood on the south bank watching me come down, their hands on hips, faces upturned. They appeared almost nonchalant, certain that they would capture me. Some of them trotted along the riverbank, keeping up with the chute as it fell toward the river, drifting upstream.

As I prepared to go into the river, my comrades above me were doing what they could to help. Their efforts were courageous, but futile. Many of the planes in my flight were not equipped to furnish protective cover. Most of them didn't carry machine guns, just rockets and bombs. Those pilots who could strafe refrained from doing so for the moment. They just circled and watched. Sallada saw Tschudy go down in the center of a village a couple of miles downstream from me. He knew the rescue of my cocky, brave, and considerate friend would be impossible, and as the jets began to run low on fuel, my chances seemed dim unless a helicopter should suddenly appear.

And then the Ma River was rushing up toward me. I took a deep breath and hit the shimmering surface with a dull "thunk," plunging deeply into the cool, muddy water. I released myself from the parachute, and as it sailed upstream, I began swimming downstream underwater with the four-knot current.

But my beautiful escape plan began to evaporate almost immediately. The heavy flight boots hampered my movements, and I realized with some horror for the first time that I was seriously injured. I couldn't move my left leg.

What had been an attempt to escape now became a battle for survival in the murky depths of the river. I began to choke and swallow water, and I fought to reach the surface without success. My life was flowing away with the current. In desperation I popped one side of my Mae West, and in moments I was at the surface, a few yards from where my survival raft floated in the water. The parachute was about a hundred yards upstream, but its movement had not fooled the soldiers.

Immediately, I saw that there was no hope of escape. Soldiers lined the bank about twenty yards away, their rifles trained on me. As they gestured for me to come ashore, one raised his rifle and fired, and a bullet whizzed over my head. What worried me most, however, was not the soldiers. Two young men in loincloths were putting out from the north bank in a bark canoe. They were obviously trying to horn in on the capture and the reward, and I judged them to be dangerous. One was waving a machete wildly over his head, and I was in no position to defend myself. My 38-caliber pistol had been lost during ejection.

Floundering somewhat, I twisted my head to look at the two men in the canoe and then began paddling to my survival gear, which was floating about twenty yards away. Still gasping for breath, I inflated the life raft and tried to pull myself aboard. I thought I could better defend myself from the raft, but with my left leg immobile, I couldn't generate sufficient kick to get aboard. So I hung there and watched as the canoe drifted toward me. One of its occupants was leaning over the bow, an angry look on his scarred face, his arm raised, and the machete in his hand. The soldiers on the bank, apparently aware of my plight, shouted at the two heroes in loincloths, but the canoe kept coming, and when it nudged into me, I pushed it away and shouted at them.

I saw the man in the bow wind up his right arm and swing, and I tried to duck and turn away. The flat side of the blade struck me on the back, and then the man hit me on the neck twice, cutting me deeply. I slapped at my neck and cursed him, and at that point he apparently noticed my injured leg. Grunting and sweating, the two Vietnamese pulled me into the raft, tied my arms behind me, and towed the raft to shore.

Several soldiers walked out onto some logs which were lashed together to form a crude pier. They rolled me out of the raft and onto the logs, indicating that they wanted me to stand and climb the five-foot bank. When I tried to do so, my leg gave way. While the two men in loincloths clamored in vain for the reward, the soldiers, arms outstretched, crowded forward and began dragging me onto the bank.

Dazed and bleeding as I was, my principal emotion was fury. I was mad as hell at being shot down, and even angrier at being captured.

CHAPTER TWO

What the North Vietnamese acquired when they captured me was an average product of Middle America and its values. My heritage, training, and background made me the very antithesis of everything my Communist captors stood for, and long before the battle was truly joined between us, each side understood the elements of the struggle and its classical nature.

Although I had lived a far from perfect life, my heart and soul belonged to God, country, and family long before the Navy got hold of me. My religious upbringing and my mother's strong influence shaped my character, although my father worried that my life was too sheltered.

There were people of substance on both sides of my family. My father told me he could trace his ancestry to George-Jacques Danton, the great orator and moderate leader of the French Revolution. My mother, Irene Claudia Steele Denton, could find blue blood in her lineage all the way back to Sir Roger Moore, Marquis of Drodhega, Ireland, who came to America in 1645 to escape religious and political persecution. In her family tree were Spanish and French noblemen, a colonial governor of South Carolina, a colonial governor of North Carolina, and wealthy landowners who had lost everything in the Civil War.

My father, a garrulous, big-hearted man, liked to drink and play poker despite his Southern Baptist upbringing, and it took him a while to get his feet on the ground. His father-in-law, a typical small-time capitalist, owned or operated hotels in such diverse places as Mobile, Meridian, Mississippi, Chattanooga, El Paso, and Atlanta, and my father clerked in all of them at one time or another.

We lived in hotel rooms much of the time, and I attended at least thirteen different grammar schools.

Despite their itinerant ways, my mother and father were proud of their Southern aristocratic background. My mother, a Roman Catholic, brought her children up in an atmosphere that would have a profound effect on my life.

In 1932, tired of the nomadic life, we moved to Chicago, where Dad became a bill collector and a captain in the Illinois National Guard. Aside from settling us down, the move had the advantage of placing the family near wealthy relatives, two great-aunts who had married well. One of them, Mrs. H. S. Hoover, lived in a magnificent suite in the Edgewater Beach Hotel with her husband and mother. Another, Mrs. Rivington Fisher, the wife of a noted surgeon, lived in a fashionable apartment nearby.

Thus I, often dressed in the typical Buster Brown outfit of the era, spent many Saturday or Sunday afternoons and evenings listening to the music of famous bands at the Edgewater Beach. On one occasion I was handed a baton and permitted to lead the Paul Whiteman orchestra.

I also sang in the St. Ita's choir, a nationally famous organization. When the choir was threatened with disbandment for lack of money, one of my aunts bought magnificent vestments for the entire group in order to keep the choir going.

But it couldn't last. My father was embarrassed by his own lack of wealth and determined to better his lot. He could see the war coming and decided in 1936 to move to Houston, which he predicted would become a boom town. Mother refused to go because she didn't think the children, now numbering three boys, would have the proper family life. So he went to Houston alone to work in a shipyard and also take a successful flyer in real estate. He lost his real estate gains, however, in a brief fling as a bookmaker. He later settled down and became a respected citizen of Houston, but by that time the family had broken up. Shortly after my father left for Houston, Mother took us to Mobile to live in the Bienville Hotel, leased and operated by her mother after her father's death. In 1938 my mother and father were divorced.

Except for the divorce, the stay in Mobile was one of the happiest periods of my life. For once, the family was settled down, and in 1939 we moved into a real house for the first time. I attended the elementary school at St. Mary's, and then went to McGill Institute, a Catholic high school. There, I plunged into athletic and other extracurricular activities.

I played quarterback on the football team, sang in the choir, performed in the drama club, wrote for the school newspaper, won the intramural tennis championship, was a pitcher and shortstop on the baseball team and a forward on the basketball team, and was elected senior class president.

There were early indications of my interest in the sea. When I was five years old, my mother took me to a studio to have my picture taken, and I was so enamored of one of the props, a model battleship, that I cried when I wasn't allowed to take it home with me. I still remember the ship in detail. But the decisive turn came somewhat later, when I saw a movie about the Naval Academy called *Navy Blue and Gold.* To this day I can remember the plot, and the actors, Robert Young, James Stewart, and Lionel Barrymore.

The movie started me thinking about my future. As a sophomore in high school, l believed that things were coming too easy for me and that I was inclined to loaf along. I knew that I would have to do my best simply to survive at the Naval Academy. And the service of a naval officer appeared to be something that I could give my all to without feeling that I was wasting myself. I still believe that.

In fact I never had any doubts about my country. I remember carrying the American flag at the age of seventeen during a parade in Mobile and considering the assignment a great honor. In the darkest moments of the days ahead, the recollection of the band playing the national anthem would flow through my consciousness and comfort me. Even now, tears come to my eyes when I hear those pure, sweet strains. I wish every American could share the feeling of love and gratitude that I have for this country and her people, and the sense of urgent necessity to protect her.

Force of arms is one way to protect her. Another and most vital way is through a spiritual awakening within each of us and a return to the basic values which made this country the greatest in history. In my Naval Academy years, where my sense of duty and honor were developed and refined, I copied some quotations onto the flyleaf of a schoolbook. Among them was a strangely prophetic one by David Glasgow Farragut, the Civil War hero of Mobile Bay: "There are comparatively few men from whom one cannot learn something, and a Naval officer should always be adding to his knowledge... It is hard to say what a Naval officer might not have to do."

There was one by Benjamin Disraeli: "Nurture your mind with great thoughts. To believe in the heroic makes heroes."

There was another from John Adolphus Dahlgren, inventor of the naval gun widely used during the Civil War: "The officer should wear his uniform as the judge his ermine, without a stain."

And finally, there was something from an anonymous writer: "The greatest heroes known are those that are afraid to go; but go."

Since my graduation from the Naval Academy in 1946, I may or may not have lived by those tenets, but I have tried.

And on July 18, 1965, kneeling in pain and fatigue on a muddy riverbank, I began to understand what they were all about.

About thirty soldiers crowded around me by now, but they seemed unexcited, almost bored, and they were handling me quite gently. Two of them cut the remaining gear and clothing from my body, searching for weapons. By the time they were through, I was down to my underwear. And someone had taken my watch.

Seeing that I could not walk, the soldiers placed me on a plank, and began to carry me. Then an A4 made a buzzing pass at treetop level and the soldiers dumped the plank—and me—from shoulder height and dove for cover. I passed out from the pain. The A4 came in low twice more despite fire at point-blank range from the guns across the river, and then circled away toward the south. I was on my own. My comrades had given up a rescue. As I learned later, some were so low on fuel that they had to land at Da Nang, the big U.S. air base down the coast.

I was carried to a mud hut in a nearby village. There, to my surprise, I was treated with some sympathy by the villagers. One reached out and patted me on the stomach.

My leg was numb, but my lower abdomen was seared with pain, and I welcomed the cup of tea and warm coconut milk handed me by a villager. After about two hours I was carried to a small boat and taken upriver to another village, where a young man on a motorcycle met us.

The soldiers transported me to the vehicle and put me in the sidecar, gently draping my injured leg over the side. On the way to yet another village, the driver was evidently told to honk his horn and make a scene, but he seemed embarrassed by it all and made only a half-hearted attempt at it.

The people ignored the whole affair anyway as the driver went through the village and up to what resembled a meeting hall. As the driver helped me from the sidecar, Bill Tschudy swaggered through the cloud of dust thrown up by the motorcycle. He managed to ask me if I was hurt, and then he was taken away. Although we would be in indirect contact again, it would be seven years, six Super Bowls, and a moon landing before I would meet him again.

By now, the shock from my wounds, the trauma from the shootdown, the whole bloody mess began to seep into my consciousness. I was bewildered, and the next few moments, mild enough in retrospect, didn't help.

I was put on display in the meeting hall, and numbers of villagers—women carrying babies, farmers carrying shovels and rakes, and militiamen carrying guns—crowded forward to stare at this strange bundle from heaven.

They appeared to be more curious than threatening, but a young soldier walked up and indicated that he wanted me to bend over. I guessed that he wanted me to bow down, and I shook my head no. Angry at the loss of face, the guard yanked a gun from his holster and placed it against my head so firmly that I could feel a welt rising under the cold circle of steel. The villagers seemed to disapprove and backed away gasping. I passed out.

Physically and mentally, I was in my prime when I parachuted from my A6. At the age of forty-one, my 165-pound, 5-foot-11 frame was trim, kept in shape by golf, tennis, and other exercise.

A life-time student of foreign affairs, I had received a master's in international relations from George Washington University after my graduation from the Academy, and I had read widely in philosophy, history, and religion.

I was also thoroughly grounded in the military sciences, having gone through all the training and schooling expected of a U.S. naval officer at my stage. Among other things, I was an expert in airborne electronics, as well as a recognized expert in antisubmarine warfare and air defense. In fact, I had devised fleet tactics that were regarded within the Navy as revolutionary.

In other words, the North Vietnamese had made a good catch, although the two young soldiers guarding the semiconscious figure lying on bamboo strips in one corner of the meeting hall couldn't have cared less. They squatted in the doorway and listened intently to news being broadcast over their transistor radio, glancing only occasionally at their bloody guest.

Sometime during the evening, a young, well-dressed woman carrying a plastic imitation leather purse on a long strap over her shoulder walked briskly to the doorway and looked inside. The soldiers moved away, and the woman, perhaps in her late twenties, stepped into the room and walked over to me. She motioned for me to lower my underpants, and while I struggled to get them below my hips, she filled a needle and dabbed me with some alcohol. Then she gave me two injections in the hip.

I was now beginning to recover my senses, and knew just enough French to ask her what she had given me. In a low, pleasant voice, she answered that it was quinine and water. Her eyes hardly left mine the entire time. Then she left as briskly as she had arrived.

It was about eight hours past shootdown. That was to be my way of measuring time for longer than I realized as I lay there in that insignificant peasant village.

So helpless was I from my leg injury that when the guard changed from two young soldiers to an old man sometime during the night, I couldn't even consider escaping. I could handle the man, but I could walk only with a crutch and I knew I couldn't get far. So through the night, during which I slept only occasionally, and the long hours of the next day, two men from different worlds mostly just stared at each other silently.

At one point, the old man helped me outside and stood me against a wall while he picked some fruit. Later he brought me some tea. At dusk, he led me outside again, where some soldiers were waiting with a truck. And there was an added attraction: a large white man, about 6 feet 4, in a uniform with no insignia.

The man, who I deduced was a Russian, appeared to be directing things; the North Vietnamese soldiers moved at his slightest gesture. When he saw two men helping me toward the truck he pushed them away, and I passed out again. When I awoke, I was in the back of a jeep, bound hand and foot and blindfolded, and on my way to Hanoi.

Peeking under my loosely tied blindfold, I could see the moon rising bloodred over the Thanh Hoa Bridge, built many years earlier by the French. It was part of Highway One and a main link to the south. I had crossed this bridge on my bombing run, and now I was crossing it again, the hard way. It had been heavily bombed, and the railway part was useless. From under the blindfold, I could see that the jeep was part of a huge traffic jam stacked up at the approach to the bridge as war material poured south under cover of darkness. I was amazed, and thought of the carnage a night raid on the approaches would cause. But it was still early in the war, and no one had thought of such a simple measure. I hoped they wouldn't get the idea at that particular moment.

As the jeep edged up onto the bridge, the two soldiers who constituted my guard began to jabber and appeared frightened. Later, one of them told me in halting English that the bridge had been bombed the night before and more than fifty soldiers had been killed.

Now aflame with pain from the waist down, I settled back as best I could. The driver was obviously trying to go easy over the bumps in deference to me, and I was thankful. It was one of the few acts of compassion that I would experience in North Vietnam.

And I would need everything I could get. It took eleven hours of driving to get to Hanoi, during which time I fell unconscious several times. Once, in a lucid moment, I thought I heard Tschudy's voice. I shook my head to clear it, and sure enough, it was Tschudy, loudly demanding water from his escorts. He was in a jeep parked about a hundred yards from ours. Both were waiting for a small ferry at Nam Dinh, on the edge of the Red River delta. We were also on another edge. The edge of hell.

CHAPTER THREE

My wife knew what was up the moment twelve-year-old Billy, our fourth child, came halfway up the stairs and called out that Captain Nelson was there to see her.

As Jane recounted to me years later, Captain Stu Nelson had called on a neighbor, Bobi Boecker, a few days before to tell her that her husband Don had gone down over Laos. Don had been rescued, and on that pleasant, warm Sunday afternoon in July, Captain Nelson held out hope that I would also be rescued.

"It's all right, it's all right, we're trying to get him out," Nelson called up the stairs.

Even now I relive the moments as though I had been there. Jane was silent as she came down to face the stocky, crew-cut Nelson and his pretty blond wife. There was really little to say as Nelson, ordinarily gruff and outspoken, mumbled the details. A parachute had been seen; my comrades had flown cover and had seen me fall into a river and then get safely to shore. A rescue effort was under way. That was about all.

Jane listened in stunned silence and thought back to the night before, when she had taken the children to a drive-in to see *Mary Poppins*. For the first time since I had left home three months previously, she had felt apprehension about my safety. In the middle of the movie she had begun to cry, silently. That Sunday morning she had written me a letter and then the family had gone to Mass.

Now Billy was staring at her, and she didn't know what to do. Finally she asked him to go and take care of Mary Beth, one and a half, our youngest. Michael and Madeleine, five and seven years old, were playing outside. Mrs. Nelson took them across the street to a neighbor.

Because of the time difference, it was now Monday, July 19 in Vietnam.

Jane did what her character and background told her to do; she went to church and prayed. Later she would take care of her family.

People made things easier. As the news spread, friends came to offer assistance, and Jane's sister began making plane reservations for the trip to Virginia Beach. Our close friend Kitty Clark came down from Washington immediately.

On Monday night, Captain Nelson came by with a map to show Jane where I had gone down, but even before he told her, she knew the truth. I was not going to be picked up. Captain Nelson finally said that the search had been called off. On Friday, the week was climaxed by an announcement from Hanoi that I had been shot down and captured along with Tschudy. The broadcast added an ominous note: Denton and Tschudy had been sent by McNamara personally and would be treated as imperialist criminals. At noon, while watching the news on television, Jane saw a picture of me and Bill Tschudy and cried out: "Is that Jerry?" My face was swollen and out of shape and I looked as though I'd been whipped. It was a shock, and she broke down badly for the first time.

She hoped I would be home by Christmas, but something I had said on my departure kept forcing its way into her consciousness. "The war will last a long time," I had said. To her, it sounded like an open-ended sentence.

Jane married me at the age of twenty after two years at Mary Washington College in Virginia and plunged quickly into the itinerant way of life that characterizes the military. The names are familiar: Philadelphia, where I was attached to the carrier *Valley Forge,* being built at the naval shipyard there; Newport, Rhode Island; Philadelphia again; San Diego; Hawaii; Lakehurst, New Jersey, where I took blimp training; Pensacola; Patuxent, Maryland; Nice, France; Norfolk; Pensacola again; Norfolk again; Kansas; Newport again; and Virginia Beach.

Each move became more of a chore as the family grew and Jane was delighted to settle down for a time in the big white house on Watergate Lane. It turned out to be a much longer time than she had bargained for.

And the Vietnam War was to last a much longer time than the American public had bargained for. If I had been somewhat prescient about the length of the war, that was not the case with the American public. Most people were aware, vaguely, that the United States had gradually been building ground forces in South Vietnam; first, advisers to the Army of the Republic of South Vietnam, then Marines to guard installations, then the Army, for offensive operations. By July 18, 1965, the day I was shot down, President Johnson had authorized a total of 193,000 men for ground forces in South Vietnam. But the public hardly knew there was a war on.

Even those who opposed it were slow to organize. The Students for a Democratic Society didn't hold their first antiwar rally until Easter of 1965, and it was generally ignored by the government and the public. In time, however, the protestors were to become almost as grave a problem as the military forces of North Vietnam.

For me, the fateful decision was made on September 7, 1964, more than ten months before I was shot down, when President Johnson met in the White House with Dean Rusk, Secretary of State; Robert McNamara, Secretary of Defense; General Maxwell Taylor, ambassador to South Vietnam; and John A. McCone, director of the Central Intelligence Agency.

The Johnson Administration for months had had contingency plans for an air war against North Vietnam, and by March 17, 1964, details were in place for retaliatory strikes on seventy-two hours' notice, and full-scale air raids on the North on thirty days' notice.

Then, on August 4, 1964, North Vietnamese torpedo boats attacked the U.S. destroyers *Maddox* and *Turner Joy* in the Gulf of Tonkin. The Congress three days later gave President Johnson the Tonkin Gulf Resolution, which said in part that the Congress would approve and support the determination of the President "to take all necessary measures to repel any armed attack against the forces of the United States and to prevent further aggression."

President Johnson had a slight problem with the timing of the start of the bombing, however. He was up for reelection against Senator Barry Goldwater, whose advocacy of fullscale bombing of North Vietnam had become a major campaign issue. Publicly, Johnson had been preaching moderation and couldn't afford to bomb the North until sometime after the election in November. In a campaign speech in Texas on August 29, 1964, he had declared:

"I have had advice to load our planes with bombs and to drop them on certain areas that I think would enlarge the war and escalate the war.

"Instead, the policy of the United States government toward Vietnam is to furnish advice, give counsel, express good judgment, give them trained counselors, and help them with equipment to help themselves."

A little more than a week later, on that fateful September 7, the inner circle of the administration decided to go ahead with the raids on the basis that they would bolster the shaky morale of the South Vietnamese government, which was on the verge of another coup, and put the North on notice that the U.S. meant business.

On February 13, 1965, President Johnson gave the order for the sustained bombing of the North, code-named Rolling Thunder, of which I was a willing part.

CHAPTER FOUR

Hanoi was noisy and smelly as I entered it on that hot summer morning in July 1965. Horns honked and brakes screeched as we moved through the city at morning rush hour. There was a certain earthy smell, which I later learned was from open sewage. Hanoi was short on amenities.

There was no question where I was. The men guarding me were weary from the long drive through the night, and not too vigilant, and I was able to peep from under my blindfold frequently. I could see lines of pedestrian and bicycle traffic, and there was a distinctly cosmopolitan air about the place as we drove down a wide boulevard. Automobiles were driven arrogantly, with amazing disregard for pedestrians and bikers.

Though I was still dazed, and very tired, my mind went back over what I had read about the city. Hanoi had once been the capital of French Indochina and was now the capital of the Democratic Republic of Vietnam. It reflected the influence of French architecture, with large, impressive buildings, wide, tree-shaded boulevards, and many parks and gardens.

The bustle and activity of rush hour as I arrived was somewhat misleading, however. Hanoi was still, in 1965, a rather sleepy, overgrown provincial city with a slow-moving population pedaling bicycles through relatively uncrowded streets.

Automobiles, a great status symbol which usually designated party members of standing, made up a minor part of the flow of military vehicles, bicycles, and trucks.

It was the rainy season, which meant hot, sultry, uncomfortable days for the city dweller, but the seed of life for an economy that depended on the growing of rice. Already, the early morning cool was fast disappearing. Sweat soaked my blindfold and stung my eyes as I tried to get a mental grasp of what apparently would be my new home. The city was named by the French early in the nineteenth century after Hanoi Province, which surrounds the city. The word means "inside the river," that is, the land lying within a loop of a river, in this case the famous Red River, which flows from the mountains of China and finally spreads itself fan-shaped in a huge delta on the edge of which this city of roughly 800,000 people stands.

By the mid-sixties its factories were turning out machine tools, motors, cement, and plywood, textile, and chemical products. The University of Hanoi had more than 20,000 students. The Polytechnic Institute, financed by the Soviet Union, had opened in 1956, and there was a well-developed system of primary and secondary schools, several large hospitals and museums, a huge library, and numerous theaters. All revolved around the socialist theory of government as practiced by the only political party, the Communist party.

The young, slim driver, who had tried futilely to spare me on the long trip to Hanoi, was now urged to go faster by the soldiers riding as guards, and we sped through the city until we came to a steel gate embedded in the most massive wall I had ever seen.

The wall, as I later learned, was more than twenty feet high and four feet thick. Its top was studded with large pieces of glass and extended more than five feet with barbed and electrified strands of wire.

As we waited for the gate to be opened, I attracted curious stares from some workers also waiting to go inside. As I looked from under my blindfold, a leering middle-aged woman loomed up in front of me and smacked me in the face with her purse.

Welcome to Hoa Lo Prison, better known as the Hanoi Hilton! The prison was a series of beige, stucco-walled cellblocks and administration buildings, all topped by red tile. Built by the French, it covered a full block near the center of Hanoi.

The gate finally opened, and we drove between two buildings into a large courtyard, where the jeep stopped and the driver got out to help me. As he reached down, he did something entirely unexpected. He patted me gently on the stomach and gave me a sympathetic look. But first, he looked around to see if anyone was watching.

His attitude was not to last, however. Later, like most of the North Vietnamese, he took an arrogant attitude towards the prisoners. He had some rudimentary medical training and seemed to be in charge of applying bandages. He was so bumbling at it and so arrogant that the prisoners called him Dipshit. But I believe that he was a basically decent and humane person.

And then something else occurred that I will never forget. As I was being led between the buildings, I heard a low, rather mournful whistling. I strained my ears, and glanced around for the source, which eluded me. But the melody was unmistakable. It was "Yankee Doodle." My heart skipped a beat, and a joyful feeling flowed through my body. I was not alone. Somewhere behind the drab walls, a kindred soul was lifting my spirits.

Later, I discovered that it was Lieutenant John McCamey, who was able to peep through a hole in his cell door and spot the new arrivals. He greeted each one with his soulful tune.

Shortly, I was in my new home, Cell No. 4 in New Guy Village, Hoa Lo Prison, Hanoi, North Vietnam. What I had in Cell 4 was two solid concrete beds (the North Vietnamese were big on concrete, which was manufactured in large quantities in the capital), with metal-and-wood stocks at the foot of each. The one amenity was a small honey bucket (a pail that served as a toilet) in one corner. The concrete bunks were about three and a half feet high and two and a half feet apart. The cell was nine feet by eight feet. The door had a small peephole and was flanked by windows which had been covered over by a thin layer of concrete. At the other end of the cell was a barred window, from which I could see part of the huge wall which surrounded the prison. A large, dry moat bordered the inside of the wall.

At some point during the afternoon of July 20, two days after l had been shot down, two Vietnamese came to my cell and woke me from a deep sleep of total exhaustion. One of them told me in good English that I was to be questioned. I wasn't in the mood: I indicated that I couldn't walk and was in great pain from the snapped tendon, which had come through the skin of my left thigh.

He was unmoved, and at the point of a bayonet, I crawled to a room in another part of the prison and was told to sit on a stool in front of a table behind which sat two arrogant-looking North Vietnamese.

Although I was still dazed and probably suffering from shock, the dangers of the situation began to seep through to me. The Vietnamese were going out of their way to appear unimpressed with my status as a U.S. naval officer. The bayonet was an unnecessary bit of show and the arrogance obviously put on, but l became acutely concerned with my welfare for the first time.

The rigorous training I had received in a special Navy course on how to behave as a prisoner of war had impressed me deeply, and I was determined to abide by the Code of Conduct.

Superconscious as I was of the fact that I was the first A6 pilot in their hands, I considered it likely they would make every effort to pry information from me about the new aircraft, and I was trying to muster the courage to die rather than reveal anything of military or propaganda value to them. Frankly, I intended to be as much of a pain in the behind to them as possible, and hoped this would convince them that torture would be useless.

Strangely, they never did torture me to obtain credible military information, and to my knowledge no one else was ever tortured for that kind of information in my initial stage of imprisonment. The North Vietnamese were much more interested in statements of propaganda value, and years later I learned that the North Koreans had taken the same approach to the crew of the *Pueblo*. Face and propaganda were their beacons. When the North Vietnamese finally did get around to torturing for military information, my time had passed. They had fliers with much more up-to-date information.

As a guard reluctantly and rather roughly helped me onto the stool in the interrogation room, I tried to hide my fear with a facial expression intended to reflect a mixture of pride and calm.

One of my interrogators was a rather plump, scholarly-looking man of about thirty. Later he told me, probably truthfully, that he had been a professor of history, Vietnamese literature, and the English language. From the eleven fliers who had been shot down before Tschudy and I were, I eventually learned that his nickname was Owl. He acted as an interpreter, but often interjected questions and remarks of his own.

The other man was about forty, and at about 5 feet 6 inches, maybe an inch taller than Owl. He was very nervous and had a rather weather-beaten face. He later told me he had been a combat pilot, but he was always careful not to discuss this around fellow officers, and I and the other prisoners thought he was lying. In honor of his pseudocombat status, he was called Eagle. He spoke English fairly well and often asked questions directly.

Owl was dressed in civilian clothes, his blue shirt open at the collar. Eagle was in an army uniform which had no insignia. They were the only two interrogators I met in my first sojourn in the Hilton.

The first four questions were easy: my name, rank, service number, and birth date, all of which I answered. The Owl leaned forward and asked, "What kind of plane were you flying?"

I gave no answer, and he kept repeating the question, louder and louder. He was getting quite agitated, so I gave him my name, rank, service number, and birth date again. After about ten minutes of this, my strength was gone and I was about to pass out. Owl dismissed me. I don't remember how I got back to my cell.

There was the same routine the next morning and afternoon, with few variations. They wanted to know where I was born, my home address, home base, name of the carrier I took off from, my bomb load. My answering technique remained the same.

In subsequent days, the routine was repeated over and over, and was now mixed with long harangues about the righteous cause of North Vietnam and the evil cause of the United States. It was all quite boring, until they began to make threats.

One day, Eagle said quite ponderously, "If you continue to refuse to cooperate in a reasonable way by answering our questions, we cannot guarantee your safety. If you continue to insult us we will have to turn you over to the civilian authorities, who will force you to talk."

Finally after one long and exasperating session, Eagle said: "If we turn you over to the civilians, they will apply severe punishment, and if that punishment results in losing a limb, they will dispose of you. They would not want to send you home a cripple."

I didn't like the way things were going. As my wound healed and I gained strength, I was beginning to get a little cocky, and felt that they were bluffing, but there was just enough edge in their voices to make me a little uncertain.

I decided to test them. When Eagle threatened me again with "disposal," as he kept putting it, I stiffened my resistance. Sitting as straight as I could, I half-shouted at them: "Are you daring to make threats against my life in contravention of the Geneva Conventions?"

Surprisingly they withdrew in confusion to a corner of the room to talk things over, then abruptly dismissed me. Even though these sessions were terribly drab (I was constantly suppressing a yawn), they were potentially dangerous nonetheless. You never knew what turn they might take, and the sound of the guard at the door at an odd hour would always bring a feeling of dread.

Then, one night about midnight, I was taken to the quiz room for the third time that day. The lateness of the hour and the excited attitude of Owl and Eagle told me something big was up, and I didn't like it at all.

I was hardly seated on the stool when Owl flourished a newspaper clipping announcing that Tschudy and I had been downed over North Vietnam. The dispatch mentioned that we were with Attack Squadron 75.

"So Denton," Eagle said triumphantly, "we know you were flying a very interesting aircraft, the A6 Intru-u-der."

They wanted me to admit it, but I didn't say anything. Then they recited a list of names of officers in my squadron, including Commander Swoose Snead, Lieutenant Don Boecker, and Lieutenant Don Eaton. I concluded that they had read a newspaper account of the rescue of Boecker and Eaton after they had ejected over Laos. Snead had greeted them and been photographed with them upon their return to the *Independence*. I had witnessed all the commotion and also had been there to greet them.

There was a hard edge in Eagle's voice when he played his best card. "Is it not true, Denton," he rasped, "that McNamara himself was aboard when you took off? Did he not personally order you to bomb civilians?"

Although I had not actually met McNamara, they thought they had something special on me, and I began to chill inside.

The next day when I was taken to the small, filthy bath-toilet building, I found and hid in my pajamas some broken glass. I would use it on myself if they really got serious about the A6. It was not that I knew anything of great value about the A6, but I believed that prolonged torture would have broken me to the point that I would reveal enough about the airplane to dishonor myself.

Not all of the interrogations were one-sided. On occasion Owl and Eagle would reveal their true feelings about certain matters.

One day Owl said, grimly, "You know, Denton, the night before you were captured, your planes killed fifty-seven of our soldiers on the approaches to the bridge [at Thanh Hoa] and destroyed many of our trucks."

The statement, and the manner in which it was given, revealed to me for the first time how much they feared the bombing. A few days later, Eagle asked me if we were going to bomb Hanoi. I quoted statements by President Johnson and Secretary of Defense McNamara to the effect that the United States would do whatever was necessary to win the war.

Eagle walked to the window, his clenched hands shaking, and looked at the Hanoi skyline.

"No! Never! You will never bomb Hanoi!"

Fortunately, the interrogations became less and less frequent, and I began to turn my attention to my surroundings. Soon I would begin collecting vital information about the prison and the people in it.

CHAPTER FIVE

The first ten days of my imprisonment were full of new experiences, few of them pleasant. I was appalled by the conditions and frequently shook my head and asked myself: What am I doing here.

The guard urinated in a gutter that ran along the outside door of the cell, so the place stank. Roaches and flies covered the walls and floor, and sometimes my body. The food, by American standards, was wretched. My stomach hurt constantly from the snapped tendon, and there was the festering wound on the inside of my thigh where the other end of the tendon had broken through the skin. I sweltered on the bare concrete bunk, clad only in my underwear. I had no shoes or sandals, and I wasn't allowed to bathe for the first five days.

Worst of all, I was alone. I longed for the comfort, security, and companionship of the *Independence,* and I worried constantly about the interrogations.

There was one North Vietnamese, however, who gave me a lift from the drab loneliness of my existence. Nursie was a breath of fresh air in a putrid atmosphere. In her early twenties, she was tall for a Vietnamese woman, and quite slender. Best of all, she was gracious, smart, and capable. I discovered all this on my second day in prison when she came to my cell with a female guard and Dipshit to inspect the bandage he had put on my leg.

At first I refused to take down my shorts in front of the women. They left the cell and seemed to be flattered that I would presume their innocence, but in a few minutes they were back. As soon as Nursie saw the bandage, she looked at Dipshit in disgust and rolled her eyes. It was much too small and was clumsily applied. She gently removed it and put on a bigger and much better one. Dipshit, abashed by her reprimand, pretended not to watch.

But the person who really helped to sustain me during those early days was Larry Guarino. He was the first American with whom I developed frequent voice contact.

It was on July 21, three days after I was shot down, that I first became aware of another prisoner in a cell near mine. I could hear the guards going in and talking to him. After much effort, I managed to drill four or five small holes in the thin layer of cement covering one of the windows flanking the cell door. Thus, I caught my first glimpse of Air Force Major Larry Guarino as he passed my cell.

Soon we were in voice communication. The huge wall and the side of the cell block made a nice channel for our voices as we called out to each other through the barred windows. He told me he had ejected from his F105 a few weeks before and was now in irons. I was shocked. It had never occurred to me that the Vietnamese would put an American prisoner in irons. What I heard next was even more shocking.

"Jerry, I'm in bad shape," he said in a weak voice. "They are giving me almost nothing to eat. I'm down to a hundred pounds and I haven't crapped in twenty-six days. I don't remember how long I've been in irons, but it's been weeks. I don't know whether I can make it."

Elation at talking to a fellow American turned to horror. I was even a little conscience-stricken because the Vietnamese had done no more than push me around on the way to interrogation. I asked him why he was in irons.

"I think it was because I was impolite at one of the quizzes," he answered. "I lost my temper and spilled a cup of tea all over the table. I was only giving them name, rank, serial number, and date of birth. They threatened me about that, but didn't do anything until I spilled the tea. Guess they thought I was being rude."

I didn't come face to face with the cocky, emotional Italian until 1970, five years later, but I came to love him like a brother during the brief period we were communicating.

The quizzes continued twice a day, but Larry said that it had been his experience that they would become less frequent. He doubted that I would be harmed, even if I was uncooperative, so long as I was "polite." Owl and Eagle were still asking questions that I refused to answer, but I was making an effort to be polite, even engaging them in arguments about the war that became quite heated at times. Larry also told me about some prisoners in a cell bordering the small courtyard of New Guy Village, which he had passed on the way to the bath. They were Lieutenant Commander Bob Shumaker, Lieutenant Commander Ray Vohden, Captain Smitty Harris, and Lieutenant Phil Butler. At various times there were one or two others. They were always making a lot of noise, Guarino said, singing and laughing, and he was suspicious of them because the Vietnamese indicated to him that they were cooperating. Shumaker had tried to get Guarino's attention as he went past, but Larry had snubbed him.

I suspected the situation was not all that it seemed. One of the guards had let me see a basket of goodies, including cigarettes and candy kisses, and indicated he was delivering it to their room. And at a quiz, Owl insinuated that the men in Shumaker's cell had a "good attitude," and thus received better treatment.

Later my suspicions were confirmed when I learned that the Vietnamese were playing off Shumaker and his cell mates against Guarino and me by pretending to give them special treatment.

Shumaker and all the others shot down earlier were very solid citizens. Shumaker was brave, but not foolhardy, and he was brilliant in devising methods of communication. Vohden had a terribly injured leg, which the Vietnamese doctors aggravated with a series of bungling operations during his first year of captivity. Nonetheless, he sought no favor from anyone and worked with the rest to improve our communications.

One thing Larry and I had to settle was the chain of command. The Code of Conduct demands that in a POW situation, command must be established on a rank and seniority basis; that is, when officers of equal rank are involved, seniority takes precedence.

Larry thought that was fine, but since he was in the Air Force and I was in the Navy, what we had was two one-man armies. Eventually, I convinced him that he was wrong. The senior ranking officer is in command over men of all services. So far as Larry and I were concerned, that was me. Larry gave in gracefully and agreed to accept my orders. Perhaps it seemed like a Mickey Mouse exercise, but the question of command soon became of immense importance.

The Vietnamese were letting Larry and me get away with murder on communications at the time, and only when we got too loud did they tell us to stop. We continued, however, by various methods.

One was whistling in Morse code, but I had to warn Larry more than once in a note about what he "said." There was a North Vietnamese officer stationed in one of the two cells between Larry, who was in No. 1, and me. Larry didn't believe me, but I had seen the officer, with a pad and pencil in his hand, through the tiny holes I had drilled. On one occasion, when I whistled a joke to Larry, I heard the officer laugh at the punch line. I believe at that point they were just trying to pick up some useful information from us.

Our regular guard was an old man in his sixties, who smoked a long pipe and seldom gave us trouble. But on one occasion he peeked into my cell and caught me standing on the window frame, casting shadows against the prison wall in Morse code. He became very agitated and pointed to the stock at the foot of the bed.

If he had looked more closely at the leg stock, he would have discovered something interesting. The stock consisted of a lower wooden frame attached to the concrete bed with a heavy metal piece hinged to it at one end. There were two spaces for the ankles, and the metal part could be swung down and locked in place, effectively pinning the prisoner.

I had been working the metal piece for several days pulling it back and forth for hours trying to break it loose. Finally, the metal gave way just above the hinge, and I had a four-foot-long, thirty-pound weapon. I kept it in place on the foot of the bed so no one would notice that it had been broken off.

It was also useful as a tool. I quickly learned that it was useless to try to pry the bars on the window apart, but I had better luck with the window frame. I used the broken end of the metal piece on the rotten concrete at one corner in an attempt to pry off the entire frame. I wasn't quite sure what I would do after that, but with constant effort, I was having remarkable success. Each day the frame got a little looser, until I believed I could pull it off when the time was ripe.

The broken stock was to cause me a great deal of trouble later on.

CHAPTER SIX

Day six in prison offered a few moments of rare luxury. I got my first bath, more or less.

The guard came early in the morning and motioned me out of the cell. I thought there was another quiz coming up, although it was a little early, but he led me on a new route past a cell that I judged to be occupied by Shumaker, Vohden, Butler, and Harris. The bath area was a covered, circular affair open at the sides. Interestingly, Nursie and the female guard were hanging around, watching as I walked into the bath area. Vietnamese women seemed to enjoy looking at the American prisoners. Because of poor diet, most of the North Vietnamese were underdeveloped, and the women obviously admired our muscular bodies and hairy chests. The two women stared at me quite unself-consciously as I walked toward the shower building.

I tested the lone shower and found that it yielded only a few drops. The guard impatiently shook his head and pointed to a full bucket of water. I just picked it up and dumped it over me without bothering to remove my underwear, and for the first and last time the old guard, usually so phleg-matic, laughed out loud.

That was the last touch of civilized living for some time, although, as Guarino had predicted, the quizzes became less frequent.

This in itself became something of a problem. There was now nothing to occupy my mind, as it wandered from one tortuous thought to another.

As I sat alone in the small, dank cell, my wound still festering and draining, sweat rolling from every pore, I thought about the prospect of long years of separation from my family.

I was also tortured by the thought of dishonor, by the fear that the Vietnamese would break me or somehow bribe or otherwise win me over. Self-doubt alternated with obsessive dread that they would frame me and convey falsely but convincingly to my family, friends, and comrades that I had been disloyal.

The loneliness was broken only by the few minutes a day that Guarino and I managed to communicate with each other. The stench and ugliness of my surroundings, the isolation, and the fear of being tortured all brought me to the edge of despair. It would be so easy to let one's mind drift, let it go blank, and in effect, give up.

To combat this, I constructed a daily routine. I would pray, exercise, plan escape, eat, nap, communicate with Guarino, and then start the cycle again at the top.

And of course, I reflected a lot on the old life and friends and family. Occasionally, my mind would dwell on the possibility that I would be moved into better quarters. I couldn't imagine anything worse than what I had. How wrong I was!

My first really bad break came sometime during the morning of July 28, while I was being quizzed. The Vietnamese inspected my cell while I was gone and discovered the damaged window frame.

Furious, they moved me to Cell No. 3. What was worse, they placed me in the leg stock for the first time. Although only the right ankle was placed in the stock in deference to my injured left leg, it was a traumatic experience.

The first time in irons is humiliating as well as terribly uncomfortable. In my case, there was to be an unfortunate side effect. While sleeping, I kept banging my left foot against the rusty stock, cutting it in several places. Because I had no sandals, the dirty water in the latrine building quickly caused an infection in the open wounds.

On my first day in the stock, the Vietnamese reduced my rations, so I stopped eating altogether to show them my determination. They immediately brought me my full ration, but I refused to touch the food. I was getting angrier and angrier. On another of my early days in irons, and with my foot still in the first stage of infection, there was an important breakthrough. On the way to the bath, I heard a voice call to me, "Go fishing!" It was Shumaker, trying to establish contact.

There were drain holes in the bath part of the latrine building. Since the guard would leave me alone for a few minutes I was able to fumble around in the main drain for a note.

It was the wrong drain, but the next day I tried the other one and found a matchstick across the hole. When I lifted the match there was a piece of string hanging down inside. On the end of the string was a note that said: "If you read this, spit as you depart the latrine door." It was written with the end of a burnt match. I spat, and thus established communications with Shumaker and the others.

I had stolen and secreted a small piece of lead, and there was enough paper lying around so that we could exchange messages daily. I wrote Shumaker that I was in irons. He was aghast.

"What the hell for?" he messaged back. As a camp veteran, he had a pretty good line on the Vietnamese. He wrote that so far they had threatened torture but hadn't done it, to his knowledge.

And we argued about where we were. I insisted that we were in Hanoi, but Shumaker and the others disagreed. They couldn't believe it at the time.

We also determined that I was the senior ranking officer, and thus camp commander. Immediately, I wrote that we should follow the military Code of Conduct. I also tried to establish some sanitary controls. We had no toilet paper at first, for instance, and we resolved to wash our hands whenever possible before eating in an effort to stop the dysentery that was already making the rounds.

I also suggested that they stop sending jokes and send me names and shootdown dates instead. I wanted a history of treatment at the camp, a map, and everything that would help in an escape plan. Shumaker sent me an excellent map of the camp drawn by Phil Butler.

I learned about Heartbreak Hotel, a cellblock across the courtyard from New Guy Village where prisoners were mostly two to a cell. And Shumaker told me about Lieutenant (j.g.) Everett Alvarez, who had gone down in August of 1964 during the Tonkin Gulf fracas.

Alvarez had led a lonely existence as the only American prisoner in Hoa Lo Prison. He was allowed to exercise in a small courtyard in one corner of the prison and had scratched messages on the wall with a nail. There was a certain poignancy to them. He marked the passing of the days by writing, "Happy Labor Day" and "Happy Halloween." There was "Have a good Thanksgiving," and "Merry Christmas." But there was no one there to read them until after Rolling Thunder began in February of 1965. It wasn't until March, when he and Shu were exercising and they established a note drop that he was able to communicate with a fellow American.

Alvarez had not been badly treated. In fact, it was reported that he had received Red Cross packages early in the game, at a time when the North Vietnamese didn't know whether or not they were in a war with the United States. But he was terribly lonely, and he would eventually spend more than nine years in prison, with his treatment to take a sharp turn for the worse.

We took every avenue we could think of to communicate with one another, including the use of eating utensils. One day I got a spoon with my meal that had writing scratched on it in tiny hand. There were some new names, and a message that said: "What, a wop in Hanoi?" It was from someone in Heartbreak Hotel who had heard of Guarino's capture.

Later, I learned that Shu and the others in his cell were on the dish-washing detail and were using that chore to collect and disseminate information. It was about that time that I learned that Shu had already spent more than eighty days in solitary.

Sometime in August, Guarino was moved from his cell because he and I had been making too much noise. That was a blow, and I became very worried about his condition. I asked Shu if he would concur in a hunger strike to protest the treatment of Guarino, but he thought it a very bad idea. I bowed to his superior experience and wisdom.

Anyway, I had some problems of my own. I wanted to get out of the stock in the worst way, and the infection in my foot was becoming serious. This became obvious even to Dipshit, who came in one day with Nursie and the female guard. Dark red streaks ran up my swollen thigh. I was passing through periods of high fever and delirium. He cleaned the foot and applied sulfa. Nursie thought this was inadequate and gave me a couple of shots. She probably saved my life. I remember grasping her hand and saying "Thank you" in Vietnamese. Her level gaze never wavered as she accepted the gesture as though it came from an elderly man.

Dipshit indicated that I should keep the foot dry, which was impossible if I were to continue to walk in the dirty water that covered the floor of the latrine.

The latrine also posed another problem. It was nothing more than five holes in concrete next to the shower. Roaches and huge spiders that I first thought were tarantulas crawled around the openings, and I was reluctant to use them. I did anyway, because using the honey bucket in my cell was even more onerous. It was too small for the American anatomy and the cell already smelled bad enough. The problem became an academic one soon enough. With exercise impossible, I became constipated.

I had finally got a thin bamboo mat to lie on, but I quickly sweated it through and it became smelly and vermin-filled. I was flat on my back almost twenty-four hours a day, still banging my sore foot on the stock and passing through periods of delirium. I was in a miserable state and decided to try to do something about it.

Before Guarino had been taken away, he had been released from irons. He had given a silly answer to some question after asking my permission. I decided on the same tactic even though it was a retreat from my rigid earlier attitude.

On August 8, my tenth day in the stock, Eagle asked me at a quiz how long it took to train a reserve Army division. I had no idea, of course.

"Oh, it takes a week, or a month, or a couple of years," I said. It was the first time I had answered a question with more than name, rank, serial number, and birth date, and the reaction was astounding. Eagle jumped up from his chair, a wide grin on his face. "Oh, Den*ton*, why didn't you tell us that long ago?!"

Owl also was delighted. He threw up his hands and said: "That's all we wanted to know!"

I couldn't believe my ears, but they immediately ordered me released from the stock. At the next quiz, I went back to no comment to their questions. They didn't seem to mind.

I was tremendously relieved, but in later years, that gambit would avail me nothing. There would come a day when the stock and that sweat-soaked, smelly bamboo mat would seem like my four-poster bed at home.

Through the hot, humid days of August, things began to settle down. There was a lot of activity in the prison as the flow of American airmen into captivity increased. We were now getting about ten a month, and I learned from a recent shootdown the reason for the increase.

Until the middle of April 1965, President Johnson had been planning each air strike from the Oval Office in the White House. But then came the

Dominican Republic crisis, during which we sent in troops, and the President was distracted. He never quite got back to personal supervision, and the military, convinced as it was of the importance of air raids on the North, slowly escalated the bombing.

One result was that I got a new neighbor in New Guy Village. Lieutenant Ed Davis arrived about the middle of August and was placed in Cell No. 2. We quickly established communications, and I learned from him that he had been married only nine days before being shot down.

CHAPTER SEVEN

There was no underestimating the effect of the Code of Conduct, both on our behavior and on the treatment we received in prison.

To understand what follows, you have to have some knowledge of the Code, which was issued as an executive order by President Eisenhower in August of 1955. It was an outgrowth of some unhappy experiences of a few prisoners of war in North Korea during the Korean War, but had its roots in the Geneva Conventions of 1949, international treaty agreements to which the United States and North Vietnam were signatories.

The Geneva Conventions were the culmination of efforts by many countries to establish principles for the treatment of prisoners of war, among other things. They recognized the change in status of a fighting man from someone who could kill or maim an opponent to noncombatant who had the right to decent treatment from his captors so long as he acted within certain guidelines. (Unfortunately, North Vietnam qualified its agreement and chose to evade the Conventions by declaring its prisoners war criminals, which meant in effect that they could treat us in any manner they wished.)

So, with the Geneva Conventions to guide the conduct of the captor—more or less—the U.S. established a Code of Conduct to determine the conduct of the prisoner. The wording of the Code is simple, although there is some confusion as to its legal status. It has none, generally speaking. It is a moral code or standard of conduct, and is not legally binding.

Even under the stresses of a Vietnam prison camp, the Code stood up well, although in practice there were some ambiguities.

Article One states: "I am an American fighting man. I serve in the forces which guard my country and our way of life. I am prepared to give my life in their defense."

An attached explanation states that it is the prisoner's duty to oppose the enemies of the United States regardless of the circumstances, whether in combat or a prisoner of war.

In other words, they had us, but they weren't going to enjoy it.

Article Two says: "I will never surrender of my own free will. If in command I will never surrender my men while they still have the means to resist."

"Means to resist" raised a serious question. If a pilot has ejected from his aircraft and finds himself surrounded on the ground by heavily armed soldiers, for example, should he literally commit suicide by charging at them?

(A study group formed to investigate the code after our return answered this particular question by noting that at some point resistance obviously becomes fanatical, and that suicidal stands are not required.)

Article Three states: "If I am captured I will continue to resist by all means available. I will make every effort to escape and aid others to escape. I will accept neither parole [freedom in exchange for an agreement not to bear arms against the captor nation] nor special favors from the enemy."

Many of the prisoners in North Vietnam hardly needed the Code's urging to escape. It was constantly on our minds. But this article was to become a major issue after 1971.

Article Four states: "If I become a prisoner of war, I will keep faith with my fellow prisoners. I will give no information nor take part in any action which might be harmful to my comrades. If I am senior I will take command. If not, I will obey the lawful orders of those appointed over me and will back them up in every way."

The explanation emphasizes strong leadership and notes that without it, discipline is impossible. And without discipline, survival may become difficult. It also says that responsibility of command *may not be evaded.*

Article Five was the most controversial article in the Code. It says: "When questioned, should I become a prisoner of war, I am bound to give only name, rank, service number, and date of birth [the Big Four]. I will evade answering further questions to the utmost of my ability. I will make no oral or written statements disloyal to my country and its allies or harmful to their cause."

The explanation notes that a prisoner, besides answering the Big Four questions, may also communicate with the enemy regarding his health or welfare, and on routine matters of camp administration. Oral or written confessions true or false, questionnaires, personal history statements, propaganda recordings and broadcasts, and self-criticism are forbidden.

The explanation also says that it is a violation of the Geneva Conventions to torture or otherwise abuse a prisoner to get information.

"If, however, a prisoner is subjected to such treatment, he will endeavor to avoid by every means the disclosure of any information, or the making of any statement...harmful to the United States or its allies."

Unfortunately, it didn't explain to us what we should do if we couldn't take it anymore. After you endeavor, what? And what does "evade to the utmost of my ability" mean? What should we do when our abilities run out?

Since the North Vietnamese were making up their rules as they went along, we had to make up ours. Eventually, we determined that we should resist until they broke us and, when we recovered, make them break us again.

After our return, a study group recognized the problem and noted that the Code provided no further guidance once the prisoner was broken. The study group recommended that our "bounce back" theory be adopted.

Article Six says: "I will never forget that I am an American fighting man, responsible for my actions, and dedicated to the principles which made my country free. I will trust in my God and in the United States of America."

No argument there.

I am proud to say that the great majority of American prisoners of war abided by the Code of Conduct to the best of their ability, even at times when probably no one would have known the difference.

Many took enormous physical and mental punishment to preserve their country's honor, and some died for it.

The Code was to take on great importance for me in October, when I was moved from the Hanoi Hilton to Cu Loc Detention Center—the Zoo.

In October on Watergate Lane the leaves on the sweet gum trees are just beginning to turn orange and red. It is usually muggy and warm, but a nice muggy-warm, the air a bit smoky, the mood indolent.

In October in Hanoi the wind begins to blow from the northeast, bringing with it the start of the dry season and chill that settles in and stays for months. The wind, light but insistent, slipped over the walls of Cu Loc Detention Center, and the chill air penetrated the cells. The prison—dubbed the Zoo because of the way the guards peered through the cell doors' tiny peepholes at the prisoners as though they were animals—was about two miles south of Hanoi. It had been a French movie colony, with a race track and swimming pool, among other things, and consisted of three or four buildings grouped together. Now it was surrounded by a large wall complete with guard towers and massive gates.

The windows had been bricked over behind the shutters. Most of the buildings had been subdivided into cells. The pool was being used to grow fish for the camp officials. The entire compound was overgrown with weeds, and piles of scattered refuse were crawling with rats. The prisoners had given each building a name and each cell a number to aid in communications.

I had been moved to the Zoo early in October along with several other prisoners as the Hilton became crowded with new shootdowns. At that stage, the North Vietnamese were deathly afraid of a rescue attempt by American forces, and even feared intervention by their own dissidents. Thus, the movement of prisoners entailed great precautions, and I was taken from the Hanoi Hilton blindfolded, the upper part of my body covered with a blanket. Guards armed with submachine guns preceded me to a jeep, where I was told to lie down on the floor for the brief journey.

Air Force Lieutenant Colonel Robinson Risner, who outranked me, was now senior at the Zoo. While the routine was little changed from the one at New Guy Village in the Hanoi Hilton, I didn't like the feel of the situation. Both sides, the prisoners and the North Vietnamese, appeared to be feeling their way toward new positions.

We were at a disadvantage because we were still a long way from a solid organization, and hadn't developed the ground rules that would serve us so well later on. At that point, however, many of us failed to realize how badly we would be mistreated.

The North Vietnamese were nervous about the war. The United States was obviously gearing up for a long struggle, pouring troops into South Vietnam and gradually accelerating the bombing of the North.

Our captors were also annoyed by our cocky attitude. They had thought we would be subservient; they were surprised by our aggressiveness. Some of the prisoners, for example, as they were being marched at the point of a bayonet to the latrine or elsewhere, would insult the guards.

I remember a prisoner one day turning to the small youth who guarded him and saying in a conversational tone: "You goddamn monkey, I wouldn't have you in my goddamn zoo." The guard, trudging along behind his charge with a huge rifle in his hands, said, "What? What?" It was probably the only English he knew.

We also communicated in the same manner as we had at the Hilton. One day Tschudy came past my cell and in a conversational tone said, "Hello, Sunday Puncher [the nickname of our squadron]. There's a note for you in the shower."

Unfortunately, some of the English-speaking guards eventually overheard the talk and put a stop to it.

My physical situation again was complicated by my foot, which had become infected for the third time. I had no bed. I was sleeping on a wooden pallet on the bare floor, and the roaches and spiders were playing tag across my body every night. Also, it was getting colder at sundown, and my thin pajamas afforded practically no protection.

Thus, I was not in the best physical shape when it came my turn to handle the latrine detail. There were now fifty-six prisoners at the Zoo, and every night except Sunday, each one placed his honey bucket outside his cell door. A prisoner from his cellblock would then consolidate them into three or four large buckets and take them to a central location on the edge of a large rocky field overgrown with weeds. Then one prisoner would have to carry the twenty or so buckets, two at a time, about fifty yards through the field to a large hole with a steep slope slippery with feces, where the buckets would be dumped.

My turn came at the height of my foot infection, when between periods of delirium, I noticed my foot increasingly covered with blood and pus. I had gone just a few yards into the field carrying the two heavy buckets when I stepped on a rock. My foot hurt badly, but I went on, slid down the slope, and emptied them. Angry as hell and almost out of my mind with pain, I limped back through the field with the two guards, "Gunga Din," a somewhat dull-witted character with a pistol on his hip, and "Teenager," who had a rifle. When I stepped on another rock near the edge of the field, I threw down the buckets and waved my hands.

"Fini, fini," I shouted at the guards. Gunga Din patted the pistol on his hip and pointed to the buckets.

"Bullshit!" I shouted. I hunched my shoulders and walked straight at Teenager, who was so surprised that he gave ground and then fell over backwards, his arms waving wildly and his rifle falling to the ground with a clatter.

Five or six prisoners were peeping out of their cells to see what all the noise was about and saw me turn my back on Gunga Din, who had drawn his pistol and stood there looking stunned. I walked about seventy-five yards to my cell and slammed the door behind me. About five minutes later I heard someone quietly lock my cell.

The next day I was brought before the camp commander called Dog, who said he had heard there had been some misunderstanding about the buckets. His manner was surprisingly mild, and there were actually some benefits from the incident. My foot was treated and the infection was cleared up. And I got a bed: my wooden pallet was placed on top of two wooden horses. My only regret was that someone else had to finish the job of carrying those goddamn buckets.

The reason I got off so lightly was that in the middle days of 1965 we were still in the "easy" period, and we were blessed by the fact that Dog was the closest thing to a gentleman I ever met in North Vietnam. In his early forties, Dog was handsome by any standards. He spoke English and French well, obviously had an excellent education, and, though cunning, was generally truthful. He was an excellent administrator, and he also had a droll side, which was very unusual for a Vietnamese.

Just before Christmas, he had a violin rendition of "Smoke Gets in Your Eyes" played over and over on the central loudspeaker. It was his way of reminding us that some of the POWs had been shot down in flames. Jerome Kern's music was just a warm-up for the main event, however. As I had guessed, the administration soon began using the loudspeaker for propaganda messages.

Many of the prisoners at the Zoo were in two-man cells, but I was still in solitary and communicating by tap code, notes, and occasionally voice with the others.

I worked for Risner by passing on new names and shootdown dates of other prisoners and by generally helping to strengthen the organization. From my corner cell in the building called the Office, I could whistle the name to Ed Davis, who was in a building we called the Barn in the cell next to Risner. And on Sundays I would shout out the Lord's Prayer at the top of my lungs after asking everyone in hearing distance to join in. In those days, the Vietnamese chose to oppose this only with threats, which I ignored.

But on October 24 everything began to go wrong. The North Vietnamese found contraband material in the cell of Colonel Risner, one of the toughest and most honorable men I've ever known, who at that time was constantly at work to improve our situation and harass the North Vietnamese. On that day, the guards found in Risner's cell an iron bar which he had been using to drill holes in the wall. They made a big deal of it and purged everyone's cell. I lost a bandage on which I had been writing, a list of POWs, and my stub of lead, but that was minor-league stuff. Risner was the one in the big leagues.

Unknown to me at the time, they moved Risner to the Hilton and began a torture routine that lasted for twenty-six days. They wanted a confession of some sort, but he resisted. Eventually, they got him to say something. One day much later, I was in the latrine and overheard them doctoring his tape prior to playing it on the radio in May of 1966.

They moved me into Risner's old cell in the Barn. My corner cell in the Office was left vacant, so the Barn lost communication with the Office and the rest of the camp. My new cell had a solid steel door, and beyond that, a solid wooden door.

While I was ignorant of Risner's ordeal, I was aware that something was going on. The guards were becoming meaner and the officers more wary and oppressive. I couldn't quite put my finger on it, but the atmosphere was changing for the worse.

Somewhere, a silent hand was tightening the screws.

CHAPTER EIGHT

November 1, 1965, just a few days after the Risner purge, became a landmark date for the prisoners at the Zoo. The North Vietnamese began to starve us.

Until then, the food had been good as prison food goes. Cabbage, greens or pumpkin, eight to twelve ounces of bread or a bowl of rice twice a day. Sometimes there was a side dish of chicken knuckles, and most delightful of all, we usually got one banana a day. Only recently, I had told a new arrival, Lieutenant (j.g.) Dave Wheat, who had also flown off the *Independence,* about the quality of food, remarking that on some days we actually got *two* bananas. Almost immediately, by coincidence, the Vietnamese cut out the bananas.

But that was only the beginning. Our rations at the Barn were cut to practically nothing, and the Vietnamese were no longer washing off the night soil, the human fertilizer they used on their crops.

On that first day, November 1, when I was led out to get my food, I found a bowl of soup sitting in the dirt instead of in its usual position on the door-step. It was cold and full of grit blown into it by the wind. And there were only two shriveled, thin pieces of cabbage in it. Floating in the water and sprinkled on the leaves were pieces of the "fertilizer."

At first, I carefully picked the solid pieces out of the soup before eating it. But with the cold days of November sapping my strength, and without enough food to sustain me, the day came when I just grabbed the bowl and gulped down whatever was in it.

WHEN HELL WAS IN SESSION

Shortly after capture, my weight had dropped from 167 pounds to about 140, and by the second week in November I was down to 120 pounds. What bothered me the most was the open-ended aspect. How long would it last? Would they really try to starve us to death?

As I shivered in my cell in the coldest November Hanoi had known in years, hope waned and depression threatened to take over. I prayed and worried about my comrades.

In about the third week of November, a large delegation of North Vietnamese politicians toured the camp. A big man in his middle forties, well dressed and well fed, entered my cell one cold day. He stood hands on hips, his small, hard eyes gleaming, and looked at me huddled forlornly in one corner.

"Well, Denton, do you know that you are eating shit?" he asked in English.

I didn't answer, and tried to give him a hard look back.

Obviously, I was already well marked as a troublemaker.

"So you want to continue eating shit?" he demanded.

Finally, I found the strength to pull myself laboriously to my feet.

"Well, I hope there is some protein in it," I said.

He was not pleased with the answer. He nodded smugly and said, "You should be reasonable, or you will continue to eat shit!" Then he abruptly turned and left.

While I merely was being starved, others at the Zoo were even worse off. The North Vietnamese were going back and forth between the junior and senior officers, applying pressure and trying to find out which would break the easiest. They were in the junior officer period in November, and Ed Davis, in the cell next to me, was being treated particularly roughly. Ensign Ralph Gaither was also under pressure.

Davis had been put in heavy leg irons and rear handcuffs because he refused to give the North Vietnamese biographical information. My food was sumptuous compared to what he was getting. For a couple of weeks in November he was receiving one small piece of bread a day and a cup of water. In the last week of the month, they cut out the bread, and Davis was down from 165 pounds to about 110.

I liked Davis. He had helped me during one of my periodic foot infections and was always cheerful and cooperative. He had been shot down in his Skyraider a few days after my capture and, as he later learned, was thought to have been killed. It was eleven months before his wife found out he was still alive.

A slender, fresh-faced person in his middle twenties, Davis reminded me of the typical all-American youngster. He had an excellent voice, and one day in September not long after his arrival in New Guy Village, I heard him singing "Fly Me to the Moon" in a low, resonant tone. The tender melody floating so gently through my dank cell seemed out of place, but it was welcome.

Now he was slumped in his cell slowly starving to death. The North Vietnamese not only wanted biographical material; they wanted him to sign a paper agreeing to follow all their orders. He continued to refuse and one cold night late in November, I heard two guards come into his cell. I put my ear to the wall. There was no conversation, just heavy grunting as they beat him with their fists. An occasional groan filtered through the wall. Then there was a steady "thump, thump." The guards had become more agitated and were beating his head against his wooden pallet. Then there was total silence, and in a minute or two, I heard the guards leave.

After a few minutes, I heard Davis scratching on the wall with a nail. The scrapes were painfully weak as he told me in Morse code what they had done. His arms were now bound from his shoulders to his elbows behind him, the ropes drawn as tightly as the guards had been able to pull them. Somehow he had found and grasped his nail, and now, with his back to the wall, he was scratching the message that the pain was unbearable in his shoulders and back.

There was a final word: "Agony." Then I heard his irons clanking as he writhed on the floor. He was losing control and screaming in pain.

Other nearby prisoners heard him too, and it was more than we could stand. We began beating on the thin metal doors to our cells with whatever we had handy, and after a while the guards came and took Davis away.

I was afraid that we would never see him again, but in about an hour he was back, painfully scratching on the floor near the wall. He told me they had taken the ropes off. He had given them a sketchy verbal biography. But they did not make him sign the paper agreeing to follow their orders.

The next day I could hear him sobbing, and I got on the wall and asked him how he felt.

"Commander," he scratched back, "I've been doing some soul-searching. If I had it to do over again, maybe I could have just held out five minutes more."

He was taken to another camp on December 4, and I didn't see him again for more than seven years.

The food improved dramatically early in December. Full portions of bread and rice returned, and they were now washing the feces off the cabbage and serving the soup hot! My mother frequently told me that the simple pleasures were best, but I had to go ten thousand miles to discover its truth. I can remember warm tears running down my cheeks the day I got my first hot food in more than a month. I tried to confess to my neighbor that I was crying for joy, but my tapping was interrupted by his own frantic knocking on the wall. He was confessing to me that he was crying for joy.

Later, I found out the reason for the change.

Secretary of State Dean Rusk had proposed a bombing pause, which had thrown our captors off balance. They thought it might be the prelude to peace talks, and perhaps our release. How many times in the ensuing years this was to happen! The course of the war always determined the nature of our treatment.

We drifted through the chilly days and cold nights of December toward Christmas, going through the daily routine: arise at 6; leave cell with guard to go to latrine; use shower; eat; pray; try to communicate; pray; eat; try to communicate. Finally, blessed sleep in the cold night.

Christmas was marked by a piece of turkey in addition to special food, and I was even given a second blanket. Until then, I had alternately slept and shivered throughout the night.

In January, with much fanfare from the prison administration, we received a medical examination. It was mostly a farce. I read the eye chart all wrong just to see what would happen, and when I had finished, the chubby little doctor said briskly, "That's fine," and made a mark on his notepad.

One of the doctors was curiously open with me. While I was alone with him, he confided in a roundabout way that the doctors in North Vietnam were underpaid and were not accorded the same respect he understood doctors received in other countries.

At one point he leaned over and whispered in my ear, "Do you like to play tennis?"

"Yes," I replied.

A childishly proud grin spread across his face, "Oh, I do too, and I'm quite good at it. I wish that we could play, Denton."

The outcome of the medical examination was as expected. A doctor told me the men weren't getting enough to eat and were suffering from malnutrition.

"No shit!" I said.

As we suspected and hoped, the medical exam was no more than a face-saving exercise to improve our diet. They pretended that the exam had led to the amazing discovery that we were undernourished and weren't holding our own. We got more bread and rice starting about the middle of January, and more protein. In my case, it was sufficient to prevent further loss of weight, but that was about all.

Still, it was an improvement. The torture and beatings abated, and the interrogations became less frequent. They still used threats to induce us to cooperate, but generally failed to carry through on them.

At one of my few quizzes in January, I was told by "JC," an officer, that I would be attending a press conference and that the guards would use the standard rope trick, the one they used on Ed Davis, to make me answer questions. Immediately I began preparing myself mentally to resist. Although I knew our captors had relaxed somewhat, the experience with Davis had taught me not to underestimate their capabilities.

On a chilly evening about the middle of the month, a jeep came for me and took me on a twenty-minute ride to a rather modern room that looked as if it had once been a film studio. Waiting for me were a number of officials seated around a long, green table, including "Dog," "Rabbit," and "Fox," plus a couple of officious-looking civilians.

I was supposed to snap to attention in recognition of the high rank and importance of the group, but I was more interested in establishing my own rank and importance as a U.S. naval officer. So I walked stiffly to a chair designated for me and, without looking at anyone directly, sat down. Someone turned my head to the side, and while I did my best to look defiant, they took a couple of snapshots and briefly ran a movie camera. I was bracing myself to refuse to answer their questions and accept the consequences when someone tapped me on the shoulder and said, "Okay, get up and leave. You are finished."

My sense of relief was immense.

- - - - -

Dean Rusk's bombing pause was just that, and when the bombing resumed in late January, so did the intensity of the interrogations. I was not being quizzed at all, but I was getting reports that some junior officers were being threatened for biographical information. I told one of these men by tapping not to give any information, and his quizzes stopped. I began to think the torture had been a brief experiment.

I was taking a hard line on the biographical material because, shortly after my transfer to the Zoo, I had been tricked into giving some information during a seemingly harmless conversation with Dog, who had asked me if I would like to write to my family.

I was too anxious, and did not think through all the dangers of the ensuing conversation. I knew Shumaker and some of the others had written home, and in the Navy survival school the instructors had said that this was permissible.

I thought Dog was making a sincere offer, and after a pause I said, "Yes, I would like to write home."

"Well," Dog said in his superior way, "I am not sure that I will allow you to write. You have a bad attitude. What special reason do you have for wanting to write? Only those with special reasons are allowed to write."

Dog was stalling, and I could sense a trap. But I fell right into it. "There is no special reason to write," I said, "but I have a wife and seven children and I want to tell them I am well." Dog said, "Ah, we respect a man with seven children." The discussion was terminated, and Dog left with a smug look on his face.

Later, from a new shootdown, I learned the awful truth. An announcement had been transmitted over the Hanoi radio that Tschudy and I had sent a joint message saying that we would be glad when the war was over so that I could get back to my seven children, and Tschudy to his seven-month-old baby. We had sent no such message, but we had each unwittingly given them a piece of information, and they had used it against us.

Beyond that, there was another reason for not giving biographical material, even false or harmless information: When you give a little, you begin to give yourself away. Thus, we had to resist at every step.

Although I had been starved, humiliated, left without medical care, and placed in irons, I wasn't quite prepared for what was to happen next. On February 7, after several increasingly unpleasant quizzes which Owl and Eagle said were unsatisfactory, I was taken to a building next to the swimming pool, which we called the Auditorium. It contained a movie projection room, a fairly large hall, and a punishment cell. Dog told me they were going to crack down on me because I had been organizing resistance and was refusing to cooperate.

"Your arrogant attitude is going to cause you a great deal of trouble, Denton," he said, and I took him seriously.

I was marched to the Auditorium and through a large, breezy hall. The sound of doors opening and closing rang hollowly as I hunched against the chill that was settling in my bones. Facing the unknown, I shuffled down the hallway toward a barred cell.

As we neared the cell, Dog asked me once more if I would write a biography. I refused. He looked at me as though I was the biggest fool in the world.

"There's nothing I can do then, Denton," he said, as two guards moved toward me. Dog turned and strode away. I felt a hard, rough hand on my shoulder as the door to the cell opened. I turned and looked at the larger of the two guards as I was pushed through the door into the small cell. It was the beginning of what was to be a long and unpleasant association with Smiley, a tough, efficient guardsman much feared by the prisoners.

As he pulled me into the dimly lighted cell, I noticed that several layers of bamboo mats and blankets covered the windows, and even the door was fixed so that virtually no crack of light could get through. I heard a clanking sound as Smiley prepared the irons, and while I stood motionless, he placed me in tight rear cuffs and large, heavy traveling irons.

The term "traveling irons" was a misnomer, an ironical term for iron ankle cuffs with a five-foot, cement-filled iron bar inserted through eyes and linking the cuffs together so that one could hardly walk. They were leftovers from the French, and much heavier than ones the North Vietnamese later used.

I assumed that the guards would leave me in the room until I had been sufficiently punished, so I looked around for a place to flop down.

Instead, Smiley asked me if I would write.

"No," I said.

He raised his arm suddenly, striking me flush in the face with his fist and knocking me down. As I looked up dazedly, he reached down, pulled me up, and hit me again several times, being careful not to strike me in the eyes or mouth. I reeled at each blow, knowing it was useless to duck. I felt sick at the stomach as the fleshy, smacking sounds reverberated off the ceiling. It was my first taste of real brutality, and I was stunned and angered. The flesh over my cheekbones swelled, and I bled from the nose, but when Smiley asked me to write something—anything—I again refused. He took me by the cuffs, dragged me into one corner, and threw me down. He turned off the light and left. I heard the key turn in the lock and I was alone in total darkness.

My first feeling was a sense of relief, but as I lay slumped in one corner of the cell, relief turned to amazement at their efficiency in shutting out all light. I couldn't see anything, and became disoriented.

As the hours passed, I moved about the room on my knees, looking for an opening. Only a tiny, pencil-sized beam of light filtered through a some-how overlooked crack near the bottom of the door. In the following days and nights, that tiny beam would become my friend, a link with the outside and a point of reference for my orientation. I could see it only when within a foot of it, but I visited it regularly and spoke to it as though it were a person.

Many hours after my guards left, the door opened and the husky figure of Smiley was outlined in the doorway. He walked over to my corner and kicked me, commanding me to rise. To ensure compliance, he pulled me to my feet and hit me several times with the back of his hand, starting a stream of blood down my face. As he dropped me back in the corner like an old rag, he indicated that I must rise whenever he entered.

Bound as I was, that was no easy matter. The next time Smiley entered, I began pushing myself against the wall until I was on my feet. He beat me anyway, slapping me hard across the face and hitting me in the stomach. He indicated that I should be on my feet whenever he entered, and since he was now returning at intervals of ten or fifteen minutes, I was constantly slipping to the floor for a brief minute or two before beginning my tortuous shinny up the wall. The rear cuffs bit sharply into my wrists each time I worked my shoulders upward on the wall, and despite the chill, I sweated heavily from the effort.

They brought me food twice a day, at which time the light would be switched on and one wrist released from the handcuff so I could eat. But after one meal, I started fasting except for water. I wanted to show them my determination to resist, and I wanted to lower the threshold at which I would pass out under torture.

Bodily functions also had become a serious problem. It took a great deal of effort for me to find the bucket in the darkness. The technique was to inch around the floor until I touched it with my head. Then, since my hands were cuffed behind me, I had to struggle to get my pajama bottoms down. If there was toilet paper, I could not find it. I was revolted by my own presence.

After what I judged to be four days and four nights of fasting and total darkness, I believed that I was beginning to lose my grip. I couldn't keep my mind occupied, and the deep, insidious cold had stiffened my body and penetrated my consciousness so thoroughly that on the few occasions when I could focus my mind, all I could do was mourn my condition. My wrists had become swollen, and in lucid moments I worried that I would lose my hands, which had been without feeling for days. There was plenty of pain in the rest of my body, however, especially in my shoulders and back.

On what I believed was the fourth night, Smiley checked my cuffs with his flashlight. He gave a little grunt and departed, somewhat hurriedly. In a few minutes, he was back with some tools. He switched on the light and looked at my wrists as three enlisted men entered the cell and stared curiously at me. Smiley was worried. My wrists were torn and bleeding, and so swollen that he couldn't contract the cuffs enough to disengage the ratchets and remove them. By squeezing very hard, he finally got one cuff off, but the other was buried deep in the pus-filled flesh. Smiley held the arm up in front of me, and the three enlisted men worked on the cuff.

JC, the duty officer, who was usually so mean, came bustling through the door, his face anguished. "Denton, I am sorry about this," he said in his high-pitched voice.

Smiley, very nervous, looked over his shoulder at JC and spoke sharply to him. JC backed away, and for the next three hours watched silently as the four men worked on the cuff. They finally got it off by removing the pin that held it together. I held my hands in front of me. The fingers were black and swollen to twice their normal size. Smiley threw the old cuffs out the door. While one of the enlisted men held my arms behind me, he snapped another pair on my wrists. Then he shoved me down in the corner. In a few moments I was alone and in total darkness again.

I had thought the cuffs would be my rescue, but as the hours dragged on, I knew that everything was as before. I began to hallucinate. Unfamiliar faces appeared and reappeared, floating along in the darkness and disappearing through the door. Strange noises came muffled out of the blankets draping the walls, and I dreamed constantly of an escape in which I crawled for miles until I was found and nursed back to health by an old Vietnamese woman.

In lucid moments, I sought a reservoir of strength. To justify the sacrifice, I built an image of my country and knew that it was the best in the world. Then I would ask myself: What difference does it make? Why not give in?

I prayed. God became more than faith. He became knowledge, and I appealed to him. Then I became ashamed. Why hadn't I embraced him so thoroughly before? I went back and forth from despair to euphoria as my strength ebbed. Isolation became total disorientation. I lost track of what I was, where I was. I was being reduced to the kernel of my being; beyond that I would lose control.

On the seventh day, a Sunday, in a momentary period of alertness, I decided to give them something. I cried for help. Finally, Smiley opened the door and switched on the light. I blinked and babbled hysterically that I had to get out. Dried blood streaked my chest. Feces clung to the bottoms of my pajamas, which were completely stained with urine. I had little left.

The next thing I remembered was Dog forcing a pen into my fist. Painfully, I wrote a biography. I wrote about every hotel I had ever lived in, and said they had all burned down. I gave the names of relatives, but no addresses, and tried to concoct a mixture of truth and fiction that would deliver me from that dark room.

It mattered little what I wrote, anyway. The Vietnamese wanted just enough to justify discontinuing the torture. Years later, an officer said that my bio was "very funny." It was not amusing to me then.

CHAPTER NINE

It was late February, 1966, seven months from my capture and a lifetime away from Watergate Lane. There was a freshness, and a promise in the air. In Virginia Beach the crocuses and daffodils would be in bloom.

In the Zoo I was to remain isolated in the punishment cell until my wounds had healed somewhat. The officials were showing my biography to the other prisoners and didn't want them to know that I had been tortured for it. The tactic didn't fool anyone, however.

As I recuperated, I searched for some answers—some reason for this long ordeal.

Strangely, despite the longing for my home and family, I felt stronger and more confident than before. Although I had been broken, and had written the much sought biography, the North Vietnamese had learned little from it. I could remember the lies as well as the truths and repeat what I had written if they came after me again.

And the ordeal had toughened my resolve to resist. My first thought, once released from the dark cell, was that I had gone the limit of my ability, and was ready to fight again.

How best to resist? I needed to build up my body, but there was the necessity of physical accommodation to my new life. It did no good to do push-ups, for instance: they only strengthened the shoulder and arm muscles, making the rear cuffs more painful. Finally, running in place proved to be the best form of exercise. It was one of the small lessons that makes such a large difference for a prisoner.

But mainly, I had to build a reservoir of psychological strength. Prayer and meditation were immediate answers, but I also needed the bread of a prisoner's life, communication. This was always extremely important to us, providing the comfort of friendship and information in our common misery. Each man's strength was reflected in another's, and together we knew that we could prevail.

We couldn't touch hands, nor could we "talk" in the normal sense. And sometimes, communication was like casting a bottled note in the sea and waiting while the response drifted back days later. But our little network bound us together in common cause, and gave us the power to resist beyond ordinary physical endurance. It was a tender bond of faith and love, and we saw for the first time the true fellowship of man.

Also becoming clear to me was the infinite difference between the heartless, mindless, and godless nature of the Democratic Republic of Vietnam and the United States of America. Despite our country's faults, we have prospered and grown under the system designed by wise men two hundred years ago. The system has survived and been strengthened through civil war, assassination, racial unrest, and a president's resignation, and has continued to bestow its benevolence on the world.

In the long prison years ahead, the difference between our country and theirs would become more manifest. I was to become more disgusted with their cruelty, not only toward the American prisoners but toward their own people as well. They never considered the question of individual rights, and indeed, the individual existed only as a slave, to serve the State.

Now, in late February of 1966, I paced the floor of my cell. Although I was isolated in confinement, I felt an intellectual freedom unparalleled in my experience and a deep nostalgia for my country and my past.

I thought fondly of the teachers who had supported me and given me a sense of my own values during my formative years: Brother Claver, Sister Mary Dorothy, Sister Benigna, Sister Mary Gerard, Sister Marcella, Brother Charles, Brother Gerald, Sister Carmella, and especially Sister Mary Josephine, who had first given me a sense of self-confidence.

It was after I had talked our entire eighth-grade class into playing hooky one day that Sister Mary Josephine had told me something about myself I hadn't realized.

"It takes leadership to do what you have done," she had said. "You have to use that ability carefully." As a naval officer, and as a prisoner in Hanoi, I remembered well her words and happily accepted all the responsibilities of leadership that came my way.

There were other scenes that kept running through my mind from those early days: the crucifix on the wall above the sister's desk; the American flag in the right-hand corner of the classroom; the teacher in her black Sisters of Mercy habit; well-scrubbed, earnest faces; hands over hearts; young, clear voices speaking in unison.

In the loneliness of the cell, with my past flooding over me, my lips began to move in concert with those young voices: "I pledge allegiance to the flag of the United States of America and to the Republic for which it stands, one Nation under God, indivisible, with Liberty and Justice for all."

It told me all I needed to know about our sacrifice.

The incident of the soap during my two weeks of recuperation in the punishment cell was revealing of the psychological pressures employed by the North Vietnamese.

Soap was much treasured by the prisoners. It was a tiny link to sanity and civilization. When in punishment status, as I was, we weren't permitted to keep soap in our cell. It was available in the shower, and it was customary for us to try to steal a small sliver for use in the cell.

So when Smiley took me to the shower one day, my mind was occupied with plans to steal and secrete a piece of soap. There was a chill in the March air as I walked painfully but eagerly to the shower room a few yards from the Auditorium. As Smiley watched, I stripped and stepped under the welcome trickle from the shower head, my eyes searching the floor for a piece of soap. There were several, but my chances of hiding a portion on my body were slim; Smiley knew exactly what I had in mind and watched me carefully, his arms folded across his chest, his thin lips set in a grim line.

But I was lucky. He was called outside, and my heart jumped. Quickly I snatched a tiny piece and hid it. Smiley was back in moments and, after a quick glance at my innocent face, ordered me to approach him. There are just so many places to conceal an object on a naked body, but Smiley checked them all thoroughly. The more he looked, the angrier he got. He knew I had taken some soap, and as he probed me roughly, his scowl deepened. But he couldn't find it. He ordered me to dress and marched me back to the cell, pushing and shoving me all the way.

As we went through the door, he spun me around and ordered me to bow. I dipped my head. He told me to bow again, with more feeling. As I bent my body, I saw his eyes widen. A deep, growling snarl filled the room.

The soap was on top of my head. Smiley snatched it with a pawlike hand and hit me flush in the face with his fist, sending me flying against the wall. Then he strode from the room, slamming the door behind him.

Shortly thereafter, I was moved back to the Pool Hall, which was about fifty yards from the Auditorium cell. I was put in Cell 6, and I immediately began to acquaint myself with my neighbors by wall-tapping and talking under the door.

When I arrived, directly behind me in the double row of cells which made up the Pool Hall were Bob Lilly, a helicopter rescue pilot, and his cell mate and former crewman, Sergeant Art Cormier. In Cell 2 was Air Force Lieutenant Colonel Fred Cherry. He was suffering from an extensive and painful wound in the upper part of his body, which was covered with a cast. Caring for him was his cell mate, Lieutenant (j.g.) Porter Halyburton. Cell 7 was empty, and Navy Lieutenant Richard Brunhaver was in Cell 8. Marine Captain Howie Dunn was in Cell 5. All this was important, even the empty cells, because they were intended to break the chain of our communication. And both the position and the quality of the men were vital.

For instance, Howie Dunn was a key man in the clearing system that had been devised because of his position at the corner of the Pool Hall. His signals warned us of the approach of the guards, and he also conducted communications with the Office. A lesser man couldn't have handled it.

Brunhaver, who had a lot of guts, was in the middle of the Pool Hall. His job was to shout messages to two nearby cellblocks, the Pigsty and the Stable. Without their courage and inventive genius, we might have been stymied. This lineup lasted a few weeks. Then there were many changes in rapid succession.

Slowly I began to gather information.

I learned that about seventy-five prisoners were scattered in the various cellblocks that had been named the Pigsty, the Stable, the Office, the Barn, the Pool Hall, the Garage, and the Gate. Most were two to a cell. A few, like myself, were in solitary.

Eventually, I would become the first military prisoner in North Vietnam to spend more than four years in solitary. Only five men were to achieve that unpleasant distinction.

I also discovered that while most were putting their lives on the line with bitter resistance, some had been giving written, unclassified military information and written biographical material without first submitting to torture. One officer had written about the F4, using material available in *Aviation Week* and *Space Technology* magazines. He had not been physically mistreated but had been much threatened, and didn't want to lose a limb.

I was shocked. The prisoners were floundering and searching for direction. Risner's transfer to the Hilton left me the senior in command. It was now my job, indeed my mandate, to provide leadership. Thus, I messaged: "I am the senior officer. I am sorry we lost Risner. I must try to take his place. We will die before we give them classified military information."

Brunhaver and Dunn, by shouting and tapping, passed the message, risking torture in order to help build the system of discipline we needed to survive.

"In the case of bio's, take all you can," I messaged. "When you think you have reached the limit of your endurance, give them harmless and inaccurate information that you can remember and repeat if tortured again.

"If communications are lost between buildings, the senior ranking officer of each isolated building must take charge. In any case, the senior man in any isolated group will take charge.

"All orders by the previous commander must be followed. The new man may make changes as the circumstances dictate, but always within the framework of the Code of Conduct."

Routine administrative questions concerning medical treatment, for instance, would be permitted in writing, I said. So the messages were tossed into the sea of despair. They drifted and bobbed, swirled and tossed in the current, sometimes changing in context and even in meaning as the word was passed—painfully, dangerously, and slowly—through the cells and cellblocks of the Zoo.

Abbreviations were essential to the communication system and had to be standardized to avoid ambiguities. A typical text would be: GM LGUZ 12IN PS ALRDY HIT F BIO X5 NOW GETG THRTS F BIO X PB LTR FM HOMEX LL FOX IS NEW XOX NEW NAME LCDR RENDER CRAYTON NO OTH INFO X PB Q W SPOT SOS.

Translation: Good Morning. Larry Guarino says 12 men in the Pigsty have already been tortured for biographies. Five men are now being threatened with torture if they don't write bio's. Phil Butler got letter from home. Looks like Fox is the new executive officer of the camp. A new validated prisoner name is Lieutenant Commander Render Crayton. We have no other information on him. Phil Butler and Bob Peel had quizzes with Spot—same old shit.

And bobbing back came the answers.

Brunhaver, after two days of dangerous communication with the Pigsty, had to tell me: "Commander, the Pigsty is bogged down in argument over interpretation of your orders on writing. They recommend you give them a yes or no on writing."

"No" was the only answer I could give. Give them nothing. And they gave them nothing, until they were tortured beyond their ability to resist. Only then did they give them so much as a crumb and virtually nothing of value.

It was incredible to the North Vietnamese that people so completely under their control would flatly refuse to cooperate. Their game plan had to change. They knew that communications were at the heart of the resistance. They would try to end the resistance by breaking the chain of communications. Then they would stalk their prey, the leadership, and exorcise and punish it. They would try to sweep together the remains and dominate it.

Fox, the camp commander who was believed to be a former combat soldier, was highly intelligent and excellent at countermeasures. We, from behind our cell doors, and he, from behind a desk in the administration building a hundred yards from the Pool Hall, dueled silently but unceasingly.

The louvered doors in the cells made conversation between prisoners fairly easy, so Fox installed thick, solid doors. The windows had already been bricked up.

We increased our tapping, and because there were no peepholes in the doors, the guards would have to open the doors to catch us tapping out our codes. Fox installed peepholes covered by sliding panels, and punished anyone caught communicating. We had been using the two central shower rooms for notedrops; Fox countered by having wells provided for each cell block.

It was a murmurous struggle; we, passing our messages and organizing our resistance; they, watching warily, figuring countermoves, stalking the leadership. To an outside observer, everything would have appeared routine: the prisoners going about their pitiful business, the North Vietnamese standing guard.

But underneath, there was the desperate battle. In truth, hell was in session.

CHAPTER TEN

Despite the efforts of Fox to foil us, the communications network operated very well through most of April 1966.

Any man who went to an interrogation would send me a complete report so that we could keep abreast of what the North Vietnamese were after, and thus prepare ourselves for our turn.

A typical quiz went like this:

NV: How are you?

American: I am terrible. I want the rights provided by the Geneva Convention. I need medical attention for my festering wounds. I want to associate with my fellow prisoners. I want time outside to exercise. [The American would recite as much of the "bitch list" as his questioner would permit.]

NV: Shut mouth! You are not prisoner of war! You are criminal! If you want better treatment, you must show good att-i-tude. You show good att-i-tude, you will get better treatment. If you are reasonable, you get roommate. In meantime, we treat you like criminal.

Did you know that this week, the People's Air Defense Forces shot down on the spot twenty-nine American aggressor aircraft? [The propaganda about North Vietnamese victories would go on and on. Only the figures changed from quiz to quiz.] Do you know our people will never give up? Now I want you to write something. Here is pen and ink and paper. Write names of some of your squadron mates.

American: I will not write.

NV: [Screaming] You *will* write! If you do not write you will be punish! Here [rattling some papers], here are writings from many of your fellows who have good att-i-tude.

American: If anyone wrote, I know you forced him to write, and...

NV: Shut mouth! Go back to your room and think deeply about your crimes. Think about how you get better treatment if you change your att-i-tude.

A report to me on this type of quiz would say: SOS (same old shit). Or, if the North Vietnamese had demanded a bio from the American for the first time, the report would say: "Quiz with Dog: threats for bio." If, after a series of such quizzes, the Vietnamese had threatened punishment that very night, the report would say: "Quiz with Dog: last chance on bio." If the prisoner continued to refuse, he was soon removed from his cell and tortured.

I also received reports on men who were sick, or who had wounds that were giving them trouble, as well as any medical treatment that was received. But medical treatment was rare.

News from recent shootdowns was quickly transmitted and eagerly received. Usually, news on the progress of the war was accompanied by cheery estimates on how the fighting was going in the South and a prediction as to when the war would end. Frequently, the new shootdown would say peace would come in about six months. If the estimate was higher, the first man to hear it would try to talk the shootdown into lowering it.

Aside from strengthening our morale and preparing us for quizzes, the communications network told us who was in trouble. Sometimes we could do something about it, as in the remarkable case of Bob Purcell, a handsome, good-natured Air Force major from Kentucky.

Purcell was in Cell 1 of the Pool Room, the only cell with a ceiling door to an attic which covered most of the cells in the Pool Room. The North

Vietnamese hadn't bothered to nail it shut because it was so high, but Purcell, using his spare pajamas and a nail, had fashioned a ladder of sorts, and was regularly climbing into the attic to assist in communications.

Through the network one day, we heard that Captain Bob Jeffrey in Cell 8 was being starved for his biography. Purcell, at great risk, opened a small hole in the ceiling of Jeffrey's cell and began lowering on a string food saved from his own ration.

Purcell also opened a hole around the base of the light suspended from the ceiling in my cell so that I was able to pass food to him for Jeffrey, including pieces of bread and bananas. I have two sharp recollections of the affair; Purcell's grinning face pressed against the hole, and the day that he almost got caught.

All the nearby prisoners knew that Purcell was in the attic over Jeffrey's cell, lowering food down to him, when we heard a guard trying to slide open the heavy, rusty bolt on the door to Purcell's door. We began clattering and banging around, trying to make enough noise to cover Purcell's return to his cell while Purcell bounded and hopped across the rafters. He literally dove through the opening to his cell, crashing to his wooden bunk with a terrible noise, and we were afraid that if the fall didn't take care of him, the guard would. But by the time the guard got the door open, Purcell was calmly sitting on his bunk. He told the guard he had fallen while exercising. Had he been caught, he would have been accused of attempting to escape, with fearful consequences.

It was about this time, while I was still in solitary in the Pool Hall, that I was taken to a quiz and handed a letter from my wife by JC. He told me that I would not be able to read Jane's letter unless I wrote something for him.

I refused.

JC argued and shouted at me.

"You are a stubborn fool, Denton," he raged. "For so little you can get so much. Write!"

Again I refused, and JC threw down the letter and stalked out of the room.

Eagerly I read the letter, a long one, which sustained me for weeks. Later we would get only six lines per letter on a standard form. But every word was treasured.

About half an hour later, JC returned and again asked me to write something.

"Do what I ask and I will let you reply," he said.

I told him I wasn't interested in replying, but I would, as the senior American officer at the Zoo, write to the camp commander and complain about the treatment the prisoners were receiving. JC looked a little bewildered. I think he thought I was bluffing. Shrugging, he gave me a pencil and piece of paper and left the room.

I picked up the pencil eagerly; the mere act of writing somehow relieved the frustration of months of brutal treatment. I said I was writing on behalf of the U.S. government and used my rank in an official heading. (Use of rank was strictly forbidden by the North Vietnamese.) I protested the inhuman treatment of the men, and said that the entire world would be appalled and shocked when it learned the details. I wrote that I had been in solitary confinement for nine months, and it was too much for a man's mind to accept without damage. I signed it with a flourish and presented it to JC when he returned.

He tore it up. He said I would never be allowed to write home. Writing home would soon become the least of my worries as the North Vietnamese reacted to an intensification of U.S. bombing.

On April 2, 1966, John A. McCone, director of the Central Intelligence Agency, sent a memorandum to the White House, questioning the value of limited air strikes. American planes were forbidden to approach within 35 miles of Hanoi, and McCone argued that instead of hampering the North Vietnamese war, such strikes had merely "hardened their attitude." According to accounts that I read after my release from prison, McCone had urged heavier attacks.

"...It is my judgment that if we are to change the mission of the ground forces [from defensive operations to offensive ones] we must also change the ground rules of the air strikes against North Vietnam. We must hit them harder, more frequently, and inflict greater damage," McCone had written.

Many high-ranking military officers and all the prisoners of war I ever knew strongly agreed that a key to eventual victory was heavy air strikes. (The prisoners would learn firsthand the traumatic effect of heavy bombing on the North Vietnamese when the B52 raids began later in the war.)

A few days after McCone's memo a presidential order (perhaps unrelated) was circulated through the top ranks of the administration. It read, in part: "We should continue to vary the types of targets, stepping up attacks on lines communications in the near future, and possibly moving to attack... on the rail lines north and northeast of Hanoi."

The change in strategy was soon to be brought directly to our attention at the Zoo. On the morning of April 17 we heard a distant thundering. It rumbled and rolled fitfully and unevenly through the warm air, as though a spring thunderstorm was making its way ponderously toward us. It was coming from the guns of the multi-ringed air defenses of Hanoi as a flight of U.S. aircraft zipped in at low level toward the city.

Soon there was another sound—the sound of running feet passing the Pool Room. The wretched prisoners pressed against the doors, to peek beneath them or, if lucky, through a crack.

WHEN HELL WAS IN SESSION

Lieutenant (j.g.) Rod Knutson, now in Cell 1, could see clearly through a crack in his door, and he later described the scene to us. It was as chaotic as a Chinese fire drill, he said, and told how Monk, a good-natured but overly neat guard, had scampered past, his precious pistol wrapped in a handkerchief so it wouldn't get dirty.

Officers and enlisted men alike ran for the protection of the shelters while the prisoners cheered and clapped.

The target was about a mile and a half away. We could judge that the planes, which some could see, had hit an oil dump, because of a huge column of smoke which towered into the sky.

When the raid, which lasted only a few minutes, was over, the city's air raid sirens finally sounded. We laughed like hell, but our euphoria was short-lived. The Vietnamese, frightened and angered by the bombing, turned on us, their most vulnerable opponents, with even more vigor.

On April 20, I again refused to write. Dog accused me of "inciting others to resist" and said that I would be sent back to Hoa Lo (the Hilton), where I would be tortured until I confessed my crimes.

In half an hour, I was on my way back to the Hanoi Hilton. I had barely enough time to pass the word about my destination and the reason for my move. Although I wasn't thirsty, I drank all the water in my jug. I didn't expect to get food or water for a long time. I also learned, just before I left, the grim news that Risner had been tortured for a confession at the Hilton.

Upon arriving at the Hilton, I was turned over to a guard that I hadn't seen before. His nickname, I learned later, was Pigeye. He was a cold, bloodless professional, a master torturer who knew all the ways to apply painful techniques. He was considered an expert, and all the prisoners came to fear him.

Pigeye was a senior enlisted man in his early thirties. He spoke and wrote Chinese and spoke some English. He had probably been educated in China. His angular face was marked by high cheekbones, but its dominant feature was a thin, hard mouth that could only be described as cruel in the most classic sense.

He immediately took me to the Knobby Room, a twenty-by-twenty-foot cell that got its name from the knobs of concrete on the walls which helped to soundproof it. There was a desk on one side of the room and two ordinary, four-legged stools on the other side. I watched as he placed one stool on top of the other. He assisted me to a sitting position on the top stool, cuffed my hands tightly behind me, and left the room. I was in a precarious position, five feet above the cement floor, with no way to break my fall if I should topple off.

Pigeye had been brisk and emotionless in his actions. I knew the North Vietnamese were not fooling around. They intended to break me for a confession. I settled down for a long wait, blinking up occasionally at the single bare lightbulb that Pigeye had left burning, but mostly just sitting there staring straight ahead. I was prepared to wait them out.

It soon became apparent that they were trying to starve a confession from me. For three days and nights I went without food or water. I sat on the stools, shifting my position carefully from time to time to ease the strain on my back and shoulder muscles, praying hard.

At one point I simply had to urinate, and I carefully toppled the stools so that I could land on my feet. I opened the peep hole in the door with my nose, stood on top of the stool, and urinated through the hole. Fortunately, there was no guard around, but, unfortunately, I couldn't arrange the stools so I could get back on them. I deliberately scraped my cheek on the wall and then lay on the floor in a heap, pretending I'd fallen asleep and dropped off the stools. When Pigeye came to check on me, he let my presence on the floor pass, although he must have been suspicious of the puddle outside the door. He sat me back on the stools.

I began hallucinating during the second night. At times the knobs on the walls became faces, sometimes devils, sometimes angels. The devils would come screaming and taunting; the angels would be singing and playing their harps. My only firm and constant thought was that I would die of starvation before I would write a confession.

On the third evening, Rabbit came into the room. Rabbit was a young officer, his most memorable feature being rather prominent front teeth. He was intelligent and spoke good English. He was proud of being a party member, and if one appealed to his ego, he could sometimes be drawn into revealing more than he should. He used the standard alternating good-guy, bad-guy technique. That evening he was being the good guy. He said he thought that torture was the wrong way and had tried to alter the approach.

"But I tell you man to man, Denton," he said. "They are going to torture you tomorrow if you do not write a confession. I know you will not give in to starvation. I have told them that. They will hurt you very badly. Maybe they will kill you," he said.

I said that I would not write anything.

Rabbit argued at length with me. "Denton, my government will probably not even use the confession. Maybe no one will ever read it. My government knows that it is humiliating for you to write a confession, even if the confession is forced, and not credible. They hope the suffering will cause you to act more reasonable, but they will probably not publicize your confession. You have everything to gain and nothing to lose if you write. Your treatment will greatly improve; you will even get a roommate. Aren't you lonely after ten months alone?"

I told him again that I would not write.

He sighed and shrugged his shoulders. "We will allow you to rest some time tonight. You have until morning to change your mind," he said, and left.

I concluded that he was trying to provide me with a face-saving way to give in early during the torture the next day, by consoling myself that I had done enough in withstanding the starvation treatment. He succeeded only in increasing my resolve.

That night I was taken to Cell 1 in New Guy Village, where Pigeye placed my arms in two stocks suspended between bunks in such a position that I could neither stand nor kneel. After several hours, Rabbit came back with a guard, who took me out of the stocks and told me to lie down on one of the bunks and sleep. I was also given four crackers and some tea, but they failed to whet my appetite, as the Vietnamese apparently had hoped.

At some point, I discovered that Jim Stockdale was a couple of cells away and called out to him. I had nothing to lose. I talked openly to Stockdale and told him what had been going on at the Zoo. I gave him a message for Jane in case he got home. I wanted her to get married again. My love for her was so great that I could even love the man she married.

I explained to Stockdale that Catholics believed that martyrs go straight to heaven and I hoped God would consider my death a martyrdom because I would be killed by an atheistic government which was trying to force me to renounce my God-fearing government. I was convinced that the next day would be my last on earth, and I felt no bitterness. God had given me a full life.

The next morning, the ominous figure of Pigeye appeared in my cell door. He was accompanied by two guards. He asked me if I had changed my mind. I told him no. Without further conversation, I was pulled from my cell and taken to Room 18, also known as the Meathook Room. Pigeye and one of the other guards grasped me, handcuffed my hands behind me, and then, grunting and swearing, began beating me severely. I tried to keep my feet and appear impassive as their fists thumped into my body and face, but it was impossible. I reeled about the cell and fell down repeatedly. They kept pulling me to my feet and hitting me, but this kind of punishment always angered more than intimidated me. Bloody nose, cut lips, blackened eyes, bruised ribs: the standard preliminary before the main event.

Then there was a welcome pause. Sitting on the floor, I shook my head and focused my eyes. There was a thin rope in Pigeye's hands, and I felt something like relief. I was ready to lose my arms rather than shed my honor, and I wanted to get it over with. He pulled my shirt sleeves down to protect my arms from scars (at that point, they were still hoping to keep the tortures secret so they could say our writings were voluntary), and then he and another guard began roping one arm from shoulder to elbow. With each loop, one guard would put his foot on my arm and pull, another guard joining him in the effort to draw the rope as tightly as their combined strengths would permit. The other arm was then bound, and both were tied together so closely that the elbows touched.

The first pains were from the terrible pinching of the flesh. After about ten minutes, an agonizing pain began to flow through the arms and shoulders as my heart struggled to pump blood through the strangled veins. After about forty-five minutes, the pain began to subside and I began to go numb. I was too weak to sit up, and when I fell backward, the weight of my body spread my fingers so grotesquely that two of them were dislocated.

Pigeye was watching me closely. He rolled me over and loosened the ropes. The blood flowed back into my arms and brought with it terrible pain. He didn't want me to lose consciousness, and the pain kept me lucid.

Pigeye had begun to lose his celebrated composure by now. His face was animated and covered with sweat, and he was apparently afraid I would outlast them and beat them out of their confession. They had cuffed a cement-filled nine-foot-long iron bar across my ankles, and Pigeye released the bar from the shackles and laid it across my shins. He stood on it, and he and the other guard took turns jumping up and down, and rolling it across my legs. Then they lifted my arms behind my back by the cuffs, raising the top part of my body off the floor and dragging me around and around. This went on for hours.

They were in a frenzy, alternating the treatment to increase the pain until I was unable to control myself. I began crying hysterically, blood and tears mingling and running down my cheeks. I feigned unconsciousness several times, but Pigeye was too much of an expert for that. He merely lifted the lids over my eyes and grinned.

Finally, I had nothing left. My only thought was a desire to be free of pain. I tried to shout but I could only whisper, "Bao cao, bao cao," the words for surrender. The last thing I remembered before passing out was the smile on Pigeye's face as he continued to roll the bar across my legs.

When I awakened, I was sitting naked on the floor in an unfamiliar shower room, a guard propping me up while Pigeye watched. Cold water mixed with blood as it ran down the drain. Pigeye said, "Wash," and he and the other guard left me sitting there rolling on the floor in the water and blood. As I slapped limply at my swollen wrists, trying to restore the circulation, I heard a voice say, "Hey, ol' buddy, what's your name?"

My voice was practically gone, and I couldn't be heard over the sound of the shower. I struggled to my knees and managed to turn it off with my elbow. I said as loud as I could, "I'm Denton."

"Jeremiah Denton?"

I said yes.

"God bless you, Jeremiah Denton. You did a wonderful job at the Zoo."

He identified himself as Robbie Risner and told me I was in the shower at Heartbreak Hotel. He was in a cell across the hall.

I said something to the effect that I wasn't doing a very good job now.

"You are only human," he said.

The guards were coming back, and we stopped talking. Pigeye and the other guard, Pimples, took me back to Room 18, where an official, Mickey Mouse, was waiting behind a desk. They sat me on a stool and I fell off. They propped me against the wall. Mickey Mouse told me to rest for a while. Mickey Mouse put a pen in my hand. I couldn't hold it. They gave me something hot to drink and tried to get me to tape. My voice was too weak and they gave up. Mickey Mouse told me to rest for a while.

I woke up on the floor with Pigeye standing over me, a rope in his hand. I was propped up again and Mickey Mouse tried to put a pen in my hand. Then they saw that one finger on each hand was dislocated and they popped them back in. I didn't feel a thing. They closed the fingers of my right hand around the pen and Mickey Mouse told me to write. He dictated some phrases about aggression and bombing. I tried to write, and thought I did, but I learned the next day that I was only making rough spirals on the paper.

They kept gesturing and threatening me with the rope, and I managed to say something into a tape recorder about "heinous crimes...Yankee imperialists...aggressors..." They told me this was not good enough and I must rest some more.

The next thing I knew I was waking up in Cell 1 of New Guy Village. When I could talk, I tried to raise Stockdale, but it was Risner who answered, he and Stockdale having switched cells. I told him what I had done, and he tried to comfort me. But I was numb. Just numb.

They came for me the next day and I saw the spirals I had made. By holding the pen like a dagger, I wrote the same words that I had spoken into the tape recorder. They wanted me to tape again, but my voice was too weak. They gave me coffee laced with liquor and tried again. This time my voice was stronger and they settled for it. Then they returned me to my cell, and I slept for a long time.

CHAPTER ELEVEN

Cat was the officer in charge of the entire North Vietnamese torture program. He was aloof from camp administration and military routine. His job was to subdue us and, failing that, to exploit us. He was vain and egotistical, and the sight of him strutting around the various camps in uniform or in his stylish civilian clothing was enough to bring murder to a prisoner's eyes. He bragged frequently of having had extensive experience with French POWs, and was probably personally responsible for some deaths.

Cat was a slender man in his middle forties. He spoke English and French well, but with a less cultured accent than Dog. He was highly intelligent, literate, and well read. He knew the party line and followed it. A sinister but somewhat handsome face was accentuated by a merciless nature. He loved his work, in contrast to many other North Vietnamese who loathed the torture or simply closed their eyes to it. He and Pigeye were a great team. One day his overconfidence would do him in, but that wonderful moment was far in the future.

As soon as my mind began to clear after the April 20-23 torture period, Mickey Mouse kept me up three nights in a row indoctrinating me with the "truth" about the war. His efforts were childish, and would have been funny had they come under other circumstances. I couldn't understand why he was wasting his time, but Cat soon gave me the reason and it horrified me.

"Denton, you are going to meet with some members of the press," Cat said one day early in May.

"Use your head, Denton," he warned. "This interview is very important. Be polite and do what you are told. Remember what punishment you have received in the past. I need not say more." I knew what he meant, and I wasn't ready to challenge him yet. "I'll be polite, but that's all," I said.

Cat had a great deal at stake, obviously. Many others would be watching my performance, and if I didn't behave, Cat's reputation would suffer.

I still hadn't recovered from the horrible experience in the Meathook Room, and I was trying to muster the strength to take more torture rather than attend the press conference. On the night before the interview, I managed to communicate with Robbie Risner in the nearest occupied cell. I asked his opinion of my alternatives.

He said he found it difficult to advise me, and when I reassured him that I was willing to accept more torture, he said he thought it probably wouldn't help. He recommended that I go to the conference and try to render it harmless, then take the consequences. He said he would be praying for me.

"I'll go," I told him, "and blow it wide open."

The next day, I was handcuffed, and blindfolded, and taken in a Jeep on a ten-minute drive to what looked like a gentlemen's club. There were rugs, inlaid stone floors, and expensive looking furniture. Pigeye was by my side, a rope in his hand, glaring at me. They put me in what had once been a women's powder room. Pigeye handed me a bottle of beer, but I poured it away when no one was looking. I wanted the beer, but I needed all the presence of mind I could muster.

After what seemed like an endless wait, Pigeye took me onto a veranda and pushed me through some French doors into a large room. I blinked against the glare of a battery of floodlights and looked into the heavy face of a Japanese reporter, who grinned at me from behind a huge pair of horn-rimmed glasses and then motioned me to a chair in front of a table filled with sweets.

There was a scraping and a slight murmur as the audience, a group of North Vietnamese officers and civilians, pulled their chairs forward. I saw Cat, Mickey Mouse, and Rabbit, among others, and they were all trying to look pleased and threatening at the same time. The reporter gestured at the table and asked me to smile, but I just stared at him. My plan was to look as distraught as possible. I also was going to answer his questions in a manner opposite to what the North Vietnamese wanted, but I had a feeling it would fail. They would dub the words, or find some way to fake the whole thing. And I was terribly afraid of the torture certain to follow. I decided to be polite and wait for an opening.

The reporter asked some routine questions about my background and then launched into a diatribe about the bombing. I didn't listen to what he was saying. I gazed dully around the room as though in a daze. The blinding floodlights made me blink, and I suddenly realized that they were playing right into my hands.

I felt my heart pounding; sweat popped out on my forehead; the palms of my hands became slippery. I looked directly into the camera and blinked my eyes once, slowly, then three more times, slowly. A dash, and three more dashes. A quick blink, slow blink, quick blink.

T...O...R...

A slow blink...pause; two quick ones and a slow one; quick, slow, quick; quick.

T...O...R...T...U...R...E...

While the Japanese droned on in a high-pitched voice, I blinked out the desperate message over and over.

TORTURE...TORTURE...

A change in the inflection of his voice warned me that he was asking an important question. I asked him to repeat it.

"Denton, what is your feeling toward your government's action?"

I licked my lips and thought my answer over carefully.

"I don't know what is going on in the war now because the only sources I have access to are North Vietnam radio, magazines, and newspapers, but whatever the position of my government is, I agree with it, I support it, and I will support it as long as I live." It was his turn to blink.

There was a faint, uncomfortable stirring in the room as the audience leaned forward, not sure of what I had said. Instinct, and the tone of my voice, had told them something had gone wrong, but they couldn't quite figure out what.

The reporter cleared his throat. The smile, which I thought had been glued on, left his face.

"What was that you said?"

"Whatever the position of my government is, I support it. I'm a member of that government, and it is my job to support it, and I will as long as I live."

The reporter cleared his throat again and glanced around nervously.

"Thank you," he said, and I was dismissed.

I arose stiffly from the chair, and Pigeye led me back to the powder room. He had no idea that anything had gone awry. This time the wait was much longer. The Vietnamese were briefing my next interviewer on me.

When I reentered the room a chubby man and a plump woman were sitting on a large sofa. The man introduced himself as Wilfred Burchett, an Australian journalist. The woman, a Russian, was introduced to me as Mrs. Burchett, but she wore no ring. The two of them had been conversing in Russian when I walked in, and I understood enough of the language to know she asked one of the officers how long I had been in prison.

As I later learned, Burchett was an itinerant writer who scavenged about Communist countries looking for stories he could sell to Red newspapers and magazines. While Mrs. Burchett looked at me engagingly, Burchett entered into an exchange with me about the war. Bolstered by the success of the previous interview, I ignored my North Vietnamese listeners while defending the United States against Burchett's clever and well-schooled arguments. We dueled for perhaps a half-hour before I was taken back to the Hilton.

Burchett seemed to be somewhat surprised at my knowledge and background in international relations and lost his cool toward the end of the conversation when I implied that he was a cheap traitor who knew in his heart that he was prostituting his talents for money in a cause that he knew was false.

Rabbit came into my cell the following day, the transcript of the press conference in his hands.

"Denton," he said, shuffling through the papers, "you are not being polite when you imply our media lie."

I mumbled something about that being the case, and refused Rabbit's request that I change a couple of my statements.

"Denton, you are going to be sorry," he warned as he left.

I reflected on the TV performance and wondered why the roof hadn't fallen in on me. I concluded that my captors hadn't caught on yet. Perhaps they were taken off guard; under the circumstances, they could not have expected me to do what I had done.

I assumed that the North Vietnamese would refuse to let the film leave the country. Astoundingly, as I learned years later, the tape got to Japan with only a few minor cuts. The only explanation I can offer is that the North Vietnamese would have lost too much face if they had refused to give the material to the reporter, especially as it was given in such a thoroughly controlled atmosphere. The reporter made out pretty well. His videotape was bought by a U.S. network and received wide circulation. Eventually, this information would get back to the Vietnamese and I would pay in blood for it.

But it was worth it. Naval intelligence had picked up my torture signals. It was the first clear message U.S. intelligence had received that we were being tortured. The North Vietnamese probably learned of the signals for the first time on the day in November of 1974 that I received the Navy Cross for the blinks.

The ax still hadn't fallen two days after my brash performance, and I was told I would be interviewed again. I was appalled that my previous behavior had not dissuaded them from another interview, so this time I would make sure.

The interviewer was another rotund writer, this one from Chile. I gave him short shrift. He asked me if I had any message and I said, "God's will will be done."

Then I got up, without permission, and walked from the room. The North Vietnamese let it, too, pass for the moment.

Apparently, it took them a few days to study the transcripts and my behavior and decide on a course of action. Their opportunity came when I was caught talking through a window at Heartbreak Hotel to Air Force Major Sam Johnson. They could have caught most of us talking at any time, but they wanted to use the communications charge as justification for what they were going to do next.

Cat, Rabbit, and Mickey Mouse came to my cell shortly after I had been caught talking. They were beside themselves with anger and embarrassment.

"Denton," Mickey Mouse said in a voice trembling with rage, "you have committed many crimes. You will be punished." He put me in handcuffs and jumbo traveling irons, then threw me in a corner and left. This was no big deal. I was elated that this was apparently all they were going to do, and as I sat in the corner staring at my hands, which were cuffed in front of me, I considered how I would convince them that this punishment was enough.

I could hear Pigeye arguing with Mickey Mouse that I should be treated more severely, and when I heard Pigeye returning, I spat on my hands and rubbed the spit on my forehead. I hoped he would take the spit for perspiration and believe that I was suffering. I even threw in a few moans.

Unfortunately, I thought to add a little more spit to my forehead, and Pigeye caught me at it. I looked up just in time to see his face reflected in a partially open, swinging glass window and saw his expression change. He strode into the room, grasped me by the cuffs, and pulled me to my feet. He was holding a three-sided ruler in his hand, and he lashed out suddenly and struck me in the face with it. Then, very deliberately, he jabbed me in the kidneys and worked my face over with the ruler for five minutes or more until my lips, nose, and the area above my eyes were bloodied. He sat me on a stool and shackled one ankle to the end of the traveling iron. With the help of two other guards, he crossed my legs and shackled the second ankle to the bar in an exercise that took more than twenty minutes. Then they cuffed my left wrist to the bar. It is one of the worst forms of torture. There is no way to describe the excruciating pain in the ankle area without experiencing the rig.

I writhed and groaned on top of the stool throughout the long night. I said the rosary over and over again, slowly for the first few hours but faster and faster as the pain intensified. In the early morning hours, I prayed that I could keep my sanity until they released me. I couldn't even give in to their demands, because there were none. It was pure revenge.

After an eternity, Mickey Mouse appeared with Pigeye at the door and the two of them sat down while a guard released the handcuff from the bar. Mickey Mouse shouted at me to walk to the desk where he was sitting. This was too much even for Pigeye. Looking at me huddled and helpless on the floor, Pigeye told Mickey Mouse that I couldn't walk—even a fool could see that. Mickey Mouse blinked at his subordinate and told me I would have to give him a statement in writing. I agreed.

He had me copy a statement which said that I had many times led pilots to bomb the churches and schools of North Vietnam. He also made a long speech about how I had always refused to answer a military question. Now, he said, I must write a paper on the command and control of an aircraft carrier.

I had no resistance left, and had to agree. I would write a paper full of ridiculous information. I figured they would accept anything, and during the next three days I wrote thirty-six pages of the silliest nonsense I could think of. I was right. They never asked me about the paper after I turned it in, nor did they ever torture me for military information. Also, they never invited me to another press interview.

On June 2, I was taken back to the Zoo. The following day, JC told me that I would have to read the news over the camp radio. I refused, and JC told me I would again be tortured. He left me in the Quiz Room to "think deeply," and I broke down and wept in fear, anger, and exhaustion.

But after several hours alone, I was taken back to my cell.

Just a few days after my press conference with the Japanese reporter, millions of people in the United States were watching it in their living rooms.

It was May 10, 1966, Mother's Day. Watching with Jane were my father; stepmother; Bill Sallada and Bill Bowers, who were on the flight when I was shot down and who had performed so bravely over the Ma River on my behalf; their wives, Betsy and Kay; my children; and Jane Tschudy. A friend had called Jane the morning before to tell her that I had been interviewed and that she thought the tape of the interview would be shown on television. Jane called some Navy officials and they found out that ABC had bought the tape and would show it the next evening. Other networks would show excerpts.

Everyone was struck immediately by my haggard appearance and the tense way I sat on the edge of the chair, hands clenched between my knees.

Jane wondered about the way I looked at the camera and blinked my eyes, over and over.

"What is wrong with him?" she murmured to my father.

As she recounted to me many years later, my voice was low except for when I told the interviewer that I supported my government in whatever it undertook. She knew instantly that I had planned the statement and she worried at the price I would have to pay for making it. She spent a sleepless night, tortured by those twin devils, fear and uncertainty, reflecting on a face and a voice that had come to her suddenly out of a void and had just as quickly vanished.

It had been a difficult year for Jane. Her concern for my welfare was relieved somewhat by the duties of a mother with seven children, and she spent some time working on our house on Watergate Lane, which we had moved into shortly before my shootdown. At that point, she and Jane Tschudy were almost the only ones in the area with POW husbands, and the two women formed a deep and lasting relationship.

She also kept in touch with Navy and State Department officials in Washington on my status, but those offices knew little more than she did. For the moment, she and the other wives were leaving the fate of the prisoners in the hands of the Vietnamese and the United States governments. U.S. policy was to keep silent on the subject. The reasoning behind this policy was outlined more or less in a letter sent to Senator John Sparkman of Alabama by Vice-Admiral A. McB. Jackson, Deputy Chief of Naval Operations.

Admiral Jackson assured the senator that all efforts had been made "to effect the release of captured personnel through the American Red Cross, the International Committee of the Red Cross, and sympathetic third countries."

Then followed a paragraph which discussed the U.S. policy of silence concerning prisoners of war in North Vietnamese and Viet Cong hands.

"While of course the U.S. government and the Navy are not insensitive to the plight of prisoners of the Communist regimes or to the worry it brings their loved ones, it must be recognized that to the degree this is built up as a public issue, it imposes a higher price for the release and safe return of such prisoners."

This policy would change radically in 1969, and the change eventually would have an immensely beneficial effect on our condition.

Despite a rather remarkable document that Jane had received from the Navy, and a long letter she had received from me in February, in which I said I was being treated well, she knew instinctively that the prisoners were being tortured.

The document, which implied humane treatment for the POWs, was obtained from a Viet Cong file in the lower Mekong Delta region by the South Vietnamese national police and was billed as a Viet Cong training paper relating to the understanding and treatment of American prisoners. It was translated into English, poor grammar and all, and sent to the United States. Captioned "Experiences on American Soldiers' Psychology," it read in part:

> *American soldiers have been deceived twice presumably Korea and Vietnam by the American Bourgeois class, so they have a deep illusion with the capitalist democratic systems and their doctrines...*
>
> *Proud of being the citizens of the strongest and wealthiest nation, they are hard to be awakened and join the class revolution.*
>
> *They are highly depraved, they are subject to be selfish, enjoy the unhealthy fun, sexual pleasures, and crimes.*
>
> *The most suffering things they consider are: far from families and*

wives and loved ones; they often hope to get back home before Christmas or birthdays; they like colorful pictures.

American soldiers are fairly well educated; officers and older soldiers travel many places so they appear well-mannered. Most of them are enthusiastic Protestants or Roman Catholics, Christmas and Pentecost mean a lot of importance to them all.

American Imperialists win their loyalty by material means: high pay, high life, encourage sexual fun, etc. Also, by reactionary political indoctrination such as learning military tradition stories, blind patriotism, believing God, slander Communist doctrines.

They never leak out military secrecy, nor confess their criminal deeds, report their personal records; they also refuse to sign peace-appealing documents.

Our common policy toward the POW is clement, release them after good treatment and handling.

As for those officers and important men, we should try to keep them. Should treat them and provide them with rations better than Vietnamese POW; fully utilize them in the international propaganda....

Tell them to write their families and how they were treated by the revolutionary forces. Contents of their letters should acknowledge the righteous cause of our revolution...

All comrades are advised to inform on the experiences on handling, indoctrinating, releasing and utilizing the POW and provide us with stuff that are useful for propaganda.

The document was dated July 2, 1963, a little more than two years before I was shot down. When I read the document years later, I was struck by the rather wistful tone, particularly where it states how the loyalties of American soldiers are won by material means. In the seven years and eight months

I spent as a prisoner, I never met a North Vietnamese who I didn't believe would trade his system for ours.

Early in 1966, the war was escalating in several directions. The carriers *Kitty Hawk* and *Enterprise* were now at Yankee Station, their planes striking targets at Vinh, Thanh Hoa, Nam Dinh, and the railyards near Haiphong, the port that served Hanoi. While heavy fighting continued in the Central Highlands, despite monsoon weather, South Vietnamese troops revolted against Premier Nguyen Cao Ky and some seized control of the air field at Hue.

As the North Vietnamese told us over and over on the camp radio, Ky was having trouble with Buddhist insurgents and sent troops to Da Nang to crack down on them. The United States announced that it had lost 243 planes over North Vietnam since February of 1965, but the North Vietnamese, of course, said that this figure was far too low.

There were hints of future action in statements by the U.S. leadership. Admiral David L. McDonald, Chief of Naval Operations, wanted to mine the Haiphong harbor, an action that President Nixon would take in 1972, and the Navy said it was considering reactivating a battleship for use off Vietnam. Eventually, the battleship *New Jersey* was taken out of mothballs and sent to Indochina for a few months.

And as the war continued in Vietnam, life went on in the United States. Cleveland was leading the American League by three and a half games in the middle of May, and San Francisco was ahead by two games in the National League. Muhammad Ali was in training for his second fight with Henry Cooper in London. The second Super Bowl would be played the following January. There was a slump in auto sales, and Senator Barry Goldwater said Richard Nixon was the logical choice for the Republicans in 1968. There was a peace march in Washington on May 16, and when some in the crowd waved Viet Cong flags, they were attacked by two youths wearing swastika armbands.

Air Force Lieutenant Colonel Thomas P. Stafford and Navy Lieutenant Commander Eugene A. Cernan were preparing for the flight of Gemini 9, which would involve a two-and-a-half-hour space walk by Cernan, and Luci Johnson was preparing for her August marriage to Pat Nugent.

Hogan's Heroes and *The Man from UNCLE* were the latest TV hits.

It was announced that Ho Chi Minh was seventy-six on May 20.

All this was unknown to me, except for Ho's birthday, which was celebrated by the guards.

On May 12, two days after Jane had seen me on television, she received a letter from President Johnson:

I wish to share with you and your seven children sincere pride in the courageous statement made by Commander Denton of support for the United States and for our policy in Vietnam. It has given me renewed strength.

Jane and the President could only guess at the price.

CHAPTER TWELVE

June 1966 began quietly enough by prison camp standards, but there was a strange and ominous mood at the Zoo, a feeling that a purge was coming. How soon, or what form it would take, no one could guess. But it soon became apparent that the North Vietnamese were stepping up the pressure for information. From their radio we learned that men shot down in the morning near Hanoi were giving their confessions in the afternoon.

One POW tapped out a complaint to me about the fast service the North Vietnamese were getting from some of the airmen. He hadn't been tortured yet, and I told him to give the airmen the benefit of the doubt. He might find that he, too, had a limit, though I said I hoped not.

A few days later, he tapped out to me: "Sir, I have an apology to make..."

They had got to him and made him confess in less than a day. They were now in a hurry.

They were also escalating the stakes in the carrot-stick technique, telling us that under certain circumstances those who cooperated would be allowed to go home. Those who did not might face war crimes trials, with death or postwar incarceration as possible punishment. They began a major camp radio buildup on the theme that we would soon be required to choose between the "good path" and the "bad path."

At first, this simplistic approach didn't bother me. I thought it went without saying that no one would accept their "deal," but their determination caused us some problems as their campaign developed.

One of the prisoners they started with was Fred Cherry, still suffering terribly from wounds he received when he was shot down. He was singled out because he was black. They raged at him about how he should despise his white oppressors, and they gave him promises of early release if he would cooperate. They left his door open and gave him orange juice and coffee so we would think he was cooperating. His cell mate, Porter Halyburton, tapped to me that Fred thought they were going to frame him and send him home early, as if he had cooperated with them. It worried him so much that he couldn't sleep at night. I tapped to Halyburton that Cherry shouldn't worry. If he was framed, we would clear his name when we returned home. Eventually, however, they gave up on him.

An announcement over the camp radio that there was a Buddhist revolt in South Vietnam caused some problems. Some airmen began arguing politics, and I was afraid this would develop into a running battle and damage morale, I passed the word that an enemy prison camp was no place to criticize national policy, and the arguments ceased.

Upon my return to the Zoo on June 2, I had asked the prisoners to pray that Jim Stockdale, who was under constant pressure at the Hilton, be returned soon to the Zoo, where the demands on him would be less concentrated. On June 4, Stockdale came to the Zoo and was placed in the Garage. He was senior to me, but couldn't exercise command over the camp because there were two Thais in an intervening cell who couldn't speak English, and a link with him couldn't be established. Later, however, the Thais would be of great help to us.

Meanwhile, I retained command of the Zoo, and it was a difficult responsibility. Crisis was routine. There was always someone in trouble from his wounds, the starvation diet, illness, or torture. I was helpless to aid anyone. All I could offer was sympathy, which, in our condition, had some value, but not much. I had long since learned that whatever I demanded, the

Vietnamese would do exactly the opposite with a "Who do you think you are?" attitude. This was often accompanied by a beating to emphasize their point. Personal disaster hung over my head continually. It was now certain torture if we were caught communicating. But, like most of the others, I was at it constantly, trying to bolster morale.

I learned that two officers, who had been tortured to the point of unconsciousness at the Hilton and were now cell mates at the Zoo, were advising new shootdowns to give in quickly, that there was no point in resisting.

I passed the word to them: "We must all lie down in front of the train and slow it down. We must do our best each time we are tested. That is the only way to defeat their aims." I asked the officers to countermand their orders and tell everyone to resist. They apologized and passed the word.

The North Vietnamese could break anyone into giving them something, and some of the men were in deep despair because they had been unmercifully tortured into giving biographies and confessions. I passed the word for them to get themselves together. "The line is, if you are broken, don't despair. Bounce back as soon as you can to the hard line."

Bounce back—it became our way of life.

I also received a question on bowing, one of the basic requirements. (The North Vietnamese had "taught" one prisoner to bow by tying a rope around his neck and yanking on it repeatedly until he got the message.) I messaged, "If they don't have you bagged, don't bow." But I had to admit to them that I was bowing (I was trying to save my energy for more important resistance) and couldn't condemn others for doing so.

You could get away with a slight bow of the head, depending on the mood of the guards, but some of the prisoners were so beaten down that they routinely bowed from the waist. There were some, however, who accompanied the bow by spitting, or an obscene gesture. This usually earned a punch in the jaw at the very least.

There were about seventy-five prisoners of war at the Zoo at any given time, but it was difficult for me to keep up with them because the Vietnamese were constantly moving them around, between cells, and from camp to camp. Some men were less able to endure torture than others and were more timid at communicating, but no one was really collaborating, despite much torture and many tricks.

For instance, a guard would come to my cell and start to hand me a bowl of meat. As I would reach for it eagerly, he would pull it away suddenly and say, "Sorry. Mistake." Then he would pretend to deliver it to another cell. But I was still recovering from the damage they had inflicted on me in May, and on the whole I was left pretty much alone. I couldn't carry the honey buckets except by slinging them across my forearms, and my hands were so crippled that one day, when I was told to wash my blue cotton sweatshirt, I couldn't do it. The guard hit me, but when I continued to stand there helplessly, he washed the shirt himself.

One day they came to me with thirty-two military questions which were very specific and intelligently phrased. I had taken a course in the Russian language at the Naval Academy, and judging from the sentence construction, I was certain the questions had been written by a Russian.

Shumaker and I were taken to separate quiz rooms, where he managed to tap a question: "What are you going to do?"

I tapped back that I wasn't going to answer the questions. I would rather go back in irons.

"You'll have company," he responded.

The two of us just sat there for three days, staring at the pen and paper on a table. Each night we would be taken back to our cells, the paper still blank.

On one of those days in the quiz room, Smiley came in with a light-bulb in his hand. The light in the ceiling was burned out, and an administrative inspection crew was coming. Smiley pulled a stool under the light and climbed up, but he was too short to reach the bulb. He was quite upset and looked around nervously, almost frantically, for a way to change the bulb.

Finally, I stuck out my hand and indicated to him that he should give me the bulb. He looked at me suspiciously and hesitated, but when he heard footsteps coming toward the room, he gave me the bulb. I climbed on the stool and put it in.

Smiley, who was always very impersonal toward the prisioners, looked at me strangely for a few seconds, took the burned-out bulb from me and walked from the room.

Meanwhile, the questions went unanswered, and after three days, Shumaker and I were returned to our cells. While I wasn't being tortured, others were, and a growing list of taped confessions was being played over the camp radio. I well knew the cost in blood. With these confessions and the constant warnings, they were actually fueling our resolve to resist. One night, they rather stupidly made a hero out of me.

Rabbit came on the camp radio with much fanfare and said: "Attention, all criminals. You know how diehard and obstinating Jeremiah Denton is. Well, we have succeeded in forcing him to confess his crimes. Those of you who remain obstinating will be forced into the same disgrace."

Then my faltering, weak voice came through the loudspeaker as I read the confession which had been extorted from me, and Hanoi Hanna, the English-speaking propagandist of Radio Hanoi, said smoothly: "That was the voice of American war criminal Colonel Jeremiah Denton."

Shortly thereafter I received a message from the Pool Hall. "We want to express our admiration for the man who is keeping his cool under this kind of pressure. We are proud to serve under your leadership," it said. It was one of the happiest moments of my life.

The wave was cresting over a camp under seige. Tired, frightened men peered through tiny cracks with bloodshot eyes, looking for signs of the Apocalypse.

It came on July 6, 1966. The North Vietnamese, enraged and frightened by increased bombing, began torturing wholesale and at a frenzied pace.

I had been in solitary for nearly a year. In that time, I had got fleeting glimpses of maybe a half-dozen Americans: Bob Shumaker, Bob Peel, Larry Guarino, Ed Davis, Phil Butler, and one or two others. Now I would see more than I wanted, under the circumstances.

July 6 was hot from the beginning. Humid air lay like a wet blanket over Hanoi, heavy, depressing, deadening. I flopped listlessly in Cell 1 of the Pool Hall, until about four o'clock, when I heard sounds of increased activity.

Instinctively, I disliked it. Any change in routine usually meant trouble. There was some nervous tapping between cells as the prisoners began to sense the different atmosphere. Even the guards, making their rounds, were more tense and curt than usual.

As darkness fell, Smiley came to my cell, flung open the door, blindfolded me, and took me to a quiz room filled with other prisoners. I was handcuffed to another American, and suddenly I was wild with joy. Gently, I pressed my knee against his, tapping out my name. Back came an answer. "Peel." Air Force Lieutenant Bob Peel had lived in a cell next to mine briefly in the Pool Hall and now lived in the Pigsty.

The prisoners, handcuffed together two by two, were put in the back of trucks, where we communicated by tapping on the knee of the man next to us. There were sixteen men in my truck, and as we moved ponderously through the streets of Hanoi, I got all their names.

After about a half-hour, the convoy stopped in an alley off a main square, where we were unloaded and our blindfolds removed. As I blinked against the glare of headlights in the growing darkness, guards with pistols crowded around while JC and Mickey Mouse told us that the people of North Vietnam wanted to demonstrate their anger towards us. They warned that if we communicated or otherwise misbehaved, we would be killed.

As other trucks were unloaded, I counted about forty Americans lined up in handcuffed pairs. In front of me was one of several trucks loaded with news correspondents, still cameras, and movie cameras. As we moved off, I gave the victory sign in front of one of the movie cameras.

The heat swept off the black asphalt in waves as our ragged group started down the street between two columns of people. At first, the crowd was sparse, well dressed, and relatively quiet, obviously high-ranking party officials. As the crowd got thicker and louder, a guard shouted: "Bow your heads!"

The words shot through me like a streak of lightning.

I shouted: "You are Americans! Keep your heads up!"

As my command rippled through the ranks, the guards prodded us with bayonets to get us to bow. Then they used their rifle butts, without success. As we trudged down a broad avenue, the crowd became nasty and threatening, and the guards, now troubled, became too preoccupied with crowd control to bother with our lack of bowing.

A middle-aged woman stood with a basket of rocks, and as I passed, she fell in behind and made me her special target. Four or five egg-sized rocks whizzed past before one struck me squarely in the back of the head. I fell flat on the ground, dragging Bob Peel down with me. I shook my head, and with Peel's help got to my feet in time for a Vietnamese man, perhaps eight inches shorter than I, to dart out of the crowd and deliver a sharp left hook to my groin. I was engulfed by nausea as the man ran back into the crowd, my curses for his cowardly act following him.

People now filled the broad sidewalks and spilled into the streets, striking at us with their fists. We began to stagger and fall from the immense strain and the blows as the protective cordon of guards broke down.

Out of the corner of my eye, I could see the man who had attacked me running through the crowd. He found an opening and came at me, his face twisted with rage, his fists clenched. I tried to dodge, but he got me again in the groin and knocked me down.

When I got up, I looked into Peel's bloody face and said: "He's not going to get me again!"

And right there, in the middle of that frenzied, murderous crowd, Peel and I practiced coordinating his left arm with my right, which were handcuffed together. At the count of one, we stook a stance. At "two," I threw a left jab. At "three" we swung an uppercut together with our manacled hands. Spot, our officer-escort, saw us swing and understood what we were up to. I shouted to him, "If that son of a bitch comes out again, I'm going to kill him."

He hesitated for a moment, and I could see the look of indecision in his eyes. It could have been the difference between life and death for us. But Spot saw the danger, and as the man came toward us again, he grabbed him by the shirt, shook him hard, pistol-whipped him across the face, and threw him back in the crowd. That was the end of my personal assailant, but the danger had not passed.

The crowd was now flailing us from both sides, and the guards were fighting a losing battle. The prisoners, some crawling on their hands and knees, were kicking and punching their way through the mob. We turned left at some point, and above a solid wall of howling people, the lights of a soccer stadium shone eerily through the muggy air.

The only thing that saved us was the stadium gates. We fought our way through the final thirty yards, using elbows, knees, and cuffs as weapons, until the guards pushed us through and closed the gates against the mob, now wild with rage because its prey had escaped. This was not the way the North Vietnamese had planned it. The Hanoi March had gotten out of hand.

While the bloody prisoners flopped exhausted on the cinder track bordering the field, the guards smiled and jabbered among themselves, relieved that it was over. For a while they didn't even try to stop us from talking. That respite soon ended, however, and on the return trip in the truck, we were blindfolded and guarded closely again.

Back at the Zoo, JC, upset and excited by my behavior during the march, slugged me while I was still blindfolded and cuffed to Peel. Then I was returned to my cell. But in a few minutes an officer came to my cell, told me to drink some water, and turned me over to a guard who took me outside to the Office end of the compound. He blindfolded and gagged me with two filthy rags which had been used to bind my sandals during the march. He then pulled my arms behind me around a tree and handcuffed them.

From various sounds, I guessed that I was one of several men bound to trees. The guards began drifting away, and I tried to take my mind off my predicament. My wrists and back ached, my groin was sore, and blood continued to run from various cuts on my body. Grit from the rag filled my mouth. I thought: Well, here I am, a sinful man tied to a tree by savage enemies, like the thieves tied to the cross next to Jesus.

"Lord," I prayed, "forgive me."

I found that despite the gag, I could make a muffled coughing sound. I coughed twice, five times, paused, then once, then four times. My initials, JD.

I was a little shaken when the coughs coming back identified the man on my left as "JC," but before I got carried away I realized with a smile it wasn't Jesus Christ but Jerry Coffee.

After several hours, I heard the sounds of men being removed from the trees and taken away. Now, at last, this horrible affair would be over. I had to lean against the tree for support as a guard removed the cuffs, gag, and blindfold. But instead of being returned to my cell, I was taken at bayonet point directly to a quiz room, where Fox and JC were sitting behind a long desk. I was prepared for the worst, but to my surprise JC summoned a guard to wipe my face, which was covered with blood, grime, and sweat. The guard blinked, as though he couldn't believe what he had heard, and gave my face a cursory swipe.

JC told him to do a better job, and this time the guard wiped my face carefully. Then JC told him to leave the room. The guard went and stood outside by the door. Fox leaned over and whispered to JC, who went to the door and told the guard to go across the road. This byplay was unprecedented, and my hopes picked up sharply. JC sat down and acted as an interpreter for Fox, who knew little English. Fox wanted to know what I thought of the march.

My eyes widened, and I felt the adrenaline begin to flow. Suddenly all the emotion pent up by a year's imprisonment and brutal treatment erupted.

"You fools!" I half-shouted. "It's the biggest mistake you've made. Parading prisoners in the streets is a return to barbaric times. I have nothing but contempt for your utter cowardice. The spectacle of helpless prisoners being paraded through the streets will bring a wave of criticism from the world."

The words came tumbling out. I paused from time to time to give JC the chance to translate. Ordinarily, such talk would bring a punch and a "shut mouth," but not this time.

Finally I stopped, and JC asked respectfully if I was finished. I said I was.

Then Fox said through JC: "I have something to say to you and I request that you remember it for a long time. These words are important. Do you understand?"

I said I did.

"The march was not the idea of the Army of Vietnam. The march was the idea of the people," Fox continued. Again he asked me if I understood, and repeated the whole thing twice.

I understood perfectly. He was trying to tell me that the Communist party had ordered the march and that the army didn't agree with it.

It was, I later deduced, a manifestation of a deep split between the army and the party. The army was concerned that the United States would send paratroopers into North Vietnam and was trying to protect itself against being tried for war crimes should the country be conquered. Such was the North Vietnamese state of mind in 1966 as U.S. troops and equipment began to pour into the South. I believe it would have taken only an extra push by the U.S. to have ended the war right then.

CHAPTER THIRTEEN

Through the month of July 1966 the North Vietnamese stepped up their "make your choice" policy, promising good treatment and early release on the one hand, or more torture and the possibility of a war crimes trial on the other.

Inevitably came the questions from the prisioners. What should they do on the choice? Suppose they were tried. How should they handle it? I passed the word that they should either make no choice at all, or simply say that they would continue to observe the Code of Conduct, regardless of the consequences.

They also continued their campaign against our communications system. About the middle of the month we were kept in our cells on some pretense for a couple of days. When I was finally allowed out to take a bath, I came around a corner and nearly ran into a bamboo fence that hadn't been there before.

I gasped audibly and my shoulders sagged. I heard a snicker behind me and turned to see Fox, who had been waiting to watch my reaction. He was not disappointed.

The fence was a severe blow to our system, making overt communication between buildings too risky considering the consequences of being caught. However, the Vietnamese outsmarted themselves by moving the prisoners frequently from one building to another, allowing us to maintain contact of a sort.

On July 20, the first anniversary of my arrival in Hanoi, I was placed in rear cuffs and stocks for five days. They were trying to soften me up so that I would make a "good" choice.

During the long, hot, helpless days in cuffs and stocks, when l could only twitch the flies and mosquitoes off my body, I occupied my mind with thoughts of the past. I closed my mind to the frequent blare of the loudspeaker in my cell, and tried to ignore my personal discomfort. I was convinced it would be a long contest, and I searched for sustenance. Thus, my thoughts turned to Ed Overton.

Overton was my coach at McGill Institute in Mobile. As my athletic mentor, he naturally had my special attention, and he taught me many lessons. One was especially pertinent to my present predicament.

During the big game of the football season in my senior year, I played my best at quarterback, but we lost. I came out of the contest physically and psychologically exhausted. My mouth was busted up; one tooth was knocked out; the bridge of my nose was cut and bleeding. Overton paid me a tribute at our first practice after the game when he told the team: "Denton rose to the occasion. He has that in him. If all of you had played like he did, we would have won."

Then I remembered another speech Overton had made at the start of the season: "To be a champion, you have to pay the price every minute, day in and day out."

I had not paid the price in extra training, extra study, or extra effort to deserve being called a champion. Athletics wasn't that high on my list of values.

But now, in a filthy cell in North Vietnam, the recollection of Overton's "pay the price" reminded me that this was a deadly game, and that the stakes involved the values that were highest on my list. I realized that I had to pay the price, day in and day out.

In the months to come, most of the American captives learned how to play the game. They understood the price and paid it. They were prisoners under barbaric conditions, but they had their own spirit, and they prevailed. In an important sense, their captors became their prisoners.

Clausewitz, the Prussian military strategist, wrote in the nineteenth century: "It is not the loss in men, horses, and guns, but in order, courage, confidence, cohesion and plan...It is principally the moral forces which decide here."

My principal battle with the North Vietnamese was a moral one, and prayer was my prime source of strength.

Another source was my country; no sacrifice was too great on her behalf. The nation is only as strong as the collective strength of its individuals. National interests, objectives, policies, and commitments depend on adherence to the nation's principles. Founded on faith in God, the United States has been blessed as no other nation. The main tenet of that faith is "Love God; love thy neighbor as thyself." Because of our faith, we have managed to cooperate effectively to achieve great prosperity and security. While prosperity and security are not everything, they are evidence that "A good tree shall bring forth good fruit."

Although the United States has never been the richest in natural resources, or the most populous country, it has produced for its people, and for much of the rest of the world, a bounteous harvest—both materially and morally.

Democracy and freedom are rarities; hard to attain, harder to preserve. The pages of history are littered with freedom's stillborn, people who rose against their oppressor, only to have sweet victory stolen from their grasp by another oppressor.

But we are different. The strength of our nation is more than a material strength. We are a strongly moral people, and our country is based on spiritual strength. Lose that and we lose everything.

The Declaration of Independence has established certain moral confines, and governs in a manner consistent with the spirit under which our nation was founded: Love God; love thy neighbor as thyself.

God is denied by the Communists, and this denial is reflected by the way they treat their own subjects. Their system derives its strength from discipline imposed by the State. Ours derives its strength from the collective self-discipline of our individual citizens.

Such thoughts would carry me through the night, until I heard in the predawn distance the rattling sound of the Hanoi streetcars beginning their first circuit. Then my thoughts would again turn to surviving another day.

- - - - -

The North Vietnamese wanted me to rewrite my confession and put it into a special form which they had devised. I refused, and after I was caught communicating again, a guard came to my cell and pointed to his wrists, then made a circular motion with his hands. He wanted me to put on my long-sleeved shirt and roll up my gear. This always meant a move and, for me at this time, almost certainly more punishment.

Fox told me I must stop inciting others to resist, and I was taken to my old punishment cell in the Auditorium, where I was placed in rear cuffs and traveling irons for the night. Then I was taken to the Gate, a building that had been used as a supply room and was now divided into three cells and a couple of utility rooms. In the cell to my left was Air Force Captain John Borling. Beyond him was Air Force Captain Darrell Pyle.

My cell was large, about twenty-five feet by fifteen feet, but that was about all you could say for it. There was no ventilation, and the early August sun turned it into a steam oven. We were required to remain in full dress, which meant underwear and pajamas which were too light for winter and too heavy for summer. Eventually our bodies became covered with boils. There were no amenities, nothing to sleep on, and worst of all, no mosquito netting. We were in rear cuffs, with ropes around our ankles.

I passed to Borling and Pyle a technique, which I had learned from Ed Davis, of removing the cuffs with a nail. They used the method effectively to free their hands when the guards were away. Ironically, I was unable to find the right-sized nail to open my cuffs. Within a few days, however, I invented a different method of opening the cuffs. Unfortunately, I was caught clicking the cuffs back on one day, and the guards soon procured a heavier type of cuffs, made in China, from which no one could escape.

After about three weeks, I was taken back to the Auditorium. My arms were tied tightly behind me, but not so tightly that the circulation was cut off. The guards had become masters at rope tying; that is, they knew how to produce constant pain without causing permanent damage. But I had also learned a few tricks, including a method of undoing the ropes and then re-tying them when the guards approached. This usually worked well, and I could achieve a brief respite, especially during the night. But there was no predicting my captors.

One night there was a heavy thunderstorm, and at about three o'clock in the morning, I decided it was safe to undo the ropes and maybe get an hour's sleep without them. Suddenly a guard, "Happy," came plowing through the torrential rain, lantern and flashlight in hand, to check on me. I heard him fumbling at the door, and didn't have time to tie the ropes in back of me, so I tied them loosely in front. I looked up as though half-asleep when Happy opened the door and shined his light into the cell. He grunted and started to close the door, then did a double-take. Puzzled, he came closer and looked at the ropes. He hauled me up by the ear and led me into the hallway, where he could get a better look. Pointing and gesturing, he wanted to know if he had tied the ropes in front. Of course, I nodded. Happy then gave me practically his entire English vocabulary.

"Bullshit!" he shouted. He reared back and knocked me against the wall. He then retied my arms behind me tighter than ever.

The next day two guards came to my cell and, after knocking me about, began raising me off the ground by my arms, which were still tied behind me. They kept this up for what seemed like hours, and I don't know how my arms didn't pop from their sockets. The pain was so intense that finally I could take it no longer. I gave in and copied my confession onto their standard form. It was small comfort that it had taken them three weeks to get it.

This was a new approach. They were now spreading the harassment and torture over a longer period of time, trying to wear us down. I didn't like the method. If I was going to be tortured, I wanted it over with quickly.

Early in September, they tried yet another gambit, when "Lump," a civilian with a large tumor protruding from the middle of his forehead, was introduced to the Zoo. He was a highly intelligent man who spoke excellent English and was well versed in psychology. Obviously someone of importance in the hierarchy, he boasted that he was a frequent negotiator for the Democratic Republic of Vietnam in trade sessions with other Communist nations, and that he had just come from a meeting with an East German group.

Lump began taking the soft-sell, good-guy approach with the POWs in quizzes, and probably suckered some of them, although I felt certain that he would eventually resort to torture if he didn't get what he wanted.

I had not yet recovered from the brutal arm-twisting session, and when Lump asked me to write something, anything, I consented and wrote on "superstitions" among pilots, a topic he suggested.

I wrote at length on the logical proof of the existence of God, using examples from the order of the universe, and Lump accepted my work. When I refused to write something more of a similar nature, he remained calm. But I knew this was only the beginning.

I had been taken back to Cell 1 of the Pool Hall late in August, and about the middle of September, Navy Commander Jim Mulligan was moved into Cell 3. Mulligan, who had been shot down on March 20, 1966, had been a shipmate of mine on the carrier *Independence* in 1962, and we were good friends. But his condition worried me. Dave Hatcher in Cell 2 tapped to me that Mulligan had been a "ball of fire" at the Barn, but now was quite different.

He was debilitated by mistreatment, was seriously ill, couldn't eat or drink much, and was so weak that he could barely tap. Hatcher tapped to me that Mulligan looked like a survivor from a Nazi concentration camp and weighed no more than 100 pounds.

We in the Pool Hall were a sorry lot, in general. Navy Lieutenant Commander Jack Fellowes in Cell 10 couldn't use his arms. The North Vietnamese thought he had knowledge of the EA6, an electronic version of the A6, and had used the ropes on him so severely that his arms were permanently damaged. The especially sad part was that Fellowes actually didn't know anything about the EA6. Fellowes was also an old friend from the early sixties, and was one of the toughest men in prison.

In Cell 10 with Fellowes was Air Force Captain Ron Bliss, who had a serious head injury. Bliss and Fellowes took turns caring for each other. In Cell 5 were Air Force Major Quincy Collins, on crutches, and Air Force Major A. J. Myers.

Air Force Major Alan Brunstrom and Navy Lieutenant Commander Render Crayton were in Cell 6; Navy Lieutenant Commander Dave Burroughs was in Cell 5; Purcell in 7; Navy Lieutenant Commander Jerry Coffee and Navy Lieutenant Larry Spencer in 8; and Ray Vohden with Air Force Major Norland Daughtrey, whose arms had been mangled in a high-speed ejection, in 9. All were debilitated, and many had serious and mostly untreated injuries.

It became evident that no one would be spared in the quest for biographies and confessions. They were now torturing badly injured men.

Our resistance remained resolute, and in the middle of October, Lump demanded information from me on camp communications. He told me they knew I was inciting others to resist, and he lost his composure for the first time, threatening me with torture if I didn't cooperate.

I refused, and a special rig was devised for me in my cell. I was placed in a sitting position on a pallet, with my hands tightly cuffed behind my back and my feet flat against the wall. Shackles were put on my ankles, with the open ends down, and an iron bar was pushed through the eyelets of the shackles. The iron bar was tied to the pallet and the shackles in such a way that when the rope was drawn over a pulley arrangement, the bar would cut into the hacks of my legs, gradually turning them into a swollen, bloody mess.

I couldn't move my legs; I couldn't turn my ankles; I had to remain in a sitting position at all times with my legs absolutely straight. The pulley was used daily to increase the pressure, and the iron bar began to eat through the Achilles tendons on the backs of my ankles.

After five days and nights in the rig, I decided to give them something harmless, hoping that the gesture would allow them to save face and release me. I wrote that we had talked to other prisoners while pretending to talk to the guards, and had also shouted under the doors. Lump shrugged and ordered me back into the rig. He was angered by my attempt to deceive him and determined to break me.

The punishment was so gory that each day Happy, after tightening the ropes, would still be weeping when he went to the next cell to let Mulligan out to empty his bucket. For five more days and nights I remained in the rig. My back got one respite in that time. I managed to lean against my bucket which I had maneuvered into position on the pallet, and relieve the strain enough to get some sleep. Even a roving guard took some pity. He saw me leaning against the bucket but didn't report it for eighteen hours. By the fifth morning, I was nearing despair. I offered myself to God with an admission that I could take no more on my own. Tears ran down my face as I repeated my vow of surrender to Him. Strangely, as soon as I made the vow, a deep feeling of peace settled into my tortured mind and pain-wracked body, and the suffering left me completely. It was the most profound and deeply inspiring moment of my life.

A few minutes later, Happy and another guard came into my cell and the two of them began pulling on the rope. Blood began to flow heavily from my legs. I felt nothing, though I still bear the scars and have frequent spasms in my legs from the ordeal.

I looked up at Happy as if to say: Why are you doing this to me? Happy stopped pulling on the rope, apparently asking himself the same question, cried out "No! No!" in Vietnamese. He ran headlong from the room and into Lump, who had been standing just outside the door. Lump ordered him back, but Happy refused in a high-pitched, half-hysterical voice. A loud, screaming argument ensued, and when Happy returned he loosened the ropes.

The next morning, I was taken from the rig by Happy, who avoided my eyes as he applied medication to the larger gashes in my legs. He also helped me roll up my gear, and since I couldn't walk, he and another guard held me between them and walked me back to the Gate, where I was pushed into my old cell. I soon determined that there were no other prisoners in the cellblock. I was again isolated.

In the fifteen months that I had been in Hanoi, I had been through six major torture sessions, five of them in the last six months. I was exhausted, but for the first time I felt as though I had really beaten them. They had not got even a face-saving gesture.

My hands were cuffed behind me at the Gate, but when the guards tried to put traveling irons on me, my ankles were so swollen that they had to settle for ropes. To avoid the embarrassment that knowledge of their failure to break me would bring, they kept me in total isolation.

The North Vietnamese were having other problems. They were still recoiling from their own excesses in July, and the prisoners were resisting longer. The resistance was so stiff that they were running out of torture equipment, and Monk had to spend several days in the road, in front of my cell, taking apart a huge metal sign and cutting it into pieces with an acetylene torch to make more traveling irons. These were lighter, less uncomfortable irons and went into wide use.

From my cell at the Gate, I could see through a crack which I had created by forcing a wooden panel in the door sideways. The opening gave me a good look at the camp, and I was thankful because it gave me a view of the heroic resistance of Air Force Captain Frederic R. Flom. He was in a cell in a detached building across the road from me and about twenty yards to my right. The building looked like a garage. Its concrete floor was lower than the road in front of it, and rainwater ran under the door and collected in a large puddle underneath his pallet. November was cold, windy, and rainy, and Flom, whose severely broken arm was in a cast, was virtually at the mercy of the elements. He was also at the mercy of Frenchy, whose brutal beatings were plainly visible to me.

I guessed that Flom could use some encouragement in his isolated misery, and on one unusually quiet night I whistled some patriotic songs, hoping he would hear them. Unfortunately, in the middle of "Stout-Hearted Men," a guard caught me and reported me to Frenchy, who roused himself from his bed to punish me. He was in a bad humor even for him, and punched me around for several minutes before departing, leaving me bloody.

In a few days, Flom was moved out, and three skinny cows took his place.

After about a month, I got a new neighbor in my cellblock. At first I couldn't tell who it was, although I had seen him being moved in, and I immediately got on the wall and tapped, "Who are you?"

The answer came back: "Coker. Who are you?" I tapped back my name and waited for a greeting, but none came. I continued to tap without getting an answer until I was fairly booming on the wall over and over: "Why won't you tap? Why won't you tap?" Finally Coker tapped, "I do not think you are Denton."

I was puzzled and a little angry. Who in the hell did he think I was? Then I realized that he thought it was some kind of trap. The North Vietnamese on occasion had attempted, somewhat crudely, to trick the prisoners by tapping, but I considered myself much too smooth an operator to be mistaken for a North Vietnamese. For the next twenty minutes I tapped to Coker an account of our duty together in VA 42 and recalled many mutual acquaintances. Convinced, he tapped to me, "I didn't recognize you when I saw you through a crack in my door. You were picking up your chow. You don't weigh a hundred pounds."

On December 7, I heard three of the guards, Pierre, Flash, and Happy, arguing outside my cell. Lump still wanted information from me and had ordered more torture. I thought Happy was telling the other two guards that using the rope trick on me would do no good, but in a few minutes the three of them came into my cell, bound my legs, and applied the rope trick to my arms. By now, I knew I could beat the rope trick by accepting the pain until I passed out. Of course, if the ropes weren't removed after a certain period of time my arms would suffer permanent damage from lack of circulation and would have to be removed. I would take that chance.

After the guards left, I crawled to the wall and tapped my condition to Coker. Then I lay on my bed. As unconsciousness approached, I felt my arms, wrists, and hands go numb and my shoulders began to hurt. I crawled on my knees to the door, and through a crack I could see the three guards pacing back and forth, glancing occasionally at their watches. They also knew the dangers of the ropes, and apparently weren't prepared to risk loss of my arms.

After nearly an hour, they came into the room and removed the ropes without a word. Pierre kicked me in disgust. That night, I peeked out the door at the heightened activity outside. Many others were getting the rope trick.

But the next day, December 8, 1966, I watched through my crack in amazement as twenty-six sets of cuffs and traveling irons were taken from various cells and stored in a room a few yards from my cell. It was the signal for what was to be a major change in the North Vietnamese torture program. They apparently had given up on trying to subjugate the mass of prisoners with camp-wide torture. Biographical information was still being forced from some prisoners, but it soon became apparent that the pressure was off, to a degree.

Our resistance had forced the Vietnamese into brutal measures, and word had leaked out. The United States and other countries had reacted violently to such outrages as the Hanoi March, and this reaction had its effect in the higher councils of the Democratic Republic of North Vietnam.

Torture was still used for punitive purposes, even at times on a camp-wide basis for such things as escapes and the discovery of sophisticated command and communications systems. Prolonged spot purges against specific groups were also conducted for propaganda exploitation, and new prisoners were tortured individually for military information. But routine subjugation purges against the entire mass of prisoners did not continue. The North Vietnamese had thought the Americans would be easy touches, and when they were not, the whole program of total subjugation was thrown into chaos. There wouldn't have been much point in torturing us to death. What they wanted was to subdue us, and then win us over to the point where we would routinely do their bidding. They failed.

Had they succeeded, it would have been disastrous for the morale and substance of the United States. The vast majority of American prisoners in North Vietnam upheld their country's honor, with enormous consequences for their nation's pride and prestige. If we had come out of there defeated and bowed, our country would have too.

For the first time since April 1966, I was accorded "normal" treatment. I was stiff in isolation in a windowless, cold, and filthy cell, but I began receiving the standard cigarette ration of three a day, I was allowed out of my cell fifteen minutes a day for exercise, I got a haircut, and I was allowed to bathe and shave at regular intervals.

When I removed my clothing and looked at my arms in good light for the first time in months, I could understand that George Coker was not exaggerating. I looked like a skeleton.

I repaid the North Vietnamese for their consideration by planning an escape. During my previous stay at the Gate, I had discovered I could open the large double door to my cell by working loose the metal piece securing the hasp, to which the large padlock was attached. This was my first real chance to work out a feasible escape plan, and I had the circumstances, time and determination to try.

All the doors to the rooms at the Gate were secured in the same way, and I told Coker in the next cell how to force open his door. But it scraped on the concrete and made a loud noise, so I figured that the best thing for Coker would be to work his way through the ceiling of his cell, come across the roof at night to my cell, and go out with me.

All the instruction to military men advised that no one should go out by himself, for various reasons, so it was important that we go out together. Also, Risner had previously passed word that no one should go without outside help, meaning someone like a friendly guard. When Coker asked me about the order, I tapped to him, "I know Robbie well, and under the circumstances, I believe he'd agree with me that God is our outside help."

George was tough, but he thought little of our chances. "You want to commit honorable suicide," he tapped to me.

But I told him how we could steal two bikes from a storage shed, use a pallet for a ladder to go over the wall, and be on our way. I was not sure about our physical strength for such an undertaking, and when Coker finally bought my plan, I agreed to wait until the Tet holiday in February of 1967. Our strength would be somewhat restored, and most of the guards would be drunk.

But I was moved from the Gate long before Tet and never had the same kind of door again. Coker and George McKnight later used the same door-opening method to engineer a successful but brief escape.

On December 13, there was a spectacular air raid on the truck park on Highway One about a mile from the Zoo. By looking through the crack in my door, I could see the planes, mostly F4's and F105's, diving down and whipping their bombs out toward the park as they passed over the Zoo. The raid lasted fifteen or twenty minutes, and the thud of bombs was mixed liberally with the sound of shrapnel falling in the street from the heavy antiaircraft fire.

As the planes banked over the Zoo, I could actually see the pilots in their cockpits. I watched in fascination and with mixed emotions. On the one hand, I feared for their safety in that sky full of fire, and on the other, I envied them. In a few minutes most of them would be back in the security and comfort of their bases, where they would sit down with their friends and eat a warm, full meal, something I hadn't seen in a year and a half. I reached up with my hand as if to grab a wing and hitch a ride back with them.

A few days later there was another raid close by, but behind my building, so that I couldn't see it from my door crack. Frenchy, just outside my cell, was looking up in horror. He thought Hanoi was being bombed, and would be destroyed. Actually the target was a railyard and there was little collateral damage, as I learned later.

On Christmas Eve of 1966, George and I exchanged "Christmas cards." As closely as I can remember, I tapped to George Coker: "May the consoling peace of the Infant King unite you and your family on this Precious Night."

George was young and one of several children from a close-knit, God-fearing family. His "card" to me was similar, and touched me deeply on that Silent Night.

CHAPTER FOURTEEN

January 23, 1967, was a day to remember. The North Vietnamese gave me a cell mate for the first time, not out of solicitude, but because they were in the process of executing a major intercamp shuffle. They had to put me in with someone else temporarily, and there they had a choice. They could give me someone with whom I had no previous contact, or they could give me someone I had already "contaminated" through previous covert association.

They chose the latter and moved me in with Jim Mulligan in Cell 3 of the Pool Hall. The happy interlude was to last only three days.

I had glimpsed Mulligan hanging up his clothes on the day in April 1966 when I had urinated out the peephole of the Knobby Room at the Hilton. I was groggy at the time and couldn't get a clear look at him, but I knew instinctively he was someone I liked.

Mulligan had been shot down over the southern part of North Vietnam while attacking a small bridge in March 1966. He was flying a single-seater A4 off the carrier *Enterprise* at the time and had injured his arm during ejection. He could still barely use it when I moved into his cell at the Pool Room. It was to cause him trouble for many years.

He was also suffering severely from intestinal problems and had to spend several hours a day on the bucket. He was weak and emaciated from his long ordeal and weighed about 100 pounds when I moved in with him.

The father of six children, Jim had served in World War II and had been recalled for the Korean War. After that, he decided to stay in the Navy. Mulligan couldn't have been a better choice for me to room with in North Vietnam. He was full of good humor under the most adverse conditions, and whenever he or I would start to complain about something, he would smile and remind me of something that his wife Louise had once told him.

"If you didn't have a sense of humor, you should never have joined," she had said.

Jim is a garrulous person, and he literally overwhelmed me with conversation while bringing me up to date on activities that had occurred while I was isolated at the Gate. He had also been in solitary since his shootdown, and his desire for conversation and information was endless.

I was overjoyed, of course, but somewhat dazed and mentally sluggish. I had trouble absorbing everything as we talked in hoarse whispers through the long hours of the night. Jim told me that his plane had gone down in flames after his ejection and that he had barely got out alive. He was badly treated on capture, and still bore scars on his arms from the gasoline-soaked ropes which had been used to bind him.

I knew almost immediately that our situation was temporary. Happy had brought us a bucket which had no top and was full of holes. I complained, but when he left it anyway, I knew we would soon move again.

Sure enough, on January 26, we were moved back to the Hilton, where a new section had just been opened to accommodate the increasing flow of prisoners. Little Vegas, in the northeast corner of the Hilton, had been specially designed to foil communications among the prisoners. There were no common walls between cells, and large hallways further divided the cell blocks. I was moved into a tiny cell in the Stardust, one section of Little Vegas. There was just enough room to stand between the wooden bunks and the wall.

Despite the enemy's efforts to isolate us, we quickly discovered ways to communicate. Voices carried well between cells at the Stardust, so we talked under our doors. In addition, we could still use the outer walls for tapping, and we devised a good system of "clearing," the term we used for warning each other of the presence of guards.

Sounds carried so well that Stockdale could lie on his bunk in his cell across from me and send messages by thumping on his chest in code. Because of the position of my cell, I could talk more safely under my door than he could, and I relayed all information to and from him, including the names of the men who were killed in a fire on the carrier *Oriskany.* Many of his friends were among the dead.

After about two days, I was caught communicating again. I was moved to the Mint, the punishment section of Little Vegas, and placed in leg stocks. There were two huge windows high off the ground in my cell. This would have been great in summer, but now, early in February 1967, the chill air of the North Vietnam winter was a constant source of discomfort.

Nonetheless, the windows had some redeeming features. The leg stocks were removed after two weeks, and I found that by getting on my bunk and then shinnying up the bars of the windows, I could see outside. The view was restricted, of course, but it had been so long since I had had more than a glimpse through a crack, that the view opened a whole new world of wonderment for me.

I could see part of the huge wall around the prison, a guard tower at the corner of the wall by my cell, and even the tower guard, tommy gun in hand. At the end of the street was a lot where the North Vietnamese were accumulating portable concrete air raid shelters, and I watched workmen moving the shelters about. The tower guard was usually looking toward the street, so I was unobserved.

Air raids were frequent at this time. We were told to get under our bunks during the brief strikes, but mostly we strained for a glimpse of the planes.

After the raids, I usually received a report from Mulligan, two cells removed, on the air battles which took place within his view.

While I was adjusting to new quarters, prison life went on. Stockdale, newly moved to a central location in the Thunderbird, was running the Hilton with a firm hand. His orders were cogent, effective, and easy to follow. The prisoners could talk out of their windows at naptime, when the guards were least effective, and through the wide spaces under their doors. And there was the usual tapping and note passing. We were now quite adept at countering practically every move by the North Vietnamese and their mastermind, Cat.

There are some remarkable lessons to be learned under duress, and in seven and a half years, you learn a good deal more than you can remember. I have discussed this with Stockdale, who suffered as much as anyone in Hanoi, and I recount, with his help, some of those lessons.

The North Vietnamese game plan was very simple. They brought the full power of the system to bear on one objective: Break our will. We are reminded again of Clausewitz: "War is an act of violence to break the enemy's will."

The torture was programmed; there was a purpose in each move, and one method followed another to a single end.

They would first attempt to impose on the prisoner a feeling of guilt. Punishment would follow. Then we were to apologize for our sins against them. Then we would atone by performing a service for them, a written biography, a taped confession, anything they could use for propaganda.

Propaganda had a high value for them, but the highest value was the destruction of our organization. And our highest value was the preservation of that organization. Without it, we were just a collection of individuals, doomed, eventually, to succumb. But we learned to outwit our captors even though they held all the cards, because our will was superior.

There was an organization in practically every prison. Periodically it would be broken down and a purge would follow. But we would rebuild, knowing that we would be caught again and would have to pay another horrible price. We learned to live with it, and grow stronger, until their organization was under more stress than ours.

By putting their organization under pressure, we acquired useful information on the way they thought and operated. One day Stockdale, challenging Rabbit on various matters, said, "You're so proud of being a party member: what are the requirements to be a party member?"

Rabbit, caught off guard and under pressure, replied: "There are only four. First, you have to be seventeen years old. Second, you have to be smart enough to understand the theory. Third, you have to be selfless. And fourth, and most important, you have to be a man who can influence others."

It occurred to Stockdale that the fourth part was the very thing they were trying to find out about us. They were looking for the leaders in order to isolate them. In their own ranks, they institutionalized influence over others with party membership. In our ranks, they kept the leadership in solitary confinement and called them war criminals.

As Stockdale relates, one day he overheard the North Vietnamese conferring about some prisoners, and when a particular name came up, one said, "Don't bother with him he's harmless."

The man was a perfectly honorable officer who adhered strictly to the Code of Conduct and took his punishment for his stand. But the North Vietnamese, judging him a man who had no leverage with the other prisoners, dismissed him as a threat. As Stockdale put it, a smart fighter knows his enemy, not only by rank but by clout.

So we had to stand up to their assault, and they had to stand up to ours, and it was a constant game of measure and countermeasure.

By the spring of 1967, Stockdale had built an excellent organization that was, to a large extent, keeping the prisoners together in their common cause. He had paid dearly for it.

During my stay at the Mint, the North Vietnamese went on a kick to build the health of the prisoners, which had become dangerously poor. Various administrators were coming through frequently to check on the food. We were even allowed seconds on rice, which was augmented with maize, and the overall quality of the food improved slightly. Most of us began regaining weight.

But while they gave with one hand, they took away with the other. They were now after new prisoners for operational military information and were stopping at nothing to get it. They were not even worrying about leaving scars. Some men died, and many barely survived.

The cell between Mulligan and me at the Mint was sometimes used for men hot off the griddle, and we spent hours trying to console the tortured prisoners. They were all new shootdowns, and besides sympathy, they needed information on various communication and resistance methods.

My own situation had improved somewhat. I wasn't being tortured, although I was still a bit fuzzy-minded, and I had developed a debilitating cough, which was not helped by the northwest wind that came through the two big windows over my head and swirled constantly through the cell. I passed the time by climbing up to the windows and watching the traffic, mostly military, on the street beyond the wall. There is something enormously satisfying in watching people going about their business in a normal way. I could see some trees and shops, people on bicycles, and women going past, carrying baskets of vegetables or loads of clothing. I noticed that the civilians passed military men without a nod or a look and surmised that the people and the soldiers were not getting along.

About the middle of February, I received word that the prisoners were being taken to a so-called Tet quiz. When my turn came, I was taken to a well-decorated room with a large table covered with a clean, white tablecloth. I was given some candy and a letter from Jane, and three smiling officers asked me how I was. "Terrible," I said, and they changed the subject.

The lights were very bright, and I suspected someone was taking movies. The officers tried to get me to smile, but I put on a sullen look, despite the sweets and the beautiful but necessarily restrained letter from Jane, which was about four months old.

Also on the table was a book containing drawings on Vietnamese history. They invited me to thumb through it. One picture showed a man, supposedly a "puppet" of the former French regime, grasping the naked breast of a peasant girl. It was about the closest one would get to sex in a North Vietnamese prison, and that page was much smudged by the fingerprints of other prisoners. It was an amazing departure from their usual heavy-handed and stereotyped form of propaganda.

This is not to say that sex was ignored as a weapon. On some rare occasions, they tried to entice prisoners by offering them a woman. To my knowledge, no one ever took them up on it. If they had, the Vietnamese would have certainly advertised their success.

The young women who worked in the camps as cooks or watergirls seemed to be fascinated by the American prisoners, and each appeared to have her favorite. But prisoner-women relationships were usually confined to an exchange of meaningful glances, more sympathetic than sexual in nature.

One day in March, the peephole in my door was opened from the outside, and a big brown eye appeared. The eye slowly rotated as its owner surveyed me and my cell. Then it disappeared, and before the peephole was closed I placed my own eye at the opening for a survey. Standing there, her nose slightly wrinkled from the sight and smell of my cell, was a girl.

There had been some conversation on the camp radio about U.S. efforts to obtain International Red Cross inspection of the prison camps, and since the girl was wearing a civilian blouse instead of the standard army shirt, I hoped she might be a Red Cross representative. But as I watched her more closely I realized that she was just another watergirl.

I then suspected, because she had been so brazen, that she was a plant, another trick by the Vietnamese to gain information or cooperation. As it turned out, I was wrong again. She had simply taken an interest in the prisoners. By sign language she asked my age. I signaled forty-three. She signaled that I didn't look over thirty-five. I showed her a picture of Jane and the children, which had arrived in Jane's letter. By pointing to my heart and then to Jane, I indicated my love for my wife.

Greta, as the girl was called, made frequent visits to the peephole, spending as many moments as she could before the sound of an approaching guard would cause her to close the peephole, shoulder her two buckets of water, and move on. Several times, when the tower guard was dozing, she climbed halfway up the ladder to the tower outside my window, and from there she would look into my cell and make sympathetic gestures in an effort to cheer me up.

Once, when she was angry with me for some reason, she climbed on the ladder and shook her fist at me, then delivered a series of karate chops at me. As I watched, completely bemused and confounded, she put on a fake smile and stomped away. But she later relented, and occasionally, as she carried water during the day, there would be a thump on the door from her carrying pole.

As the winter of 1967 softened into spring, I was offered the chance to see a priest in private. I accepted, and was taken one day to a room in the Riviera in Little Vegas where I was introduced to Father Jean Baptiste, an activist prelate often used by the North Vietnamese in photos and newsreels to illustrate their broadminded attitudes.

As I sat in front of the elderly priest and his interpreter, I gazed at the deep lines creasing his face and wondered at the compromises he had had to make and the suffering he had undergone. Obviously, it had been necessary for him to surrender on many issues in order to stay with his people.

I was permitted to ask any questions I wished, and the first was: "Is the Catholic Church in North Vietnam accredited by the Vatican?"

"Of course," he answered.

(Years later, I learned personally from Pope Paul VI that this was a lie.)

I asked him how he could reconcile his religious views with the atheistic government he served. He answered: "We are permitted to worship God as long as we do not interfere with the state."

This answer and his other statements were carefully rehearsed, and obviously being noted by the interpreter. As we talked, air raid sirens began wailing and we could hear rumbling sounds approaching as the rings of the Hanoi air defense began opening up. Prompted by the interpreter, the priest asked: "Do you know this is Easter? Why is it your planes bomb on Easter?"

Actually, it wasn't Easter, but I gave him a straight answer anyway. "We are trying to help South Vietnam in self-determination and bring them freedom so they can truly worship," I said. I went on at some length about the justice of our cause.

To my surprise, the interpreter, after a slight pause, relayed my answer to the priest. From his subtle reactions, I believe the priest agreed with what I had said. The interpreter then left the room and Jean Baptiste granted me absolution by simply requiring me to say the Confiteor. I said it in Latin, overcome with emotion, and grasped his hand, placing it against my forehead. We both wept. When the interpreter returned, the priest turned away from him and smothered his sobs by drinking a glass of water.

Lump had once said to me on one of his good-guy days that North Vietnam couldn't afford to have freedom "the way you have it." Now the North

Vietnamese were trying to show me that there was still some freedom of choice in their country, and that there was some viability in the Church. Although I deeply appreciated the opportunity to see Jean Baptiste, I refused in the future to take part in any North Vietnamese-sponsored religious ceremony unless they promised that there would be no talk of politics. They refused, saying that they couldn't guarantee what a priest might say. Any religious ceremonies in which POWs were allowed to participate were designed purely for propaganda.

Near the end of May, a guard came and told me to roll up my gear, and with Mulligan, I went to a quiz room where Flea, an officer who often showed the effects of drugs or alcohol, told us that we would again be put together in a cell. He said we both had a bad attitude and that the move was no concession, but the camp was so crowded that we couldn't be kept in solitary.

So Jim and I moved into a tiny cell in the Stardust. The shutters on our window were kept closed, and we were so hot and tired that we could hardly talk and couldn't eat at all. Very shortly, our condition became so poor that the shutters were opened and we could get some air.

At the end of June 1967, the North Vietnamese discovered the meaning of a slogan we often used, "BACK U.S." Actually, it was an acronym put together by Stockdale, each letter standing for a phrase. The B, for instance, stood for "Don't bow in public," the K for "Don't kiss them goodbye," meaning there should be no complimentary statements for our captors as a price for release.

This infuriated them, and they reacted against this "dark conspiracy" in typically brutal fashion. The crackdown would soon involve me, and my few weeks of relative peace would come to an end.

A guard had been posted full-time in front of the cell in which Mulligan and I had been living, and I had to be extremely careful with communications, especially in view of Mulligan's condition. He was so debilitated he could barely stand, and on one occasion he confessed to me that if he had to go through the mill one more time, he didn't think he could make it. The North Vietnamese were sparing no one, and screams of the tortured in the night were commonplace.

Nonetheless, I had obligations, since I was in command of my cellblock. One day I was talking out the window of the cell to Scotty Morgan, who was relaying messages from newly captured Red McDaniel. McDaniel, three cells away, was caring for some badly injured and ill prisoners, whose names were being passed along with some personal messages. I asked eagerly, "Does Red have any messages for me?" (Red and I had been friends for years.)

In the spring of 1965, the year I was shot down, my son Bill was playing in the opening game of the Little League season. The opposing team had walked the previous batter, a tall, rangy lad, to get to little Bill. The bases were loaded, it was the last inning, and I was literally breathless as Bill came to the plate, took two pitches, and lined the third one over the center-field fence for a home run.

Now the message came back from McDaniel: "Your son is burning up the Little League again!"

I half-shouted, "Hot dog!" It was a costly error. So absorbed had I been in the conversation that I didn't hear a warning cough. A guard had been sneaking along the inside wall, and he jumped out and nailed me and Hubert Flesher, who was clearing from another window. Considering the current Vietnamese attitude on communications, I knew that I was in for more than irons, I was taken immediately to a quiz room, where Rat, an officer, accused me point blank.

"We have caught you! Who were you communicating with?"

"No one," I answered. "I was just calling out my name. Mulligan warned me not to do it, but I did it anyway. He had nothing to do with it."

"You sure?" Rat asked suspiciously.

"Yes, I'm sure," I answered. Rat knew I was lying because the guard had told him I had been talking for five minutes or more, but he accepted my explanation and Mulligan was not bothered.

They wanted me to confess what I had actually talked about, and I was put in rear cuffs and a double set of traveling irons and taken to the latrine-bathhouse, where I was told to kneel in the hot sun. The bathhouse was concrete and uncovered, and the four walls reflected the rays of the burning sun. I guessed that the temperature was 120 degrees or more. As I knelt and sweated under the noonday sun, I could hear Flesher somewhere nearby, screaming and moaning. I closed my eyes and said the rosary.

My physical condition was poor, and as the hours went on I would fall over. The guard would come and drag me around the rough concrete by my leg irons until I managed to get on my knees again. I weakened rapidly, and to make matters worse, I had to move my bowels. It is peculiar the way the mind works under certain circumstances. It was not relief from the sun that I wanted most right then. It was not food, or water, or even removal of the cuffs or traveling irons. What I wanted was toilet paper.

I was already so filthy and uncomfortable that I didn't feel I could stand one more discomfort, that of defecating without the luxury of toilet paper. And there was no way that the silent, sullen guard outside would provide that amenity.

As the long minutes passed, my need became more pronounced. So as I kneeled in the sun, my head bowed, fever raging through my body, I once again turned to my source of strength. I prayed, almost apologetically, for a small favor.

When I had completed my request, I threw my head back and peeped under my blindfold at the sky. As I looked up, I saw a large leaf, swirling and fluttering in the heavy air and heading my way.

I watched fascinated as it took a sudden dive and landed practically at my feet. It was large, about nine inches long and six inches wide, and pleasantly furry on one side. Perfect!

I twisted my body and picked the leaf up with my cuffed hands, tore it into four pieces, and worked my way to the nearby bucket, where I put the pieces to use.

Another prayer had been answered, but I was still in deep trouble. The combination of long hours in the sun, hunger, and general abuse had produced a high fever. I had become allergic to the irons, and my ankles had reacted by swelling around the leg shackles. I was in such poor shape that even the guard noticed and brought a doctor. He ordered me taken to the Riviera, where the traveling irons were removed with some difficulty.

I was still in punishment and was required to sit on a stool for several days and nights, blindfolded and in rear cuffs. I kept falling asleep and waking up on the floor with a new bump on my head. My fever got so high that the doctor ordered me out of punishment. My life was in jeopardy.

I was incoherent when I was taken to a big, airy cell in the Thunderbird at Little Vegas, where the rear cuffs and blindfold were removed and my clothes taken off. There I lay semiconscious in my shorts until Abe, a hateful guard whose angular, Lincolnesque features had earned him his distinguished nickname, came into my cell and demanded to know why my outer clothing was off.

I was too dazed to answer, and he made me put them back on. Then he slapped me around until Flea came in and stopped him. "Denton," Flea said as Abe left the room, "that man is a savage. I will take care of him one day."

I had been in punishment for five days. It was now July, and I was approaching my second anniversary as a prisoner. I was so out of it that about every ten minutes I stupidly pounded my initials on the wall. Exasperated, Bob Peel, who was in irons in the next cell, messaged, "Okay, okay, we know you're in there."

On July 8, with my fever down, I was taken back to the Stardust, where Mulligan thanked me for not implicating him. I discovered that the Vietnamese were pressing harder than ever to stop communications and to break our organization. The "BACK U.S." purge was on. The North Vietnamese were taking in four or five prisoners at a time for questioning and torture, and while Stockdale was being worked over for the names of key people, he had told them, "You'll never break us. There is no way to break our organization because the senior man will always take charge."

As the days dragged on into August, the "BACK U.S." investigation intensified and the guards became particularly vicious. One day Pimples, an especially obnoxious guard, spat through the peephole and hit Mulligan flush in the face. His Irish temper got the best of him and he spat back, then turned to me and said: "Hah! Got him right in the eye!"

"Jim," I said, "you better take a crap whether you have to or not because they're going to come back and punish us." In a few minutes, guards came and put us in irons.

Early in September, Abe, who lit cigarettes for the prisoners with a wick made out of toilet paper, came to our cell on his rounds. Instead of lighting my cigarette through the peephole, however, he stuck the wick in my face and burned me under the eye. I backed away and went to the corner of the cell, fuming. Mulligan wanted to wipe my face and treat the burn, but I said no. "This is the chance to get Abe's ass," I said.

When I went to the bath later, Flea asked me about the smudge. I looked at Abe and said, "Ask him." We never saw Abe again, and we heard later that he had been sent south. The guards could torture, beat, or kill us, but only under orders. Flea was one officer who would not allow gross violations by the guards.

The communications purge was now in full swing, and some of the prisoners were being hurt very badly. I was moved to the Mint, where I was placed in rear cuffs, traveling irons, gag, and a blindfold. Howard Rutledge, who was in the next cell and with whom I had little contact, became angry with me because I would tap only my initials, but he apologized when he learned that I was blindfolded and couldn't "clear" myself.

Frequently, through the long days of early September, I could hear other prisoners screaming and groaning as they were worked over. A guard jumped on George McKnight's stomach so violently that he defecated. The guards then gagged him with his shorts. Others were beaten nearly to death. Air Force Lieutanant Colonel Norm Schmidt went to a quiz in an angry mood, and in the context of the times I knew that was dangerous. He never returned, and his remains were brought to the States in the summer of 1973.

Late in September I was called to a quiz with Flea. He ordered me to kneel, lectured me for about fifteen minutes, then asked me questions which I refused to answer.

"Denton," Flea said, "I think that no matter what we do, you will not tell us about Stockdale and the organization. Is that right?"

"That's right," I replied. "If you get rid of him, I will take over. If you get rid of me, the next man will take over."

I was amazed when he questioned me no further and had me return to my cell. He was trying to tell me something. I didn't know what, but I knew it wasn't good.

Sometime during the evening of October 25, I was taken from my cell to an alleyway just inside the Hilton wall where I was blindfolded by Sarge, a rather slow-moving, slow-thinking guard who spoke some English. He told me to kneel on the ground with my head bowed while other prisoners were brought out, blindfolded, and told to kneel. By various signals, I determined that Rutledge and Coker were among five or six others waiting silently for something, we didn't know what.

As we waited in the chill air, I heard a shrill voice nearby. It was Greta, arguing with Sarge. I heard her approaching at a fast pace, heard more arguing and a slap as Sarge struck her. But she kept coming, and in a moment I could feel her hand on my shoulder. I remained still and quiet. This was a serious loss of face for the guards, and the consequences could be disastrous.

I heard Sarge moving away, apparently to report Greta's actions. While he was gone, Greta stood there with her hand on my shoulder, talking to me in soothing tones, as a mother would talk to her child. After several minutes, the guards came and dragged her away. Then I was pulled up by the ear and pushed into a truck with the others.

I never saw Greta again.

Eventually, I ascertained that there were several other prisoners in the truck, with two guards for each prisoner. We were sitting on dozens of lengths of thin pipe, and as the truck rolled and bumped through the dark streets of Hanoi, the pipes shifted beneath us and pinched with every bump.

I had no idea what was up, and I was uneasy. The silence was broken only by the rattle of the pipes and the heavy breathing of the truck's occupants. The thought ran through my mind that we could be on the way to better conditions, or we could be on our way to our deaths.

For one prisoner, the latter would be the case.

- - - - -

After about fifteen minutes, I felt the truck going up a steep, rough slope, probably a driveway, and then come to a stop. We were taken from the truck one by one and, still blindfolded, led about twenty yards into a building. I was told to stand still for a few moments and then was led down a long walkway. Behind me I could hear the rattle of irons and the sound of doors closing. Then silence again. I felt a hand on my shoulder, turning me around. A guard shackled me with a pair of traveling irons. Then my blindfold was removed.

I blinked. My mouth fell open in disbelief. I was looking into the dark shadows of the tiniest, most barren cell I had ever seen. I heard a voice behind me. "How do you like your new home?" It was Rat. He was smiling.

"No one can stand this," I said, trying to keep my composure. But it would be my home for more than two incredible years.

CHAPTER FIFTEEN

Alcatraz.

It was the name Shumaker gave to the new home for the eleven men who had been singled out for "special treatment." Alcatraz meant solitude, filth, hunger, and despair, and many other things that even now the ten survivors are sometimes reluctant to talk about.

It was also a badge of honor. Each man had earned his way in. There were, of course, men elsewhere who possessed equal credentials but had been so clever or lucky, that they had escaped this final horror.

And horror it was. The cells were tiny: a standing area forty-seven inches square, plus a raised pallet area the length of a man's body. The pallet was nothing more than bamboo strips laid side by side. Mine had a nail that protruded near my right shoulder blade. There was no window, and the only ventilation was from a few small holes drilled in a steel plate above the door and a six-inch space under the door, which was recessed. A dim bulb, ten watts or less, provided the only light. Most of the time there was only darkness and silence.

My possessions consisted of a toothbrush; a water jug; a cup; soap; a washrag; two blankets; a bucket; two sets of underwear and two shirts; a turtleneck sweatshirt; a torn mosquito net; and a pair of sandals which were only pieces of rubber with a strap. I didn't get socks until much later.

When the heavy wooden door closed behind me on that first night, and the bolt slid into place with a thump, a choking feeling welled up in my throat. The cell was so tiny, so dark. I could hear little crawling sounds as the roaches and spiders reacted to their new roommate.

My first thought was to contact my comrades, and I put my ear to the thick brick and cement wall and tapped. Behind the dark facade, the communications had already started as the others tapped out their names in the night.

Howard Rutledge, in Cell 1 at the far end of the cellblock; Harry Jenkins next; then Sam Johnson, Bob Shumaker, Ron Storz, Nelson Tanner, George Coker, George McKnight; and then me, with an empty cell between me and McKnight.

Opposite Shumaker's cell were three more cells, set at a right angle to our cellblock. In them were Jim Mulligan and Jim Stockdale, with the cell between them used as a storeroom.

Alcatraz, in a busy section of Hanoi not far from the Red River, was practically across the street from the Plantation, where some American prisoners were being kept, and was actually a part of the complex housing the Ministry of National Defense of the Army of North Vietnam. The Alcatraz compound itself was small, perhaps 2,500 square feet. One high wall on the east side was topped by barbed wire and covered with broken glass embedded in concrete. The other walls were lower and less secure. In a large pen, in one corner, several pigs were kept. One to three guards were on sentry duty at all times.

Our situation had been presaged more than a year previously, in May of 1966, when Mulligan had been taken to a quiz with a senior general, who had explained the "make your choice" program. The general said he understood there wouldn't be many who would accept a program of cooperation, but those who did would get good treatment and would be sent home. There would be a vast majority who would not cooperate but who would not cause great trouble.

And there would be a small group who would lead the resistance. The general called this group "Hard-core diehards." They would be shackled, receive poor food, and be isolated from the others, he said, and when the war was over, they would not go home.

We were the "diehards," and it was easy to determine why each of us was in Alcatraz.

Howie Rutledge had killed a man with his pistol during his capture when the man had charged him with a weapon. Rutledge despised the North Vietnamese and didn't try to hide it. He was extremely clever at communicating and paid for it; he was among the top four or five prisoners in the amount and intensity of torture and mistreatment he received in prison. His retentive memory and quick mind helped make him a superior leader, but mainly it was his indomitable will that made him a marked man.

Harry Jenkins, in the cell next to Rutledge, was famous for his daring raids off the carrier *Oriskany*. Skipper of an attack squadron, he had got a good deal of publicity for his exploits before he was shot down; he had had more than his share of torture and mistreatment. A tall, rangy man with prominent ears and beetle brow, he had the best sense of humor of anyone at Alcatraz.

Sam Johnson looked like a Texas cowboy, and in fact he was from Texas. He was a strong resister and a good trooper, despite a badly twisted arm which he could barely use. He exerted a steadying influence on everyone around him.

Bob Shumaker was in a class by himself. The sandy-haired Californian was a temperamental genius who was slicker than anyone at inventing new ways to communicate. He was so slick, in fact, that the Vietnamese seldom caught him, but they could tell by the patterns of communication that he was outfoxing them. An athletic ex-boxer, Shumaker had missed the astronaut program only because of some lymph nodes near his ear.

Ron Storz was a tall, gangly New Yorker, with long arms and legs, prominent ears, and a permanently mournful expression. He showed early that he would be one of the toughest. Once he refused to put his heels together during a quiz at the Office and the guards practically shredded his body with a metal rod. At Little Vegas he would pass notes containing the tap code to new shootdowns by slipping them in their rice while he was picking up his own food from the chow rack. He was constantly homesick and, unlike most prisoners, was pessimistic about the war. He knew it would last for many years, and didn't believe he would survive.

Nelson Tanner had made the North Vietnamese a laughing stock, and they never forgave him. After being tortured, Tanner had given them a biography which included Clark Kent as squadron commander and other comic strip characters as members of his family. The overeager enemy had publicized the biography, and the resultant horse laughs had made them furious. Tanner set the record for consecutive days (123) in irons. He was a balding, thickset Tennessean, about five feet nine inches, with a round face and big neck. He was stolid, quiet, strong morally and physically, and unrelenting toward his captors.

Young, baby-faced George Coker was just too tough for the North Vietnamese to handle. Strong-minded and doctrinaire, he was scrupulous in his attitude toward them and simply wouldn't talk to them. His advice to new shootdowns was: "Look them in the eye and say No!" He wrote good poetry, was an excellent bridge and chess player, and was strictly moral in everything he did. He had engineered an escape with McKnight, which undoubtedly earned him some points toward Alcatraz, but my guess is that he would have been there anyway because of his resistance.

George McKnight, a slim six-footer, had been a boxer in college. He had intense eyes, deeply set in a long, lean face. He was a brave man who, in my judgment, was among the top five resisters in prison. When he wasn't plan-

ADMIRAL JEREMIAH A. DENTON

ning an escape, he was thinking up new ways to foil the enemy. He, Stockdale, Rutledge, Risner, and I each spent more than four years in solitary. Ernie Brace, a civilian pilot for Air America, was the only other American prisoner to achieve that dubious distinction.

Jim Mulligan, a six-foot Irishman, had of course demonstrated time and again his willingness to sacrifice himself for others, and was always a vital force in the resistance. His constant good humor and his ability to laugh in their faces was a tremendous irritant to the North Vietnamese.

Jim Stockdale, who had been the air wing commander aboard the *Oriskany*, was considered a "high-grade criminal" by the North Vietnamese, and his "BACK U.S." program had frightened them. To add insult, he had once given the BS signal during a filmed confession and the signal had got through. He had limitless physical courage, and I remember watching him back in our Naval Academy days serving as cannon fodder while he was a junior varsity player against the huge Navy football team. Despite his relatively small size, Stockdale was always on the attack against the biggest players he could find.

His leg had been dislocated at the knee during shootdown, and the North Vietnamese, citing to him a slogan, "Politics before medicine," had refused him treatment. The result was that he was in intense pain for many months and his leg eventually froze at a right angle. From his central location at the Thunderbird, in the Little Vegas areas of the Hilton, he had run a vigorous, successful resistance operation until the "BACK U.S." program had been traced to him during a torture purge. Because he had led the prisoners at Vegas so well, he had become the No. 1 target. He was the senior officer at Alcatraz and in command.

Three of the eleven at Alcatraz, Johnson, McKnight, and Storz, were in the Air Force. The rest of us were in the Navy. The ages ranged from Coker's twenty-six to Stockdale's forty-four and my forty-three, but most were in their middle to late thirties.

- - - - -

The prisoners of Alcatraz would begin to stir during the dark, quiet, early morning hours. The lids on the buckets would rattle, and the sound of coughing and spitting would echo unpleasantly through the small compound. And, if the wind was right, the street noises of Hanoi—trolleys beginning their rounds, the subdued noise of motors—would drift hollowly into our dazed, half-conscious world.

About six thirty I would hear the sound of keys rattling as the key guard opened the door to Stockdale's or Mulligan's cell, removed their irons, and took them to the head one at a time. Since the rattling keys meant that eventually I would be fed, my mouth would begin to water.

There was a wide space under nine of the eleven cell doors, and the prisoners in those cells would come to their doors and stand while a guard reached underneath and unlocked the irons. Some of the prisoners would move around contrarily or kick at the guard, and the guard would twist his irons to teach him a lesson. In the evening, when the irons were being replaced, there was often more trouble. Each prisoner had his own set of irons to which he had become accustomed, and the guards would frequently mix them up. There would be howls of anger until the prisoner got his proper set.

After about a month, the guards began sliding the irons under the doors after the evening meal, then watching through the peephole while the prisoner put them on and locked them. After about a year, a few of us learned to click the locks without actually locking them. Depending on the alertness of the guard who was handling us, we would try our luck and go the night with one leg free. The irons, which were two ankle cuffs and a sliding bar, were uncomfortable and restrictive; having even one leg free was a big relief.

During the morning rounds, I would spend my time peeping under the door to see who was visiting the cement hole across from my cell to empty his bucket, and listening to the message he was scraping out. Listening for messages was a big event each morning, and if I missed any part I would tap to McKnight and get him to fill me in.

The scrapes went something like this: Scraaape, scraape...pause... scraaape, scraaape, scraaape...pause...scraaape...scraaape...pause...

The prisoners, huddled in their cells, would translate.

"Hi!" the scrapes might read. "Looks like rain today."

The first man usually commented on the weather, since the others couldn't see outside. This was of much interest although I'm not sure why, because we would spend at the most ten minutes outside.

Other messages might read: "HBSJ." Happy birthday, Sam Johnson. Or "HAHR." Happy anniversary, Howie Rutledge. The anniversary would be in reference to his shootdown date.

Such was our long association in prison that we knew everyone's important dates, and would scrape like hell with our bamboo strips, one eye on the suspicious guard, to salute the birthdays and shootdown dates of everyone in camp as they came up. Shootdown dates, incidentally, were an important part of our prisoner identification. On contacting a new prisoner, the date would be included in our salutation if we had time. For instance, I would tap to a newcomer, "Denton, 18 July, 1965," sometimes with a twinge of realization that the date was rapidly receding into the past.

We would take every opportunity we could to communicate. I had the latrine duty and would clean up after the others. This meant I had more time to send messages, a not inconsiderable luxury.

Bob Shumaker got the sweeping duty, and with his head down in a cloud of dust, he would furiously sweep the greetings and news, pass on messages, tell jokes, and complain, until the guard gave him a kick for taking too long.

And from the cells would come the muffled coughs, snorts, and hacks that brought him the answers and comments of his constituency.

In October, the days were still long enough so that I would trudge the cement path to the cistern in pale morning light, shivering against the chill. But as the days shortened, there would be only darkness and gloom as I stripped, doused cold water over my body, soaped it, and doused again before washing my shirt and pajamas in the same water and hanging them up to dry. Then I would take down the clothing I had hung on the line the morning before and trudge back in my shorts to the cell with my empty bucket.

And always, I could feel the eyes on me, watching from under the doors as I went past.

A guard would come and give me the first of three cigarettes we were allowed each day. Previously, I would throw my cigarettes away on occasion in protest against the treatment, but now in Alcatraz I would smoke that first one eagerly, trying to mask the hunger gnawing at me. By the time breakfast was shoved under the door, about ten thirty, I was literally drooling. The food was meager, soup with some greens and occasionally a piece of pork fat, and rice, and I would leap at it and gulp it straight from the pewter plates. I was hungry again as soon as I finished eating, and it wasn't until about four thirty that the next meal was shoved under the door. In more than two years there were few times when I wasn't desperate for food.

Aside from our scraping and sweeping, most of our communicating came during the quiet hour after our first meal when only one or two sleepy guards were on duty. Then our cellblock became a madhouse as everyone got on the wall.

We didn't establish regular communication with Mulligan and Stockdale in their separate block for about two weeks, when we worked out a system of flashing under the doors. There was about a six-inch space under the doors of the main cellblock, but only about a half-inch under Mulligan's and

Stockdale's doors. Nonetheless, we could communicate with them by inter-rupting the light under the doors with our hand, a method we transmitted to them by scraping on the bucket one day.

Thereafter, Stockdale and Mulligan would transmit messages by flashing to Tanner in the middle of my cellblock, and Tanner would tap them to us, which made him the center of a three-way communications network. The system was ponderous and took great effort, courage, and patience on the part of Tanner, but it worked.

The North Vietnamese were leaving us pretty much alone at this time. We weren't being tortured, and even the young, illiterate guards appeared to accord us a grudging respect. They were kept in hand by the camp adminis-tration and were ably led by the key guard, a young intelligent man who was entrusted with most of the camp keys. We had some respect for him, and I was a little disappointed to learn one day that he was stealing cigarettes from the storeroom between Mulligan's and Stockdale's cells. He had a long bamboo pole with which he reached into the room, knocked the cigarettes on the floor, and worked them under the door. We called him CS, for Cigarette Stealer.

Actually, the first few months in our new home were not so bad. It would be worse later, but for the moment the pressure was off, and the terrible fear of torture was lifted. Although we were getting cuffed about occasionally for various infractions of the rules, the principal objective seemed to be to leave each individual with the impression that he was completely isolated from his kind, the only American in camp. But of course, it soon became apparent that this was unrealistic, since we were constantly communicating.

There was a tacit understanding that unless these communications be-came overt, they would let them continue. I don't believe they ever quite caught on to the flashing, but they knew that the scrapes and sweeping meant something. One day, as I was cleaning the latrine and transmitting,

Rat came up behind me, and with a wry smile said, "Denton, that is a very long message."

As Christmas approached, Rat came to my cell, stuck his head in the door, and said, "Denton, what would you like for Christmas?" Befuddled, I looked up and mumbled something about a letter from home. He smiled and closed the door, and I wondered if this was another trick. I heard him going through the cellblock, asking the same question, and I got on the wall to get a full accounting. Most wanted letters, and some wanted medical treatment. All, of course, wanted food. When Rat got to Rutledge's cell, he poked his head in the door and said, "Ah, Rutledge, what would you like for Christmas?"

Rutledge's quick answer was typical of him: "A cup of coffee and a bus ticket to Saigon!"

Surprisingly, Rat delivered on most of his promises. I got a letter from Jane and an enormous meal which included turkey, an egg roll, a spiced salad, and caramels. I felt bloated when I had finished.

On Christmas night, Rat came to Mulligan's cell, and with a big grin said, "We take you to Catholic service tonight." Mulligan thought there might be other Americans there, and it would be an opportunity to tell them where we were. He was taken to the Plantation, where he attended Mass with twelve other Americans. He recognized Jerry Coffee and passed the information to him that there were eleven Americans isolated in a prison two blocks north of the Plantation. Other prisoners didn't learn fully about Alcatraz until Christmas of 1968, a year later.

Christmas to us meant the rarest of treats, treats so humble that in days past we would have considered them absurd. We spent all of Christmas Eve composing greetings to each other, and the night was filled with the quiet tapping of trapped men wishing each other peace on earth, good will to all. I sang carols in a low voice that in the deep silence carried to the others. There was one more special treat in honor of Christmas. Rat allowed Shumaker to draw some chessboards on scraps of paper. They were passed out to us on Christmas. Rat had said we could play only with ourselves—knowing full well that behind the walls we would tap our knuckles and fingers raw playing the game with each other.

At Alcatraz, I had already invented the vocal tap code, and now I made up a variation of it for the chess moves. By various signals, including the usual coughs, sneezes, and hacks and an occasional rattle of the lid on our buckets McKnight and I played every day. A lid would rattle, there would be a cough, then silence as one player would decipher and study his opponent's move. Then, sometimes, a loud "You dirty bastard!" would burst forth as the player would discover what his opponent had done to him. Other prisoners, listening in on the game, would laugh until the guard rattled the bolts on the doors and shouted, "Silence!"

After a week or so, Rat opened the door to my cell and looked in at me. "Ah, Denton, how do you like playing chess?" he said.

"Wonderful," I replied flatly, not wanting him to know how much I truly enjoyed it.

"Well Denton, how would you like someone to play with in your cell?"

"Wonderful," I replied, this time with feeling. I was too surprised and overjoyed to be suspicious.

"Ah, Denton," he said, raising his eyebrows and smiling, "I don't mean boy. I mean girl!"

Groucho Marx couldn't have done a better job of wiggling his eyebrows than Rat did at that moment.

"I'm married," I said, and turned back to my chessboard. Rat took the rejection in good grace and seemed almost respectful at my answer. As soon as he had closed the door, I got on the wall and took a poll, asking if others had ever got the same kind of offer. Three yeses came back.

After about two weeks, however, we decided to make Rat promise that all the prisoners in Hanoi would get chessboards, and when he wouldn't, we reluctantly turned ours in.

So the long, silent days and nights drifted past into the cold, rainy months of January and February. The drizzle and chill were constant, and sometimes a storm would fill the cement gutter and cold, dirty water would flood into the cells, carrying dead cockroaches and rats. Even the tempo of the attacks on the power plant nearby slowed as the weather closed in and chilled our very souls.

Communications remained the heart of our existence. Without that slender and infrequent link with the others, I think I would have lost my mind. I came to truly love them and developed a fierce pride that we had been singled out. Aside from an occasional room check and quizzes, the North Vietnamese left us alone. Even the occasional quiz, which was no more than an attitude check, was a welcome break in routine. Rat actually ran the camp and conducted most of the quizzes, but Slopehead, who was generally in charge of camp maintenance, sometimes pried his way into the act, to Rat's embarrassment. Slopehead conducted his quizzes dead drunk, his head rolling from side to side as he tried to form a coherent question.

We were in relatively good shape during those early months. I kept my body sound by running in place in my cell and kept my mind occupied with religion and with communicating. We all had our own ways of keeping our minds occupied. Daily we would recite to ourselves the name, rank, and serial number of every prisoner we knew about in Hanoi. Most of us constructed homes in our mind and worked mathematical problems. Mulligan ran a mental computer. Once he passed the word that at 8:24 A.M. on Sunday, five percent of the week was gone. Now and then, when someone was trying to communicate with him, he'd flash, "Call me later, I'm working on something."

We made up menus for the day. Every evening, Mulligan would construct a dinner for Stockdale, patiently working through the soup and salad, the roast beef, parfait, and even the brandy Alexander and proper cigar. Shumaker was especially good on breakfasts, and each morning we would eagerly await his offering while the guards were ladling out our miserable fare. Food was constantly on our minds, and we frequently saw the guards picking out the few tiny bits of meat and pig fat before the meals got to us. This was a steady source of irritation.

All of us sorted through our lives. I began thinking through the names of my former squadron mates, my Naval Academy classmates, high school friends. Then, grade by grade I went, remembering names, faces and personalities until one day I was sorting through the first grade and recalling with amazing clarity names and faces I thought that I had long forgotten. I'd laugh to myself over some childhood prank, or weep over some nostalgic reminiscence. I remembered a toy airplane I had received on my third birthday, and tried to bury myself in the swirling, pleasant memory.

Others were going through the same process. Mulligan recalled walking down a dirt road past a cemetery with his grandparents and asking what it was. They told him, and he repeated the word. His grandmother was amazed. "He's not even three," she said.

Mulligan discussed the phenomenon with Stockdale, who tapped to him, "We are regressing. We're going back to our childhoods."

Later, the process would accelerate until some of the prisoners actually began losing control of their bodily functions.

Most of us had horrible nightmares, and there would be a calling out and crying in the night. Once, Stockdale had such a violent and uncontrollable nightmare that the guards came in and beat him. They thought he was trying to communicate.

On nights when I couldn't sleep, I had my own special game. I made pets of the lizards that clustered around the dim light over the door catching insects. The lizards were a species called geckos, and there was one I was especially fond of, a male I named Bullmoose. He was quite a lover, with his own harem (they made love upside down, hanging from the ceiling), and I became absorbed in his elaborate and lengthy courtship ceremonies. The geckos would have three or four young, and because of Bullmoose's ardor there was a periodic population explosion, with the young competing with each other around the light for insects.

The weaker young would eventually lose out (even their own mothers would chase then away) and fall to the floor gasping for breath. I would care for them, swatting mosquitoes with my bamboo fan and feeding them to the unfortunates. I would have to be careful about the swatting, however. They wouldn't eat a dead mosquito no matter how hungry they were. But this welfare state approach didn't work for long. The baby geckos soon forgot how to catch their own food, and as they became older their instincts took over; they became shy and stayed away from me. They would hang on the wall away from the hunting grounds and starve. One by one they would fall to the floor, twitching and gasping until they expired. Force feeding didn't work.

The adult geckos were amazingly quick. They would leap from the wall, snatch a flying insect in midair, and splat against another wall where they would hang on and devour their prey. Once I saw a gecko swallow an enormous horsefly and sit for hours without moving, digesting his victim. On another occasion, Bullmoose captured a dragonfly and worked it around in his mouth until he got the bottom end moving down his gullet. The dragonfly's wings were still flapping as they slowly disappeared into Bullmoose's mouth. This cooled his ardor, anyway. He didn't move for a week.

Unfortunately, the geckos were unattracted by the small, sluggish flies which covered my ceiling and walls by the hundreds. Other cells, farther away from the latrine, were less infested. The flies were easy to kill since they hardly moved, but I would get tired of squashing them. Once I counted 250 kills before I quit, and there were plenty more still alive.

It was sometimes so quiet in the early morning hours that when I swatted a mosquito there would be three distinct little "thunks": one when I hit it, and softer ones when it hit the wall and then the floor. The geckos would hear the sounds, and by the third "thunk" one would be scurrying toward the floor. He would have to hurry because there was a spider down in one corner of the cell just over the bottom of the door who could also apparently hear, or feel, the sounds. He too would scurry toward the floor after the flopping mosquito.

And now a third party would enter the fray. Ants were always patrolling under the door and invariably made first contact with the mosquito. Then a struggle ensued. It was usually one, two, three: ants grab mosquito, spider takes it away from ants, gecko gobbles spider and mosquito.

It was like watching a football game on TV.

CHAPTER SIXTEEN

In the spring of 1968, we celebrated Easter weeks ahead of the rest of the world. We didn't know when it was to fall (April 14 as I discovered many years later), so we guessed, and chose a Sunday in March. I said that we should pray for a sign that would deliver us from our long ordeal.

I composed a poem in three stanzas. One stanza I "recited" on Holy Thursday, the second on Good Friday, and the third on Holy Saturday. Almost all of us at Alcatraz had a deep belief in God. Thus, each stanza was eagerly awaited, and the following morning the others would scrape back their comments on my effort.

The poem was titled "The Great Sign." It represented a conversation on Holy Saturday night, about thirty hours after Christ was crucified, among the three women who found the stone rolled back from Christ's tomb on Easter morning.

I made up the first stanza for Joanna, one of the holy women. It went:

His manger birth drew kings in awe,
His smile the former blind men saw,
In Him divine and mortal merged,
Yet He's the one the soldiers scourged.
The second stanza I composed for Mary, the mother of James:
He praised the humble and the meek,

The grateful deaf-mute heard Him speak,
His face was love personified,
Yet He's the one they crucified.
The third was spoken by Mary Magdalene:
Now our tears with doubts combine,
How could He die yet be divine?
We must dispel this faithless gloom,
Let's pray at dawn beside His tomb.

The poem illustrated as well as anything the desperate hopefulness of the prisoners in our dark and lonely cells as we looked for a "Great Sign."

And the sign came on April 1, when, early in the morning, Rat flung open the door to my cell and half-shouted: "Denton, we have defeat you! There will be no more bombing! Johnson has quit!"

Using our "180-degree" rational, we assumed this meant that the North Vietnamese had made a tremendous concession to Johnson, who in turn had ordered a halt to the bombing. We concluded that peace should not be far off. To me, and to many of the others, it was the sign for which we had been looking. It had come too close on the heels of our fervent prayer to be coincidence.

We held to our hope for a long time, although Mulligan began to waver after a while. He began to believe the end of the bombing meant we would sit there for years and rot. Eventually, I also began to waver, but neither one of us expressed our doubts, and it was a full year before I would completely lose faith in my "Great Sign." In the meantime, our purgatory would continue.

A camp radio was finally installed at Alcatraz early in the spring of 1968, and it provided a few moments of welcome relief from the interminable boredom of our lives. It came on at seven o'clock each morning and stayed on for fifteen minutes. We didn't realize how much we missed Hanoi Hanna until we heard her husky voice again one morning, giving us her one-sided views. We heard for the first time about the Tet offensive, launched against major cities in South Vietnam by the Viet Cong and North Vietnamese on January 30, and which was continuing; and of course, discussions of President Johnson's real reasons for ending the bombing of the North.

Spring brought a change for the worse at Alcatraz. While the winter months had been cold and uncomfortable, we were at least protected from the wind and rain and could survive. But as the weather warmed even our survival was at risk.

It began to get hot, very hot, and our tiny, unventilated cells began to throb with the heat as the unrelenting sun bore down on the flat, tarred, and unprotected roofs. As the humidity rose, the cells became like steam closets. We crept to our cell doors and sucked like animals for air, gasping for breath.

Also, we began to hear statements over the camp radio by American prisoners critical of the war and the U.S. government, and we didn't believe they had been tortured for them. The voices were too steady, the tone too sincere. After one particularly obnoxious statement, one word came through my wall: "Barf." Some in Alcatraz would have happily cut the throats of the speakers.

And the early releases had started, with many of the released prisoners dishonoring themselves in our eyes. There was deep resentment among the men at Alcatraz that Americans had accepted special treatment, although we learned before our return home that a couple had told the truth about conditions and had helped focus attention on us. Navy Lieutenant Bob Frishman, who had lost the elbow in his right arm on ejection from his airplane, and Seaman Douglas Hegdahl, who had been swept from a warship by a wave and had been picked up at sea, spent much of their time, once they had returned to the United States, stirring interest in the prisoners of war. Frishman and Hegdahl had received permission from senior prisoners to accept early release. We couldn't say the same for some others.

The American public was slow in understanding the magnitude of the North Vietnamese torture program, and until Frishman and Hegdahl began speaking out, the prisoners were only shadowy figures to be pitied and wondered about.

Meanwhile, the heat was intensifying as May wore on, and the guards would open the doors to find us gasping on the floor, our food untouched. One day Cat showed up, and called Mulligan to quiz. He demanded to know why Mulligan wasn't eating. Mulligan was nearly out of his mind from the heat and ranted at Cat.

"You can't hurt me any more than you have already," he shouted, tearing at his clothing and baring his chest. "Look at my chest!" Mulligan demanded. "My bones are showing, I'm starving, and I can't eat. I can't breathe and you ask me why I won't eat."

Cat dismissed the complaint about the heat. He didn't believe it. It must be something else.

"Shut mouth, Mulligan!" he shouted. "You have bad att-i-tude!"

Then, because it was bad form to allow prisoners to starve themselves to death, Cat said, "If you eat, Mulligan, maybe you will get letter from wife." And he raised his eyebrows and wiggled them, as though he was offering him a woman. Then Mulligan was thrown back into his cell.

We were all fighting a claustrophobic depression and battling for survival. We would never make it through the summer. I demanded to see Rat. Surprisingly, my wish was granted and I was taken to the quiz room.

A prisoner had to be careful how he presented his case. "Demands" were rejected out of hand and the prisoner would be shoved back to his cell. So I said, "I want to congratulate you on carrying through on the excruciating treatment and putting us to a slow death by heat."

I believe Rat was honestly surprised, as I went on to describe the situation. "No, Denton, I did not know conditions were that bad. Our orders are to keep you isolated and in irons. We have no orders to kill you. We will study."

In a day or two a large crew showed up under the leadership of Smiley, my old friend from previous tortures, and set to work to improve conditions. They covered the roof with leafy branches and planted vines next to the door. The vines, which had enormous leaves, grew quickly, and by the time the leaves on the roof branches had withered, the roof was covered with a tangle of vines.

It was on the day the branches were placed on the roof that Smiley, seeing me going to empty my bucket, went into my cell and made the bed and bundled my clothing into a neat pile. As he passed me on my return, he gave me a friendly smile, which surprised me. When I saw what he had done, I knew I had been repaid for fixing the bulb at the Zoo in 1966. I wanted to thank him, but I never saw him again.

To our great relief, the work group also hammered open the steel plates over the doors. The bolts were rusted and couldn't be turned, and it took them days to complete the job, but when they were finished a welcome breath of air slipped into the cells.

So we drifted through the summer, somewhat more comfortable, but still hungry, still lonely, and still looking for a sign. There was a surge of hope when the peace talks began in Paris on May 10, but when the talks began to drag, we began to lose interest in them.

In June, Rat was replaced by an officer called variously by the names of Softsoap, Fairy, and Slick. Rat had tried to do his job and had usually kept his word on anything he had promised. Softsoap was much better educated than Rat, but much less trustworthy.

That same month we heard on the camp radio that Robert Kennedy had been assassinated. We were deeply saddened, even though we felt that his antiwar attitude had come at the wrong time and place. We didn't think we would get out of there on the strength of antiwar sentiment. We would get out when a real settlement had been reached through the application of significant force.

On July fourth we got a big meal because the American people, as Soft-soap said, had "denied Johnson's war." We got another one on September 2, the North Vietnamese national day. That was one day in the year when we could count on a big meal.

Also on September 2, I was given a routine quiz by Mickey Mouse, who had just replaced Softsoap and seemed as bored as we were. I engaged him in a lengthy debate over U.S involvement in Indochina. I was usually wary of Mickey Mouse, a hard-working Communist hardliner, and had warned the others that his appearance was sure to mean a change for the worse. But since he now seemed to be in a receptive mood, I began to elaborate on the policies of Roosevelt and Truman, both of whom opposed colonialism, and both of whom had a strong determination to contain Communism.

I said it had become clear to the United States and the world by 1947 that Russia was the real colonialist power and had proved it by its rejection or falsification of elections in Eastern Europe. The Soviet Union was an expansionist nation and the West had formed the North Atlantic Treaty Organization (NATO) in 1949 to halt that expansion. Although France was a respected ally, we had not been in sympathy with its efforts to preserve colonialism in Indochina after the war, but we preferred France and the government it had set up under Boa Dai in Vietnam to the evil of Communism and thus had supported the French.

I noted that many of the Eastern European nations that had been subjugated by the Soviet Union had revolted—Hungary, Poland, East Germany—and had been ruthlessly crushed with the help of Soviet troops.

I conceded that North Vietnam might receive some immediate gains from the organization of resources of the country under Communism, but I added that fascism or democracy—or any strong political organization—would also achieve short-term benefits. But the nations under Soviet control were being drained of their substance, and I predicted that Czechoslovakia would soon revolt and that North Vietnam would revolt in twenty years or less.

At the mention of Czechoslovakia, Mickey Mouse, who had been listening attentively, grabbed at the arms of his chair and jerked himself upright. "Denton," he half-shouted, "you have radio!"

I was stunned, and stared at him. He accused me again of having a radio which carried Voice of America, and with no further explanation called a guard. I was taken back to my cell, and while Mickey Mouse watched intently, I was stripped, spreadeagled against the wall, and searched thoroughly. Mickey Mouse finally left, puzzled and still unconvinced.

Much later I learned why he had been upset. The Czechs had indeed revolted and had been suppressed ruthlessly on August 20. He thought I was making a fool out of him with secret information, information I could have learned only from a hidden radio.

That was the only break in the string of dreary, unending days. Sometimes in the fall I invented a game which I called Five Questions to help us occupy our minds. Each day, a prisoner would put out five questions on any subject he wished. They would be passed around at rest time, with the questioner to be the sole judge as to the truth of the answers.

For instance, the questioner might ask us to name five fish that can live in both salt and fresh water. Now who would know that? Surprisingly, somewhere in the subconscious were the answers to the most difficult questions. If you had that information stored in your mind, you could usually dredge it out, and most people have heard something on just about everything, it seems. It was amazing how successful we became at answering the most esoteric questions.

Even this seemingly harmless pastime caused problems. We had become very high-strung and nervous, and arguments raged when there was disagreement over the answers. At the game's peak some of us would go off the wall and wouldn't speak to each other for days. When I got home years later, I sent a check for $100 to Harry Jenkins and a $200 check to Jim Stockdale in payment of the bets I had lost, with the admonition that they not return them. But they did anyway.

There were a couple of other developments that fall. Our captors began allowing us to exercise outside one at a time for five minutes each day, and a screen was put up around the bath area. The screen was the result of a strange incident.

Three sides of the wall enclosing the compound were high, maybe sixteen feet. But the fourth side was low enough for someone to see over if he stood on something. One morning as I was washing, I saw a woman looking over the wall at me. Until then the only outsiders I had seen were a couple of kids who had climbed into a tree overhanging a corner of the compound and had thrown some rocks at me. When I saw the woman I did a double take and quickly covered up.

She was back the next morning, peeping over the wall, and when I returned to my cell, there was a loud thumping on the back wall of my cell. I suspected a trap of some sort and didn't thump back, and in a few minutes there were loud voices. A soldier had apparently caught the woman.

I didn't see her again, but the guards made us keep our shorts on while bathing thereafter, a circumstance that made us all unhappy, until a bamboo fence was erected around the area. Such was their strange morality.

I was still wary of Mickey Mouse, and felt certain there was a change coming in our treatment. Major changes did occur very soon, and looking back on them years later, I tried to analyze the reasons for them. The sequence of events is important to the understanding.

In September and October of 1968, the Harriman peace negotiations appeared to be heading for success. Then, on October 31, President Johnson dramatically announced a bombing halt of North Vietnam. And on the first Tuesday in November, Richard Nixon was elected President of the United States.

The three circumstances added up to a belief in the minds of the political leaders of North Vietnam that the war was coming to a close, and I myself thought there was a secret agreement behind Johnson's bombing halt.

If the war was to end, the North Vietnamese wanted the prisoners, particularly the senior officers and resistance leaders, to go out on their knees, presenting a disgraceful spectacle during the release sequence.

We had discussed the election in our awkward, dangerous way. There was some division of opinion on the relative merits of Nixon and Humphrey as President, but after the election, we all expressed our happiness that Nixon had won because our captors were now quite unhappy.

Although the North Vietnamese believed that eventually Nixon would be tougher than Johnson, they continued to hope against hope that Nixon would settle generally on Harriman's terms.

The situation in 1968 was full of contradictions and ambiguities, and behind it all was the Johnson administration's difficulty in trying to come to terms not only with Hanoi but with South Vietnam on proposals which would satisfy the three parties. The peace negotiations in Paris had been between the U.S. and Hanoi, but in November the two sides agreed to allow South Vietnam and the Provisional Revolutionary Government, the Communist entity in South Vietnam, to join the talks, which they did in 1969. Perhaps this was the breakthrough towards peace which encouraged the North Vietnamese to believe an end was in sight.

In any case, they prepared for the coming release ceremonies in a savage way, and our fourteen-month sabbatical at Alcatraz suddenly came to an end.

Just before dawn one day in the middle of December, a guard hid in a bomb shelter across the cement gutter from my cell and then slipped unnoticed into the empty cell between McKnight's and mine. We had gone on the wall to each other as soon as we had awakened. At the first few taps the guard leaped from the cell and shouted to McKnight: "You communicate! You communicate!" Then he shook his finger at my door and repeated the charge to me in a high-pitched, excited voice.

Instantly, a deep chill ran through my body. They could have caught us communicating at any time, and this sudden noisy coup could mean only one thing. After fourteen months of relative peace, we were to be tortured again. I knew this would be a deadly serious matter. The others sensed the same thing, and fear immediately gripped them. I began to pray.

As we watched under our doors and listened intently, trying to figure out the next move, guards came to McKnight's cell and led him away to a building across an alley outside the compound gates. Then all was silence again. I tapped to Coker, two cells away, and we speculated on what was happening to McKnight. We concluded the worst.

The days dragged on. We waited anxiously and prayed. Several days later, in the early morning hours, McKnight came dragging along the cement walk to the latrine, where he emptied his bucket. I peeped under my door at him. He was bloody and looked terrible, but he had enough strength remaining to scrape to us that the North Vietnamese had tortured him into writing a letter of apology for his crimes.

He was put back in his cell that day and tapped to me just a few words: "Purge, I say no comm." Then there was silence. They had worked him over pretty badly.

We understood the word "purge" only too well, and we appreciated his getting word to us that he had denied communicating. Of course they weren't interested in whether we were communicating or not. It was just a convenient excuse to put pressure on us for some as yet unknown reason.

Before McKnight could continue tapping, I was taken from my cell and across the alley to a quiz room where I faced Mickey Mouse, no longer the attentive listener. He got right to the point.

"You have been caught communicating," he said, shaking his finger. "You must apologize. You must write letter to President Ho Chi Minh and apologize for your crimes."

I said I would not.

"Okay," Mickey Mouse said. "I leave you to think deeply."

I was taken to another room in the same building. Irons were placed on my legs and I was pushed against a wall, arms outstretched over my head. There I stood for two days and two nights under guard. If my arms slipped, the guard would force them upward again and press a nail hard against the palm of my hand for added encouragement.

On the third morning, Mickey Mouse came in and asked me again if I would write the letter of apology. I refused.

"We are going to get serious then, Denton," he warned. Having beaten them in my last two torture sessions in 1966, I thought I could do it again. In an effort to deter the punishment, I wrote Mickey Mouse a note reminding him of my previous success, and said that if they were determined to torture me, they would have to torture me to death. That was a mistake. It was a pledge I couldn't keep.

The next stage was rear cuffs and leg irons. A guard dragged me around the rough cement floor until the leg cuffs began tearing into my ankles. He jerked me left and right, lifted me by the rear handcuffs—the same mess all over again for hours. Then I was left on the floor for a day.

Mickey Mouse gave me one more chance to write the letter, and again I refused.

In the months since my last torture, the Vietnamese had developed a rig which was unknown to me, and it was the perfect answer to my ability to take pain until passing out. As soon as Mickey Mouse left the room, a guard slammed open the door, and held out a rope and a four-and-a-half-foot pole, pointed at one end.

"Ah, Denton," he shouted, grinning, "here is your old friend!" Actually, the pole was new to me.

Two more guards came into the room, and the three of them began tying my wrists and lower forearms together in front of me. They forced my elbows apart and forced my knees between them, and pushed the pole through the hole created by my elbows and knees. Then they tipped me back on my spine and propped my feet on an overturned stool so that my feet were raised about a foot off the ground.

In essence, I was in the fetal position, my thighs pressed against my chest so tightly that I could hardly breathe, My body was tipped at such an angle that most of my weight was on the tip of my spine. The pole was the key to the rig. If the rig was properly tied, I would pass out eventually and fall on my side; the end of the pole would hit the floor and slide out of the rig, easing the pressure on my arms and restoring circulation. The pain that came with the blood circulation would bring me back to consciousness; thus the prisoner couldn't beat the rig by passing out.

But the guards had tied the ropes poorly. They had allowed some of the loops to overlap, and by working at the rope I could eliminate the overlaps, thus loosening the rope and allowing enough circulation so that I lasted about four hours without passing out. The rig was still painful, but I could stand it. Mickey Mouse came in, obviously worried that the rig wasn't working and I would beat it, as I had promised.

He had the guards untie me and I was brought some food, but I couldn't eat it. I dawdled with the food to buy time, but Mickey Mouse became impatient, and with a wave of the hand said, "Denton, we will break you now."

I was retied, but again ineffectively, and I was able to last four more hours. Finally, a guard named Sad Sack inspected the rig, criticized the guards for their incompetence, and supervised the retying. This time the rig worked, and after an hour of agony, during which time I watched my hands slowly swell and turn black, I passed out and fell over. The end of the pole hit the floor and slipped from the rig, as intended, and the rush of blood to my arms brought me back to consciousness and renewed pain. By then, six or seven guards were in the room kicking and punching at me.

There was one big guard we called Jack Armstrong, who was much decorated and treated with deference by the others. He was a husky, strong fellow and as he swung at me I spat at him and tried to butt him. Surprisingly, tears came to his eyes and he stopped and turned his back. As I looked up in wonderment, Mickey Mouse brusquely ordered him to hit me again. Jack Armstrong turned around, dutifully gave me a little poke in the face, and left the room.

After a period of time, pain becomes an all-encompassing entity, a fiery, blinding devil that courses into every part of the brain until you would literally do anything to escape it. After three cycles, the rig became too much. It had driven me to the point where I would have happily committed suicide to escape it. I would have run my own mother down with a truck if the price was freedom from pain, but I could do nothing. I felt my heart pumping mightily to force the blood through my strangled limbs and hoped that it would give out.

I prayed to die.

After a total of about twelve hours in the rig, I called for the guard, who had been listening outside the door. In a matter of seconds there was the sound of excited voices as he passed the word that I had broken, and I heard several people rushing in triumph toward the cell. Among them was Mickey Mouse with pen and paper in hand. I agreed to write.

The next day in about three brief paragraphs, I wrote, in essence: Dear Ho Chi Minh, I am sorry I bombed your country. Please forgive me.

On December 23, I was returned to my cell practically unconscious and in high fever. I was too whipped to eat, and just slumped on my pallet.

On Christmas Eve, still very sore and with the fever still raging, I was blindfolded and walked with assistance to the Plantation, two blocks away, where I was taken to a brightly lit room that was obviously rigged for picture taking. There was a spectacular table full of goodies, including champagne, in the middle of the room.

And there, ensconced on a high-backed chair, was my old friend Cat, his eyes sparkling. He thought I had been beaten down and was now prepared to mop up what was left. An incredible conversation ensued.

"Ah, Denton," he said, "good to see you again. How are you?" I told him I had been tortured again. He ignored that. "How are conditions?" "Terrible!"

"Can't eat because of the torture." "Is there anything I can do for you?" "Only if you do it for everyone."

The conversation, such as it was, was deteriorating rapidly. Cat was getting angrier and angrier and I was getting meaner and meaner.

To break the tension, Cat politely offered me a banana, but I declined.

"All right, Denton, eat that banana!" Cat said, his voice rising as he pointed to the table.

"No."

"It will be good for you."

"If everyone gets a banana, I will take it."

He lost his composure.

"Shut mouth! You eat banana! That is an order!"

ADMIRAL JEREMIAH A. DENTON

I just looked at him sullenly and shook my head. It was an impasse, and Cat was fast losing face. Abruptly, he ordered me back to my cell.

I knew I would pay for my attitude, but I was angry as hell about the apology I had written to Ho Chi Minh.

They broke off the torture temporarily after McKnight's and my ordeal because they wanted to go through the ritual of observing our holiday season. But on January 8, I was taken across the alley for the second time, where Mickey Mouse asked me what had happened on Christmas Eve. I shrugged and told him I had followed the Code of Conduct and refused a special favor.

"You were a fool on Christmas Eve, Denton, and now you must pay," Mickey Mouse said. "You must read on the camp radio." He knew I would refuse.

I was run through the same mill for two more excruciating days, only this time Mickey Mouse left the window open and faced me toward it so the prisoners at Alcatraz could hear my screams. When I gave up, Mickey Mouse had me read excerpts from their news service into a tape recorder for about a minute, but I was so incoherent that the tape was useless.

The next day, Softsoap, holding a pole and rope in his hands, warned me that the tape was unsatisfactory and said, "You must make it sound more like you." The following day I read the news over and over again until they settled for something they thought they could play on the camp radio, but it was still screwed up. They played the tape for about twenty seconds, but when my shaky voice and gross mispronunciations brought laughter and jeers from the Alcatraz cells, they turned it off.

As soon as I was returned to my cell, Mickey Mouse tried to cash in on my screams by ordering Mulligan to read on the radio and threatening him with torture if he didn't.

"I know what you did to Denton," Mulligan told them, "and you'll have to do the same thing to me."

181

In the predawn hours of January 23, Harry Jenkins, who had been suffering from an infestation of worms, began screaming in his cell from the pain of horrible cramps. In a few minutes there was the bustling sound of guards scurrying to his cell. We were extremely worried about Harry's condition, and when we heard some scuffling and heard Harry shout, "Go ahead, hit me!" we thought he was being beaten to keep him quiet.

In a desperate effort to take the pressure off him and protest the beating, we began banging on the walls and doors of our cells and yelling. The next morning Stockdale passed the word ordering a two-day protest fast. None of us ate the next day, and during the dawn hours of January 25, Stockdale was taken away. As senior officer, he had been blamed for the ruckus. It was a year before we learned his fate.

He was taken to Little Vegas, where he was tortured severely for five days and then ordered to make a movie to be shown to other prisoners of war. The gist of the movie was to be: "We have a new president, and he has a secret plan for ending the war. A delicate situation is in the making. Take hope but act with caution. Do exactly what the North Vietnamese tell you during the release sequence and things will work to your advantage."

Stockdale resisted. Then suddenly his captors abandoned the idea. The party line changed, and the movie was never made.

With Stockdale gone, the remaining ten prisoners waited uneasily in their cells, wondering what was to come next. To our amazement, a doctor appeared on the scene with a retinue of medical assistants and solicitous guards. An English-speaking guard came to my cell and asked me what was the matter.

I said that we were all ill and that Jenkins, who was especially ill, had been beaten two nights before when he had cried for help. The guard spent some time trying to convince me that Jenkins had not been beaten and said, "There has been a misunderstanding and we will prove to you that you will get humane treatment when you are sick."

Then the doctor and his assistants gave me a complete physical with all the trappings, including a stethoscope, a light in the ears and nose, thumping on the chest and back, the whole routine. They listed all my complaints and gave me medicine for worms, a rash, and the cuts inflicted during my last torture session. They went through the cells, spending at least twenty minutes with each prisoner, and then made a dramatic exit in a shower of gauze and pills.

After the doctor's departure, we were called to quiz one by one, where Mickey Mouse explained patiently that Jenkins had not been beaten, a statement Jenkins himself later confirmed. Mickey Mouse asked if the prisoners had any other complaints. I said that we wanted to be treated under the terms of the Geneva Convention, but he merely shrugged this off and insisted that we were wrong about Jenkins; sick men would not be beaten. This was as close as the Vietnamese had ever come to an apology.

It was late in the morning when the final quiz ended, and since I was now the senior officer, the others began pouring messages at me about the fast. They were hungry. I received messages from McKnight and two others saying that they assumed I would end the fast now that we had made our point, and others, while emptying their buckets scraped messages like, "They gave up. We won," or "Let's eat!"

I felt duty-bound to continue the fast that Stockdale had ordered and which still had one full day to go, so when I cleaned the latrine area I messaged: "My order is steady as she goes."

Immediately, groans and exclamations issued from the cells, and when I returned to my own cell, I was bombarded with angry messages which in essence said that had Stockdale witnessed the events following the Jenkins affair, he would have called off the fast. They understood my feelings of loyalty toward Stockdale, but said that further fasting could not help him and would be damaging to us.

I was in a terrible dilemma, and I agonized over it. On the one hand, my feeling was that simple integrity demanded that the fast be continued. On the other hand, I knew that Storz and Mulligan in particular were emaciated and needed sustenance, and all were weak from illnesses, the recent torture, and generally poor living conditions. And the big thing was that they were all sincerely convinced of their rationale for discontinuing the fast.

More messages came in, including one that said it was the unanimous opinion that it would be idiotic to continue the fast. Camp morale and unity were now at stake, and as I heard the guards preparing for the next meal, I sent one word on the wall: "Eat!" I received the low whistles, grunts, and taps of joy with mixed emotions.

Crisis was piling on crisis. Rutledge had been pulled across the alley previously, and was still out when Mulligan was also moved across. After several days, Mulligan, looking wan and beaten, was let out to dump his bucket and scraped out, "Torture." As soon as he was put back in his cell, I was pulled and taken across the alley to a torture room.

Mickey Mouse was sitting behind a table. In a tone which seemed to reflect genuine sadness, he said, "Denton, the last time you were punish, I make administrative mistake. The heading on your statement should have read 'Request for amnesty from Ho Chi Minh' instead of 'Apology to Ho Chi Minh.' I ask you now to change the heading."

I refused to change it, and Mickey Mouse sighed and shrugged his shoulders.

"You are being fool, Denton," he said. "Think about it."

Then he left the room. As I sat there alone, I could hear Rutledge two rooms away groaning through the last stages of torture. Finally, I heard him say, "Bao cao," and heard Mickey Mouse whisper to him, "Rutledge, are you ready to write?" In the deadly silence, I heard Rutledge whisper painfully, "Yes, I am ready to write."

The next day, Mickey Mouse asked me again to change the heading. He also showed me requests for amnesty in the handwriting of Mulligan and

Rutledge, and one from a man named Larson, who I later learned was Air Force Lieutenant Colonel Swede Larson. Again I refused and told him that one day he would have to face a war crimes trial.

"You leave me no choice," he replied. "You must suffer again." He left the room, and several guards replaced him. I was resigned to the worst and wasn't disappointed.

The preliminary stage, the beating and dragging, went on longer than usual this time and continued for several days. The rig finished me off. By this time, I *wanted* to do what they asked; anything to escape the pain, and I had just enough strength to change the heading. Before releasing me from torture in early February, Mickey Mouse made me promise to copy excerpts from an antiwar book written by Dr. Benjamin Spock, the baby-care specialist. I did as he asked, copying the same material three times.

As I was being helped from the room by two guards, I looked up at Mickey Mouse and asked if they were finished with me. He rubbed his hands together and smiled and said, "Yes, Denton, we are finish." I had gone a few more feet when he stopped me.

"Wait, Denton," he said. "I forget. There will be one more thing." He came up to me and looked into my eyes. "When you are release, you must meet with our senior officials. You know what I mean."

I knew exactly what he was talking about. A room with a long, green table, North Vietnamese political and military officials.

Torture in an adjacent room until I made a satisfactory videotaped departure through that room.

My forced smiles, their grim faces. My bows, their hard eyes. My disgrace, their triumph. Yes. I knew what he meant.

The way the North Vietnamese had concentrated on me, I began to believe that they were trying to break me permanently, and I wasn't certain they couldn't do it. I was afraid that if they succeeded, they would use me to send improper orders to the others, and I wasn't sure that I could stand up to one more trip through the mill. I passed the word that if they made me send an improper order, I would precede that order with the BS, and the next senior man, Jenkins, should take charge. But that never happened.

Although my last major torture was in February, I was still being pressed to rewrite my biography. One night in March, while I was lying on the floor of the punishment room, my hands cuffed behind me, Mickey Mouse came in and woke me up. This was unusual. It was about two o'clock in the morning, and he was out of breath and shaking from excitement.

"Denton, I have something to tell you," he said, shaking me. "I know you usually don't believe me, but time will prove I am telling the truth. I have just come from a meeting at headquarters," he said importantly. "I have receive information to make provision for *two* more years."

As I struggled to sit up, he went on: "I must provide for *two* more Christmas," and he held up two shaking fingers.

"The war will go on!" he shouted, and left.

I was too beaten down to care at the moment, but later I realized that he was announcing that the North Vietnamese had just come to the conclusion that Nixon's terms were unacceptable and that, indeed, the war would go on. We would not be leaving Hanoi anytime soon.

Immediately, they stopped the amnesty request aspect of the purge which had, so far, been forced from only four senior officers at Alcatraz. They had threatened that everyone would be forced to write such letters, but now the letters would be meaningless. This corresponds to their letting up on Stockdale for the movie.

But rather than end the purge, they continued the torture and simply changed their goal from letters of amnesty to a propaganda letter to former mates.

Shumaker was cast naked in the alley outside the punishment room and whipped violently with a fan belt from an old jeep until he was covered with blood and agreed to write a letter to his squadron mates telling them how pointless it was to continue fighting. Tanner was accorded the same treatment.

And the pace of the purge also changed abruptly. Instead of a week in the torture room with rope and pole, we were now being kept in the punishment room for weeks at a time, under constant threats, but nothing else. Then they would set us day and night on stools before getting serious and applying beatings with the fan belts.

Everyone but Storz, who was in frightful physical and mental condition, was beaten. The Vietnamese, reluctant to torture Storz, hoped to wear him down with psychological harassment.

As spring approached again, despair deepened. We tried to keep our spirits up with games and poems. Coker was especially good at Christmas poetry, and Storz passed around the words to Robert Service's "Dangerous Dan McGrew," and "The Cremation of Sam McGee." I contributed what I could remember of "Gunga Din." These were our only diversions.

Everyone was extremely nervous and irritable, and while we remained united, the mood in the compound was growing black and sometimes not quite rational. Some would leave the wall for days in anger over some small matter or argue violently with their fingers and knuckles on the wall over the slightest differences.

George Coker argued for days that I should allow him to rewrite his biography as the North Vietnamese were demanding. He believed this would keep them off his back for more damaging material, such as a letter condemning the war. I would not agree at first, but when I thought he was beginning to approach the never-never land we all feared, I granted him permission. I predicted they would come at him anyway, however, for a damaging statement. I was correct, and George apologized.

He delayed writing such a statement by mashing his hand with a desk in the torture room so badly that he couldn't write. George McKnight was also under the same pressure, and he delayed his ordeal by beating his blanket and inhaling the dust, aggravating an already severe pulmonary condition.

And so the desperate battle went on.

CHAPTER SEVENTEEN

As in all other times of crisis, we relied on our religious backgrounds to give us strength and to help us accept the sacrifice of our monastic existence. I went through the Mass each day in English and Latin, took spiritual communion, and meditated deeply.

I figured that I had about a one-in-four chance of coming out alive, and about a one-in-fifty chance of coming out sane enough to live a normal life. But I had resigned myself to my fate, and thus could achieve periods of serenity. I had made peace, whatever might happen to me.

At what we thought was Easter of 1969, I composed another poem, which I titled "La Pieta." The composition and passing of it was an event much awaited by the others, and I took great joy in it. It read:

The soldiers stare, then drift away,
Young John finds nothing he can say,
The veil is rent; the deed is done;
And Mary holds her only son.
His limbs grow stiff, the night grows cold,
But naught can loose that mother's hold,
Her gentle, anguished eyes seem blind,
Who knows what thoughts run through her mind?
Perhaps she thinks of last week's palms,

With cheering thousands off'ring alms
Or dreams of Cana on the day
She nagged him till she got her way.
Her face shows grief but not despair,
Her head though bowed has faith to spare,
For even now she could suppose
His thorns might somehow yield a rose.
Her life with Him was full of signs
That God writes straight with crooked lines.
Dark clouds can hide the rising sun,
And all seem lost, when all be won!

The poem was later passed to other prisoners, many of whom memorized it. I became known as the president of the Optimist Club.

Those not subjected to the prison-of-war experience may have trouble understanding how real was the presence of God to most us.

Our tapped conversations almost always ended with "GBU" (God bless you), and at night the final exchange between men in adjacent cells would be "GNGBU" (Good night, God bless you). Christians of all denominations lost old prejudices and found brotherhood; Christians and Jews were reconciled, and most of us lived with the awareness of God's love.

One story, "Denton's Cross," which became well known in prison, will illustrate perhaps what I am trying to express.

One day in New Guy Village during the early months of my imprisonment, Ed Davis passed the word to me that he had left a gift in the latrine area. There I found a cross which he had woven of bamboo strips taken from a broom. The Feast of the Assumption of Mary into heaven was the occasion.

I was deeply touched by the cross; it was my only really personal possession, and I kept it hidden in the pages of a propaganda pamphlet the

North Vietnamese had given me along with a list of prisoners of war I had put together. Cell checks were rather perfunctory in those days, and I managed to hold onto the cross through the days in New Guy Village and into the first days at the Zoo, keeping the pamphlet hidden between my bamboo pallet and the stone floor.

But the North Vietnamese began alterations on the cells at the Zoo, making the ventilation openings smaller by adding bricks. When they came to my cell, a guard named Gunga Din came in and made a thorough search while the civilian crew waited outside. In a few moments, I heard a grunt of triumph. He had found the cross. He ordered me outside. There another guard held a bayonette at my back while Gunga Din threw the cross on the concrete and stomped it with his boot. Then he picked up the pieces and threw them into an open sewer. I was outraged but helpless as I was led away to another cell while the crew went in to work on my cell.

The work crew was an interesting group. Their leader was a stocky man in his early fifties who reminded me of one of my high school teachers, Brother Charles, a French-Canadian. He was exceptionally well dressed, in good work pants held up by a leather belt, and a shirt and leather jacket of excellent quality. He went about his business in a highly professional way along with two younger men, who carried themselves with a certain dignity, and two women, one of whom had obviously lived a toil-filled existence. She was squat and slumped from labor. Her fingers were thick and gnarled, and her face was wrinkled like a prune, although I don't believe she was much more than forty years old. I learned later that she was an expert bricklayer, and once saw her carrying a huge hod of bricks.

It took them about a half-hour to narrow the ventilation holes, and then Gunga Din brought me back to my cell. As soon as the door closed, I looked for the list of POW names in the pamphlet, but the list was also gone. In a rage about the cross, I was tearing the pamphlet to pieces when I felt a bulge among the pages. There was a cross: a new one! Overwhelmed, I studied it for a moment. It had been beautifully woven from the straws of my broom. Obviously, the work crew had made it. It had required the collaboration of all of them at great risk.

Despondency over my loss turned to glorious triumph and gratitude. Later, while outside picking up my food, I was able to cast them a discreet look of thanks. The leader gave me a nod and a smile in return.

Ron Storz, the young Air Force major who had resisted so gallantly, was beginning to pay the final price. The tall, gangly New Yorker was homesick for his wife and two children from the moment he was shot down in April of 1965, and the feeling never left him throughout the long years of his imprisonment. He was also pessimistic about the war, and believed we would never be released.

Late in May, Mulligan was flashing a message to Storz under his door when he heard a thump and saw Storz's arms sticking out underneath his door. There was a guard stationed in the cell next to Mulligan, and he called for him and then pointed to Storz's cell.

In a few minutes, the compound was crowded with guards and officers, including Softsoap and Mickey Mouse, and the doctor, who gave Storz a shot. Later, they moved him across the alley, where he was fed intravenously and received special food. One of the guards even donated some blood. But his condition continued to deteriorate. Once when Mulligan was allowed to empty Storz's bucket, Storz mumbled to him, "There's no way the war's going to end soon. We'll be here forever."

He wasn't eating. Mulligan saw this and ordered him to eat, but it was no use. He was down to about 90 pounds. Once, when the guards were walking him in the sun trying to restore him, I got a good look at him. He seemed almost translucent. On June 28, he was taken across the alley more or less permanently. There the North Vietnamese continued to treat him while trying to talk him into writing a letter requesting amnesty.

Each day when he came to dump his bucket he would scrape to me questions about the difference between amnesty and parole. I tried to explain to him that amnesty was a no-strings release, while parole involved certain concessions, such as an agreement not to bear arms against the enemy, in return for release.

His questions worried me, and when he came back to his cell for one day I passed a message on amnesty and parole which was primarily aimed at him. I said there would be no charges brought if anyone went home without making a propaganda statement if the man was in danger of losing life or limb. He could say that he "appreciated their humaneness" in allowing him to leave. Those not in such danger could go home only according to the normal rules: that is during a legitimate prisoner exchange or in the final release of all prisoners.

I wanted Storz to understand that he could accept his freedom if it were offered in order to save his life, but no one could accept parole.

We could tell by his latrine messages that he was becoming more and more irrational as the summer of 1969 wore on. The Vietnamese had given him a Bible and a deck of cards, and Softsoap had started teaching him how to play bridge. I had left him a three-page note in the latrine on how to bid, and he was constantly scraping questions to me. I would answer by flashing through the peephole in my door, or, if there was a reasonable guard present, whispering the answers.

Ron had become quite bold and was practically shouting questions at me. The guards would allow that, but they would usually look sternly in my direction and I had to be careful. One day when I didn't answer a question loudly enough, Ron said, "Well I know who my *real* friends are."

There was nothing we could do to stop his roller-coaster ride in hell.

Sometime in midsummer there was a flurry of excitement. One evening a guard went from cell to cell ordering everyone to roll up, that there would be a move. We demanded of Flea, the officer on duty, the reason for the move. We were raising so much fuss that he finally came around and told us that the Red River was rising and Hanoi was to be evacuated. I tapped to McKnight, "We're going home and they won't tell us the truth." McKnight passed the message along, and in a few minutes a reply came from Shumaker: "You're optimistic enough to buy the Brooklyn Bridge."

In the excitement, the pressure on our communications was less than usual, and in my own excitement I literally pounded on the wall the sequence of Navy orders for getting underway, ending with "Anchors aweigh!"

We waited in our cells for the order to move, and as the hours passed we began asking about the delay. Flea told us they were waiting for the trains to move us out. Then, at about two in the morning, he told us we weren't going after all and that we should unroll our gear. Mulligan was especially angry and sat stubbornly on his rolled-up gear the rest of the night, waiting for trains that never came. When the guard told him to unpack, Mulligan said, "Hell no! You said we're moving and we're moving!"

The flood scare was over as quickly as it came, and the next morning I had to message to Shumaker: "My anchor got fouled in the Brooklyn Bridge!"

In September 1969, something occurred which would change our lives immensely. We had heard on the camp radio that Ho Chi Minh was ill, and on September 3 he died. Mickey Mouse came to me immediately to warn me about the guards, who, he said, would be very irritable and unpredictable.

"You should tell everyone to be careful and not offend them at this time," he said, and I passed the order to cool it. The effect of Ho's death on the guards was disastrous. They broke into the storage cell next to mine and took drugs and wine, and while messages of condolence from other countries were being read endlessly on the camp radio, they wept and got drunk. The officers were also badly shaken, and wandered through their duties in a daze.

Ho's funeral took place about five blocks from Alcatraz, and as I listened under the door I could hear the sound of guns booming and the roar of many jet aircraft zooming in the traditional flyover. And there was the high-pitched wailing of thousands of voices as the founder and president of the People's Republic of Vietnam was carried to his grave.

We speculated on Ho's successor and hoped for a revolt. I suspected that his death would mean a change in our treatment, but I didn't know which way it would go. Almost immediately, subtle changes began to take place which I interpreted as a good sign. The camp administration was less harsh, and the purge petered out.

In October, I was caught communicating and got my first real clue on the new treatment. I was taken to quiz with Softsoap, who said, "Denton, you have been caught communicating. You know what has happen before."

"Yes, sir," I said.

"I am going to surprise!" Softsoap said. "This time you will not be punish. We still have regulation and you have broken it, and I will criticize you for it. But as long as I am in authority, there will he no more punishment for communicating."

Night had turned to day! As I stood there, a chill ran through my body and the flesh on the back of my neck prickled with a sense of joy. I tried to appear unperturbed, but I had to exert great will to keep the tears from flowing.

A guard took me back to the cell, and as soon as the door closed I got on the wall to tell the others what had happened. I said I thought the North Vietnamese might be coming off their torture line, and that our treatment would improve. The others were somewhat skeptical. Torture had become a way of life.

The next day I was again caught communicating, and off I went to another quiz with Softsoap.

"Ah, Denton," he said, "you did it again. The guard is doing his duty, but you will not be punish."

While were talking, a guard came stomping into the room and threw his arm across his chest in salute to Softsoap. It was raining, and as water dripped from his slicker, the guard rather theatrically reported that he had just caught Sam Johnson communicating.

Softsoap translated the report to me and repeated his pledge that no one would be punished for communicating. When I reported this scene to the others, they began to lose their skepticism. Johnson had indeed been caught but hadn't been punished.

We began getting breakfast, which was bread and a little sugar, and regular medical checks. We were even allowed to see each other briefly on occasion—"accidentally," of course. One day as I was coming from the bath, I came face to face with Shumaker, who was washing the dishes. We were both flabbergasted, and Shumaker tried to pretend he didn't see me.

I asked the others not to flaunt their newfound freedom; the Vietnamese could turn us off quickly. The treatment had changed so radically that some of us thought we were to be released.

Softsoap even asked me what could be done to improve conditions, and I suggested that we should be allowed to mingle and play games. He asked what games, and I suggested Ping-Pong and basketball. As I learned later, prisoners at other camps did begin playing games and mingling about this time, but such privileges didn't come about while we were at Alcatraz. However, we were getting more letters and packages, the food was much better, and the attitude of the camp administration toward us was much improved.

One day during a routine quiz, Softsoap and I discussed the justice of our respective causes, and I recounted to him the policies of Roosevelt and Truman toward Indochina, policies which I had explained earlier to Mickey Mouse. I said I could understand how Ho Chi Minh had become a Communist.

"He went to Russia for help when he believed no one else would help him to obtain freedom for his country," I said.

But I went on to explain to him, as I had to Mickey Mouse, how post-World War II events had forced the U.S. to become oriented toward containment of Communism in Europe, and how the Chinese revolution and the Korean invasion forced us to adopt the same policy in Indochina, where Bao Dai was seen as the lesser evil.

The South had infinitely more freedom than North Vietnam, even under Diem, in spite of considerable corruption and some repression in South Vietnam.

"What I can't understand is the Communist suppression of political, religious, and press freedoms," I said, and went on with my lecture about how Communism might bring short-term material gains, but in the long run the people would not be allowed to share in the fruits of their own production, because they would be funneled to Russia.

Softsoap listened for a long time, then reached across the table and grasped me by the forearm. In an emotional voice he said: "Denton, you have seen more and read more, and you know more than I do. You can make argument that I cannot answer.

"But you must understand we never have security. We always fight. We have no unity. Under French there was no security, no law for Vietnamese. If Vietnamese woman raped, or peasant murdered by French, there would be nothing that would happen to those that did it. We had nothing but corruption.

"Now for the first time we have security. We do not have other things, but for the first time we have precious security."

He paused, his eyes glistening, and asked, "Do you understand that?"

I was touched by what he had said, and only pitied him and his people.

In any case, our jailers had changed along with our circumstances. We even received a gift at Thanksgiving, a bamboo basket with a round top and lined with cloth in which we were to keep our tea hot. We had seen them piled at one end of the compound one morning, and some of us thought they were basketballs.

When the guards came around and handed them to us, I didn't know what to do with mine. I thought it was just a fancy basket. The guard finally pointed to the top and said, "Tea." Then he made a cuddling motion to indicate warmth.

As December approached, we began to sense that something was about to happen. On December 9, Frenchy came around and told us to roll up. Rutledge thought we were going to be released, a feeling unshared by the others. Ron Storz actually became violent. He screamed at Frenchy. "You lying son of a bitch, you're not going to do anything." While Storz tapped on the wall, "Don't believe him," Frenchy stood outside his cell shaking his head and shrugging his shoulders. Frenchy was noted for his mean temper, but in this case he accepted Storz's outburst. He knew he couldn't deal with him in his condition but didn't want to hurt him, either.

One by one we were taken from our cells and led to a truck in the alley, where we were blindfolded. As I was about to climb into the truck, Softsoap came up and said, "Ah Denton, this time you will not ride in handcuffs. We will blindfold, but you will not be uncomfortable.

"And Denton," he said, "do not forget tea basket." And this after years of beatings and torture.

As I wedged my way into a seat in the truck, I determined by tapping on the knee next to me that Coker and McKnight were in with me, and we tried to speculate where we were going. That question was answered in a few minutes when I felt a jolt as the truck went over a curb and I heard a familiar squeak as a gate opened. We were back at Little Vegas after more than two years in hell.

Unhappily, the change in treatment had come too late for Ron Storz. He was left behind in Stockdale's old cell. The North Vietnamese were undoubtedly embarrassed about his condition and didn't want the other prisoners to see him.

We hadn't been allowed to say goodbye to our friend, and we never saw him again. He died in April of 1970.

CHAPTER EIGHTEEN

Everyone within shouting distance soon knew that the Alcatraz gang was back.

Coker and McKnight were taken to the Mint, where John Dramesi, also a former escapee, was living, but the rest of us from Alcatraz were in Stardust at Little Vegas. I was taken blindfolded to Cell 6. After Alcatraz, it was like the presidential suite. It was large and airy, with a big back window and two sets of double bunks. This led me to believe I would soon get a roommate.

We had come in about eleven o'clock at night, and in moments we were practically booming messages off the wall to each other. We were making so much noise that the guards were in a frenzy, and Bug, the sinister little torturer who had been terrorizing the camp, warned us about it. "Denton, be reasonable and quiet. Things are going to get better," he said. Reluctantly, I messaged the others not to flaunt our communications. We didn't want to go back to Alcatraz.

The next morning, December 10, I was allowed to bathe, and as I was coming out of the bath carrying my towel, cup, and bucket, I ran into my old friend Cat, followed by a retinue of guards and officers. He was in uniform, his shoes carried a high shine, and he gave me a big false smile as he strode toward me, hand extended.

"Ah, Denton, I believe," he said, blinking in the bright sunlight. He knew damned well who I was, and I was annoyed. I ignored his hand and went to attention.

"Yes, Denton," I replied, looking straight ahead.

"Long time since I see you, Denton," he said, dropping his hand. "Yes. Not since the banana and the torture." He ignored this. "We will be having many discussions, Denton," he said, and I was allowed to pass. It seemed to me that Cat was less sure of himself during this brief encounter. His false cordiality failed to hide the worry in his eyes. The next morning I was taken to quiz with him.

The arrogance and sparkle were definitely gone. He appeared tired and distraught, and a nervous tic had developed over one eye. He settled into an overstuffed chair under a picture of Ho Chi Minh, with two huge dictionaries beside him. It was obvious that this was to be a serious discussion, without the usual harangue.

"I have some very important announcements, Denton," he said as I sat on a stool in front of his desk. "I, other officers, and many of the guards had in our rage allowed ourselves to vent our anger on the prisoners and were responsible for deviations from our Vietnamese tradition of humane treatment."

I sat there silently, bemused and surprised at this unprecedented admission.

"I have been required to make public self-criticism for my mistakes," he went on, "and from now on you will be allowed to follow the Code of Conduct. I will prove by my deeds that my words are true, and I want ideas from you on how we can apply humane treatment, including games and movies. We shall have many discussions in the future. Here are French-Vietnamese and English-French dictionaries for consultation to make sure we understand each other.

"Maybe you would like to explain to girls in kitchen about menus," Cat said, emphasizing the word *girls*.

I said, "No, we can't accept that."

Cat, the mastermind behind the torture campaign, was now almost conciliatory. "Just follow reasonable orders and don't insult guards," he said.

I accepted a cup of tea and said I wanted to talk to the other prisoners about this new era. Noting the blood that was running from around a large callus on my knuckle, Cat smiled and said, "Ah, Denton, you have ways to talk to them." He meant he would look the other way while I tapped out the conversation on the wall, but he didn't want anyone communicating outside of the Stardust. I couldn't make any promises.

The quizzes with Cat went on almost daily for two weeks. He was continually trying to impress me with the new image. I figured the North Vietnamese believed that President Nixon was going to try to carry the war to a successful conclusion, and that they might be held accountable for their crimes. They wanted us to go home in good condition. Although Cat didn't keep all his promises, from then on no one I know of was tortured for propaganda or military information. At the time, of course, I had no certain faith that he was telling the truth, but I passed the information on to the others for what it was worth.

I was overwhelmed by Cat's new attitude, but I had to be careful about what to recommend. There should be no special favors for anyone, I told Cat, and everyone must get a roommate. And we must all be allowed to follow the Code of Conduct. We would accept games if everyone were allowed to play. I also asked the whereabouts of Jim Stockdale, and when he replied, "Stockdale is tranquil," I was frightened. He wouldn't explain further.

The Alcatraz gang established communications with the Thunderbird in the first day or so and learned that Stockdale was there living with Jim Hughes. Stockdale was senior to Lawrence, but Hughes did not think Stockdale should communicate, and Stockdale had given command to Navy Commander Bill Lawrence.

Lawrence had been running Little Vegas very well, but against great odds. As his senior, I inherited command and immediately discovered that some of the prisoners in the Desert Inn were good resisters but hadn't learned to communicate. Others were receiving special favors and weren't participating in the camp structure. They were reading on the camp radio without pressure from the Vietnamese, and were getting the run of the cellblock and exercise yard and good food. Some were decorating the party room voluntarily for Christmas and Tet, and some were even making antiwar tapes.

Little Vegas was a mixed bag of about eighty prisoners in late 1969. When our group had been taken to Alcatraz in 1967, the structure we had developed became fragmented despite the best efforts of Lawrence, Navy Commander Byron Fuller, and others.

We learned that many of the prisoners were still rolling from severe torture and a few others were just plain collaborating. It was necessary for me to reestablish camp-wide resistance and unity and force some of the senior officers into the communications system. By tapping and whispering over the tops of the shower stalls in the bath, I began passing the word that there had been no torture since October of 1969 and they should begin saying "No!" to the North Vietnamese. I wanted the prisoners in the Desert Inn to stop reading on the camp radio, decorating the party room, and writing for a camp magazine the Vietnamese had started, called *New Outlook*. The Vietnamese had made serious inroads into the organization and it would not be easy to reconstruct. Fuller and Lawrence had done their best in the midst of chaos, but it was hard going.

The Alcatraz gang was furious.

McKnight, in the Mint and about twenty-five feet from the Desert Inn, called out of his window, "You rotten sons of bitches." Rutledge, who was in Cell 8 of the Stardust, thumped on his wall during the quiet hour trying to get the Desert Inn to respond, without success. He became obsessed and boomed their names, but no one would answer. I also called three of the men by name and accused them of collaborating and shouted out my window that they should follow the Code of Conduct and stop reading on the radio. They did not acknowledge. Shumaker in Cell 3 fixed up a reflector made from the top of a tin can and cleared for Rutledge while he worked on them, but it took us months to get them to respond. In the meantime, we were infuriated to see them eating outside regularly, an unheard-of special privilege.

This was one area where Cat refused to budge. When I demanded equal treatment for all, he dodged the issue. Repeatedly he responded, "I am your uncle. You are my nephew. I have good nephews and bad nephews. I shall treat some better than others, but all will be treated well. You must be patient." He knew favors were damaging to morale and unity.

I also had some administrative problems to solve. Rutledge and Shumaker, both excellent communicators, were feuding over the job of communications officer. I knew that the one that didn't get it would sulk for days. Finally, I put Shumaker in charge of written communications and gave Rutledge command of the tapping, which turned out to be a happy solution.

On December 23, 1969, I got a roommate in Cell 6, Jim Mulligan. Except for less than four months with Mulligan in 1967, I had been in solitary since July 18, 1965, the date of my capture.

There was no question that things had become more relaxed. We were allowed to exercise outside every other day, play Ping-Pong for a half-hour, and play French pool in the game room. Some of the guards even became friendly, and one in particular became a favorite of the former Alcatraz immates. We called him Ichabod. A tall, lean, young man with a big Adam's apple, he spoke excellent English and was assigned to the Stardust as a key guard, a position that carried great responsibility in the camp administration. He was intelligent, almost professorial, and had a gentle personality. He was also new and perhaps a bit too trustful. Usually when it was time to bathe, he would just open the door and walk away, leaving Mulligan and me to follow him.

On Christmas Day he opened the door as usual and walked several paces in front of us as we started out of the cellblock. On the way, I paused at Shumaker and Tanner's door, opened the peephole, and exchanged Christmas greetings with them. Ichabod caught me at it and became very angry. He said I had betrayed him and I couldn't be trusted. I told him that it was my duty to communicate, but on this occasion I had only exchanged Christmas greetings. He didn't believe me, and it took him a long time to get over the incident.

Ichabod, who was from a northern province of North Vietnam, was quite curious about life in the United States. One day while I was exercising in the yard with Mulligan, he asked me if it was true that there was racial prejudice in the United States, a question that revealed his obvious distrust of Communist propaganda. He was always interested in the truth and was unwilling to accept everything the propaganda machines turned out. I believe he was quite surprised when he received an honest answer from me. I admitted there was racial prejudice in the United States, but said this was a human tendency. Some governments promoted prejudice, but the United States did not; the official policy of the nation was equal rights for everyone. About that time another guard, Hack, came up and told Ichabod he shouldn't talk to me about such things.

Just after the turn of the new year of 1970, I went with Mulligan one day to get my food from the rack outside the door of the Stardust. As usual, I picked up a piece of bread from the basket on the floor. Big Ugly, a huge guard known for his enthusiastic torture techniques, pointed to the bread basket and nodded. I thought he meant I should take another piece of bread, which I did.

When I had returned to my cell, Big Ugly came up and pointed accusingly at my two pieces of bread. I was furious. I thought he had set me up and started to leave the cell and return the extra piece of bread. Big Ugly threw his rifle across his chest and blocked my way, but I was so angry that I charged right into him and knocked his rifle out of his hand. I put the food back on the table, then went back to my cell and slammed the door.

In about an hour I was blindfolded and dragged off to Calcutta, a tiny cell behind the kitchen area. I stayed there eight days and seven nights. I refused to eat in protest and subsisted on water and vitamins from a package I had received from Jane. It was cold, and I was suffering from an abscessed tooth and severe headache. At one point I was taken to quiz with Bug, who said I would have to apologize to Big Ugly. When I refused, he pushed and slapped me around. As the guard took me away, Bug cocked his eye in a characteristic way and said, "Tomorrow you will be torture to write like Senator Fulbright!"

The next morning before dawn, I was blindfolded and taken to be quizzed by Cat.

"Do you think it possible you misunderstood?" Cat asked. I said no. He then reminded me the bread was hot and suggested that I may have misinterpreted Big Ugly's gestures. "I want you to think about this." I was dismissed and taken back to Calcutta.

In the afternoon, a guard took me to the quiz room, where a dentist looked at my abscess and said I needed surgery. He assured me I would be treated, and I began to soften toward the bread incident. After lunch, Cat asked if I had changed my attitude.

Reluctantly, I admitted it was possible that Big Ugly was trying to tell me the bread was hot and that I would apologize if that were the case. I wrote a letter that said, "If guard meant bread was hot, then I owe an apology. If he tried to frame me, he is a despicable liar and you should kick him out." That appeared to settle the matter, and I was taken back to my cell at the Stardust. But Big Ugly wasn't satisfied. The next day he came into my cell and thrust his bayonet at me, ordering me to bow. I had to bow seventeen times. Two days later I complained to Cat, and shortly Big Ugly disappeared.

By late January of 1970 note drops were established everywhere, including the baths and the game room. Sometimes the notes would get lost (once a note dropped from a light fixture and fell on the head of a guard), and we would leave a dummy note to test whether the North Vietnamese had discovered the drop.

I stole a steel pen point off Bug's desk during one of my quizzes and concealed it in a bar of soap. They searched the entire camp when Bug discovered it was missing, but they never found it. I also dipped small pieces of cloth in Bug's inkwell when he wasn't looking. I reactivated the ink with water after it dried out, then used it for writing notes on toilet paper and the wrappings from packages we were receiving. To this day, I write in a small hand.

Meanwhile, my occasional quizzes with Cat were deteriorating. As April approached, he was still granting special favors to some of the prisoners, and others still did not have roommates. I warned him that it would cause him trouble if he persisted, and when he did, I called for a fast to begin on April 30. It was to be on a voluntary basis and would exclude the sick. I wanted it to look like a grassroots effort which had spread spontaneously. Most of the prisoners cooperated, although many of them didn't like it. They said it wouldn't have any effect. But from my Alcatraz days, I knew this wasn't so. I went three days without any food, and then went on half-rations as planned. We lost a lot of weight, which I knew would upset our jailers. They wanted us to go out plump.

On the prearranged date of May 11, after more than a week on half-rations, the fast ended. There was always a face-saving period before the Vietnamese would make a concession, but by the first days of June the fast began to pay off. Visiting between cells within buildings was allowed, and only one or two prisoners were still in solitary. All were allowed to eat outside, and exercise and play time were increased.

The new regime seemed to be taking its toll on Cat. As the warm days of May passed, his tic got worse, he lost weight, and his hands began to shake. In June he was replaced by a colonel, a no-nonsense combat soldier, who immediately called me in and said that all the prisoners would be treated the same. I never saw Cat again, but someone said he looked terrible and had lost one star off his collar.

In June, Rutledge and Jenkins were allowed to visit our cell, which helped relieve some tension that had developed between Mulligan and myself over cribbage. I fell behind in the beginning and blamed it on luck, but as time went on my advantage grew on the daily log we were keeping, which made Mulligan irritable and angry. This was balanced a bit by the fact that Mulligan beat me consistently in French pool. In the meantime, Rutledge was beating me in Ping-Pong, a circumstance that made me so unhappy that I would come back to the cell and brood, then discuss my next day's tactics against Rutledge with a sympathetic Mulligan. I had thought myself a pretty hot player but I only beat Rutledge twice, and I think he threw one of those games because I was becoming so uptight. The games had become the biggest things in our daily life.

By the searing hot days of July, Mulligan, Rutledge, Jenkins, and I had programmed our brief daily visits to give each one of us a chance to talk. Rutledge was so garrulous that he would have dominated the conversations. So everyone got a day to talk on any subject he wished. Jenkins discussed math, Rutledge engineering, Mulligan domestic politics, and I talked about international affairs. Unfortunately, even this led to trouble and we engaged in violent arguments that on occasion nearly resulted in blows. We would soon get over it, but in other cells, long-standing grudges developed and there were some slugging incidents.

Our gradual improvement continued. There was plenty of well-seasoned food. Letters came monthly. Packages arrived about every three months, although they were usually half-empty by the time the Vietnamese had screened out forbidden or suspicious material. Pressure against communications continued, but did not include physical mistreatment.

On July 2, we had a joyful reunion with Stockdale, who was moved in with Shumaker, Johnson, and Tanner. In all the years of our prison association, he had been little more than a fleeting glimpse, a tap on the wall, a voice under the door. Now he was there with us. We had a lot of information to tap, about the year he had spent in limbo after he had been taken from Alcatraz, and we began to catch up on others we had not seen or heard from for years.

We learned about a camp mystery involving Air Force Captain Ed Atterberry, who had escaped with John Dramesi in the spring of 1969. After they had been recaptured five or six miles from the Hilton and brought back, Atterberry had never been seen again. Some of the prisoners believed he was struck in the head with a rifle butt and killed that same night. They had heard a heavy thump as Atterberry was being brought in and then a series of soft slaps, as though they were trying to revive him. Dramesi had spent much of his time in prison on a forlorn search for his companion, but to date had turned up nothing. Later, on the day of our release in 1973, Dramesi finally cornered Bug and demanded to know Atterberry's whereabouts. He was told he had died of a "serious disease."

Medical treatment improved immensely. A woman dentist operated on my abscessed jaw, and in July I was taken blindfolded to a hospital in Hanoi, where a large tumor on my chest was removed. It had been growing since 1966, and I had become quite concerned about it. The surgeon did an excellent job, and the scar is hardly visible today. There were many wounded soldiers at the hospital, which was probably the biggest in the country.

I wasn't blindfolded on the trip back to camp and I looked eagerly out the window of the small truck during the fifteen-minute ride. I saw long lines of women waiting for rice, the usual bicycles and Jeeps, and I even caught a glimpse of a well-dressed woman, who appeared to be Russian, getting into a rickshaw.

By now, the entire Alcatraz gang was in the Stardust, plus Dramesi, whom we made an honorary member of our club. Stockdale took over command from me on November 1, but held it only a few days. Robbie Risner, the Korean War ace who had eight MIG's to his credit, soon arrived at Little Vegas and took over.

A few days later, Risner learned that he was outranked by Air Force Colonel Vernon Ligon, and a few days after that Air Force Colonel John Flynn passed the word that he was taking over from Ligon. In the meantime, some men from other camps arrived. They shored up the organization and helped run it. Among them were Navy Commander Dick Stratton, Air Force Lieutenant Colonel Bud Day, Navy Lieutenant Commander Jack Fellowes, Air Force Major Ron Webb, and my first contact from New Guy Village days, Larry Guarino.

We soon learned the reason for the population explosion at the Hanoi Hilton. On November 20, U.S. troops had raided Son Tay, a prisoner of war camp twenty-three miles from Hanoi, but had found the camp vacant. By chance, the North Vietnamese had emptied the camp earlier and the change had gone undetected by reconnaissance planes. The raid so frightened the Vietnamese that they decided to bring all the prisoners to Hanoi.

As I learned when I returned home, Jane thought the U.S. had bombed Son Tay. She had seen a headline in a newspaper which said, "POW Camp Hit," and had been so furious that she picked up the phone and called the White House, demanding to know if the government was trying to rid itself of the POW problem by killing them. A general patiently tried to reassure her. Several days later she learned the truth.

Jane had received the first letter from me in February of 1966, about seven months after I was shot down. It was two and a half pages, and told her I had been injured during the ejection but was otherwise well. Since then, she had received a six-line letter, perhaps once or twice a year, and knew little of what was happening to me. Her husband had become a vague shadow, a lost soul sitting in a lonely cell thousands of miles away.

I had tried to communicate the truth by slanting certain letters in peculiar ways. When I returned, I learned that phrases like "hard purge on," "irons at night but no pun(ishment)," and "Storz bad" had got through, but the Vietnamese eventually caught on to the strange writing. In November of 1969 while I was still at Alcatraz, Teeth called me into a quiz and showed me a letter I had written which was full of backward writing.

"We know you have done this before," he had said. I was afraid they had caught previous letters and were holding them. They hadn't, but I had to stop temporarily. I tried the backward writing again in 1972, when I attempted to warn U.S. intelligence about the movement of prisoners to the Chinese border and the letter had got through.

Through the years I had learned a few things about my family from Jane's letters and the pictures I was allowed to receive. Madeleine, who had just turned eight when I left home, had taken up horseback riding, and I stared admiringly for hours at a time at a picture of her in her riding habit. One of Jane's letters said that Madeleine had won a second-place ribbon in a horse show. She was especially good at the jumps.

From the double-talk which Jane sometimes used in her letters, I learned that our eldest son, Jerry, was an Army helicopter pilot in Vietnam. She also told me that Donny had received a scholarship to Phillips Exeter Academy for his senior year in high school and later had received a scholarship to Haverford College. By 1970, Jim was a student at Elon College and Bill was in Norfolk Catholic High School. Mary Beth, who was a pretty baby just learning to say "Daddy" when I left, was now in elementary school. A picture of Michael, by now ten years old, playing the piano alongside my mother, who was an accomplished pianist, brought tears to my eyes.

Despite the pictures, I had trouble visualizing what my family looked like as the children grew older, and as I had to discipline myself to fight the waves of homesickness that swept over me. But just the thought of my family helped me to retain my grip on my sanity.

Unknown to me, Jane had plunged into organizational work with the National League of Families of American Prisoners and Missing in Southeast Asia and, of course, had kept in close contact with the wives of prisoners from Virginia Beach. There were quite a few because of the large network of naval installations in the area. She and Bill Tschudy's wife, Jane, had become close friends, and Jane and her son Michael had become like members of our family.

Sometime in the summer of 1969 the wives decided to become vocal in the cause of the prisoners. Until then, they had been advised by the U.S. government to use restraint because the government thought public attention could raise the price for our release. But groups of wives had begun to organize in different areas of the country and were now questioning the value of continuing silence. After the release of Frishman and Hegdahl and the news that the prisoners were being badly treated, the government began to feel there was little to be lost by speaking out. Also, more and more the wives and other citizens were demanding action of some sort on the prisoners' behalf, and the pressure began building in all directions on an issue which had been all but ignored by the public.

Sybil Stockdale, who lived in California, began to tie the various groups together and organize them into what soon became the National League of

Families of American Prisoners and Missing in Southeast Asia. Louise Mulligan of Virginia Beach was an early leader in this effort on the East Coast. Ross Perot of Texas was one who made extensive and expensive efforts on our behalf and who has continued to help us since our return.

Jane had agonized over the situation. She didn't want to go against government policy or do anything that could damage the prisoners; but years had gone by and nothing had changed. In June of 1969 some members of prisoner families had attended a meeting at the Defense Department with Melvin Laird, the Secretary of Defense, who told them the policy of silence should change. It was time to speak out on the prisoners and exert pressure on Hanoi for better treatment and Red Cross inspection of the camps. That advice was all the waiting families needed.

One day Jane and another wife, June Nelson, walked into the newsroom of the Norfolk *Virginian-Pilot,* sat down at the city desk, and said to an editor, Ed Brandt, "We need some advice. We've never done anything like this before and we need to know how to get some publicity."

Brandt was well acquainted with the history of all the shootdowns from the area, but had been somewhat puzzled by the silence of the families, having tried unsuccessfully for years to learn even the contents of letters the wives had been receiving from the prison camps. Now there was a breakthrough on both sides, and within weeks the *Pilot* was planning a special section without advertising to publicize the plight of the prisoners and their families.

Meanwhile, by 1970, the Virginia Beach campaign was rolling. The wives needed an office, and a mobile home was loaned to them by a local businessman. From the mobile home and with the assistance of friends, the wives began conducting an all-out publicity campaign. A speakers' bureau was established, and a letter-writing campaign was continued. Billboards, bumper stickers, newspapers, magazines, and television were utilized. Jane became a board member of the national organization and was vice-chairman for one year.

Politicians were awakening to the problem and a steady stream of Congressmen went to Paris to meet with North Vietnamese officials engaged in the peace talks. Some of the wives also went to Paris to confront officials each day as they left the peace talks.

We in Little Vegas learned of the campaign late in 1970 when Stockdale received a package with one item wrapped in a POW-MIA bumper sticker, but we didn't comprehend the scope of the movement until we returned home.

In the fall of 1970, Jane and the other wives at Virginia Beach raised money to send four men—Roy Martin, mayor of Norfolk; Donald Rhodes, mayor of Virginia Beach; Billy Mitchell, a student at Old Dominion University in Norfolk; and Ed Brandt—to Paris with the signatures of 100,000 citizens from the Tidewater Virginia area on petitions requesting humane treatment for the prisoners, and inspection of the prison camps by the International Red Cross, in a venture financed by the newspaper and other generous citizens.

With the aid of U.S. Embassy personnel and Mitchell's high school French, the four men found their way to the residence of Mai Van Bo, a North Vietnam representative to France, where they demanded entrance in order to present the petitions. The North Vietnamese at this point weren't receiving delegations on the prisoner subject and called the police. The men returned the next day, this time with a delegation of Associated Press and United Press International reporters and photographers, and with the help of John Vinacor, an AP reporter who handled the translation, exacted a promise from someone at the barred door that they "would be called the next day at their hotel and receive an answer to their request for an interview."

The North Vietnamese do not like the free press. and when the men were invited the following day to come to the residence, it was with the stipulation there would be "no journalists" with them. The North Vietnamese had been intimidated by the group of photographers and reporters and didn't want a repeat of the previous day's scene, when the American delegation had risked arrest and pushed its way through the ring of French gendarmes to bang on the iron grille, covering the door until it received attention.

Martin, Rhodes, Mitchell, and Brandt met with Mai Van Bo for nearly an hour, were served tea, and debated the treatment of the prisoners and camp inspections with the North Vietnamese delegate. As they were leaving, they received the usual propaganda booklet purporting to show American atrocities in Vietnam. In return, Brandt handed the Vietnamese translator the large package of signatures.

The wives hoped that constant pressure from such citizen groups would convince the North Vietnamese of the public's interest in the prisoners, and even now, most of us believe the pressure helped improve our treatment.

The wives were also pressuring their own government for action. They had made numerous requests to meet with President Nixon, but couldn't get in to see him, although all the government officials they dealt with were quite sympathetic. They wanted to meet with Henry Kissinger, then an assistant to Nixon for national security affairs, and one day their request was granted.

About twenty wives and parents went to Washington to meet with Kissinger, but unfortunately, he couldn't attend. The families were furious when General Alexander Haig, the military liaison man to the President, showed up in Kissinger's place. Poor General Haig, standing uncomfortably at the end of a long table and faced by cold, frustrated stares, listened while a wife read him a statement.

As he shifted about, hands in pockets, one pocket split and a cascade of coins clattered to the floor. While his aides scrambled to retrieve the change, everyone laughed and the tension was broken.

Later, family members met with Kissinger every other month, an hour each time, and were much impressed. "I don't know what you did to

Haig," he said about six weeks after the coin incident, "but he refuses to come here."

Kissinger was very courteous and knowledgeable, head and shoulders above everyone they had dealt with, Jane thought, and the families were convinced of his sincerity when he assured them that the prisoners would be part of any deal with the North Vietnamese.

The families had no false hopes. They didn't believe pressure would bring about the release of the prisoners, but they hoped it would contribute to an improvement in the camp conditions and treatment.

CHAPTER NINETEEN

On December 23, 1970, Jenkins, Rutledge, Mulligan, and I agreed to pluck turkeys for about eighty prisoners. As I went through the routine of "She loves me, she loves me not," with the feathers, I wondered what was to come next in this interminable existence. It was difficult to believe that more than a year had passed since we had left Alcatraz.

On Christmas Eve, we were called in one at a time to sign for Christmas packages. The next evening there was a heavy rattling of plates, which usually meant a move, and a friendly watergirl cleared her throat loudly, a danger signal. In minutes, a highly trained, heavily armed special team of North Vietnamese civilian intelligence people swooped in and shook down the cells, searching for contraband. They even melted the soap in their search for forbidden goods. As we learned later, they apparently found a tape that had been smuggled into camp in a package of Life Savers; it contained certain information from U.S. intelligence. They also found parts of a radio receiver that a prisoner was trying to make.

The next night we were taken to a courtyard where Bug told us we would be moved in with others. With our gear under our arms, we trooped into a building in which twenty other prisoners were already bedding down. Camp Unity, which included several buildings in a rough quadrangle, occupied about half of the Hanoi Hilton. Until the arrival of some South Vietnamese military and American prisoners in the fall of 1970, it had been used for civilian political prisoners. The South Vietnamese, and some Americans from the Zoo and other camps, displaced the civilians as the Vietnamese began consolidating the entire POW system at the Hilton. The major buildings at Camp Unity were numbered zero to eight. On December 28, most of the prisoners from Little Vegas were moved into Building Seven, which housed forty-seven prisoners, the same number, more or less, as the other buildings. Nearly three hundred and fifty American prisoners were now together, although still in separate groups. Bamboo barricades surrounded the building yards, which were used for exercising, bathing, and washing clothes.

Our building had no cells and was about forty-five feet long and twenty feet wide. There was a cement platform about a foot high in the center where we laid our mats. It was large enough for all of us to sleep on, shoulder to shoulder. The platform was surrounded by a space just large enough to walk in. There was pandemonium that first night as disembodied voices and taps on the wall suddenly became flesh and blood; there was handshaking and hugging as we circulated and staked out places to sleep. Unhappily, a few former roommates picked places as far apart from each other as possible as old grudges and hatred began to surface in the changed atmosphere. Nonetheless, many of us talked the night through, relating our experiences, asking questions, laughing and joking.

There was a crisis almost immediately, however: who should be in charge of the nearly three hundred and fifty men of Camp Unity? Air Force Colonels John Flynn, Dave Wynn, Norm Gadis, and Jim Bean were being kept isolated in Building Zero, leaving Risner and Ligon, both lieutenant colonels, as candidates for the job. After some discussion it was determined that Ligon was senior to Risner in date of rank, and Ligon became commander, with Risner becoming deputy for operations. Stockdale and I were his primary assistants. Stockdale was in charge of plans and policy, and I was director of current operations.

We started immediately to organize the entire camp. We had to standard-ize communications methods and abbreviations and decide on our resistance policies. If we continued to receive reasonable treatment we would follow the Code of Conduct, be polite to the guards, and go about our business. But what if the treatment changed for the worse? Should we go on offense? We decided we would. We would march to exercise and count cadence to show that we were still military. If that didn't work, we would refuse to exercise or to eat. And if that didn't work, we would escalate to loud singing, a method of resistance they particularly disliked because they didn't want the noise spill-ing over the wall and into the streets.

Each building was also divided into flights, eight men per flight, with a flight leader to carry out the policies and handle the duties. The flight leaders in Building Seven reported to me. We had good communications with all the buildings except the one where Flynn and the other colonels were being kept, but after a week Ligon received a message from Flynn, who outranked him, which said Flynn agreed with the policies we had formulated,

The North Vietnamese were uncomfortable with our organization and tried to subvert it by giving orders to junior officers and refusing to recog-nize command structure. To make matters worse, some of the prisoners, including many who had laid low during the tough years, were harassing the guards and being uncooperative to both sides. Like the Children of Israel, we were having trouble with our own people as we neared the Promised Land and the frustrations created by years of imprisonment and torture sur-faced. They wanted to appoint their own building leadership, to establish the duty sections and tell us where to sleep. We ignored them or pretended not to understand, and they became very nervous.

We also had problems with the handling of food. The guards would come into the building and pick several men to dish it out. If they weren't included in the flight designated for that duty that day they would refuse and there would be a minor confrontation. As we moved through the month of January 1971, tensions grew.

While we were wrestling with these problems, I received a surprise visitor. It was Teenager, the young guard I had knocked over so long ago when I had refused to carry the honey buckets at the Zoo. During the intervening years Teenager had grown quite savvy. He was good at catching us communicating at Little Vegas, and was a rather good-natured thorn in the side who delighted in matching wits with us. One day in 1970 at Little Vegas, he had come into our cell to talk and we had given him a vitamin pill while he showed us a picture of Ho Chi Minh and a picture of his mother, wife, and baby. He was curious about the pills and we got the idea of getting him hooked on them so we could trade off with him on our communications. Thereafter, we gave him one pill daily. After about the fifth day, I took him aside and whispered in his ear, "We no bao cao pill, you no bao cao communications." He said okay and never bothered us again.

And now in late January of 1971, he stood at the door, his gangly arms hanging at his side, tears in his eyes. "I leave now, Den. I come to say goodbye," he said sadly. I asked him where he was going, and he answered, "I think Laos, to fight." I expressed my sorrow at his departure, and as he turned to leave he called over his shoulder, "I wish you luck, Den." We were probably the best friends Teenager ever had.

The tension between the prisoners and our captors finally came to a head. A couple of days after our move to Camp Unity we had held a church service, a practice we continued despite orders to stop. One day Bug, who was in charge of our building, delivered an ultimatum that the next church service involving more than eight people would he broken up. "How would you like to go back to treatment of 1967?" Bug warned. It was a constant threat, but after long and heated discussions, we decided to hold the service anyway. Since we knew they would pull the leadership and the participants in the service, it was decided to spread the church duties among several men. One would lead the Pledge of Allegiance, another would give the opening prayer, another the sermon, and so on. If it appeared there would be violence, Ligon would halt the service.

On Sunday, February 7, 1971, we were ready, and so were the North Vietnamese. Several guards were outside the door as we began, and in a few minutes Bug strode into the room with Ichabod and Hawk behind him. Hawk told the choir to stop singing but they ignored him. Then Coker took up with a sermon, followed by Rutledge, who quoted from the scripture, and Risner, who gave the benediction. Again and again Hawk demanded that we stop, but he was totally ignored. When Risner was finished, Ligon said, "Dismissed," and everyone started to disperse. Hawk took Risner from the room, and Coker and Rutledge were also led away. With a shake of his fist, Bug shouted, "Now you will see my hands not tied!" The three men were taken outside and forced to stand with their backs against the building while we crowded to the windows to see what was happening.

And then Bud Day began singing "The Star-Spangled Banner." As his hoarse voice rose in triumph, the rest of us joined in, our voices rolling through the courtyard and over the walls in a full, joyous crescendo. A hundred guns couldn't stop us. It was the first time in many years that I had heard our national anthem, and my heart swelled and tears rolled down my cheeks.

News of the service and the confrontation spread through the camp quickly, and I could almost feel the pulsations of emotion flowing from prisoners. That evening I invoked an old Naval Academy tradition with a slight variation. As dusk was falling, I began singing:

This is building number seven, number seven
number seven,

This is building number seven,
Where the hell is six?

Like wildfire, the chant spread from one building to the next until the entire camp was blowing out the frustrations of years with a simple schoolboy exercise. The uproar continued most of the night despite the presence of the helmeted troopers and the reinforcements that were now pouring into the camp.

The next morning we learned that Risner, Coker, and Rutledge had been taken to Heartbreak Hotel, where they were put into a single room. They had not been beaten or handcuffed. In protest of their departure, we decided to fast and refuse to leave our building. Shortly, Bug came in, backed up by a riot squad and shouted, "Give attention!" Then he called out the names Ligon, Stockdale, and Denton, ordering us to come forward. As we were led out of the building we could see hundreds of troopers, bayonets at the ready, scattered through the courtyard. We were thrown to the ground, our arms roped behind us, and taken to Building Zero. Ligon and Stockdale were placed on a bunk, where they each contributed one leg to a single pair of stocks. I got a bunk and a pair of stocks all to myself.

Risner and Rutledge were soon moved into Building Zero also, but not placed in irons. Our captors were taking great pains not to punish on the basis of the church service, but for the riot (singing), for which Ligon, Stockdale, and I were held responsible. The appearance of the hated ropes and the segregation of the leaders had a subduing effect for the moment. But the men remaining in Building Seven continued the fast until the water was cut off, a move that ended it.

A few days later there was a bridge tournament in Building Seven, and the tournament organizers were brought to Building Zero. Then a rowdy birthday party for Shumaker was held a few days later, and the leaders of this event found themselves in Building Zero. By the middle of February, almost all the senior officers were in cells in Building Zero, where they remained until a few days before release.

The North Vietnamese finally agreed to allow church services, but placed such outrageous restrictions on them that they continued to be a source of friction. In the game of action and counteraction, we formed goon squads to glare at the guards and make threatening gestures. Some of us were in stocks twenty-four hours a day into March. Others in the camp complained of this, and Bob Purcell, in charge of one of the buildings, threatened major counteraction if we weren't taken from irons. The next night we were allowed to leave one leg out of the stocks, and Stockdale remarked somewhat wryly: "If only we could get a cheery message back to the States: 'One leg out!'" He was only half-kidding. These little things meant a great deal. Stockdale, Jenkins, Mulligan, and I were the last to come out of irons.

Eventually, I was put in a cell with Rutledge, Jenkins, and Stockdale. Since there were only two bunks, we rotated sleeping on the floor except for Stockdale, whose badly twisted leg earned him a permanent berth at our insistence. Finally, Jenkins and Rutledge insisted on my taking the other bunk in deference to my seniority and over my protests. I gave up when they lifted me bodily into the bunk and sat on me.

There was one advantage in the new location: Colonel Flynn, who had been isolated, was in Building Zero. With so many of us now in the same building, he could be in touch with the rest of the camp, which enabled him to exercise command.

From information I had accumulated in Building Seven, I spent three days developing a summary of prisoner activities and camp structures going back to 1965 and gave it to Flynn. He took advantage of the unprecedented communications opportunities which now existed and organized the prisoners along Air Force lines: each building became a squadron as part of the one wing he created.

As the month of March 1971 wore on, some housekeeping problems developed. The roof over our cell leaked and when we complained to Bug, he shrugged and said, "Take much money. You have to fix." Jenkins, who had a brilliant engineering mind, constructed a drainage system from the cords of the mosquito netting. His maze of lines drained the water out of the window and through the peephole in the door. The guards were much impressed by this effective system and would come to the door and stare and ask questions.

One day in March of 1971 while Stockdale and I were still in irons, a small, wiry South Vietnamese army captain slipped into our cell while a guard's back was turned and quickly grasped our hands before dashing out. Thus I was introduced to one of the most remarkable men I have ever met.

Nguyen Quoc Dat, code-name Max, had been the subject of a brief conversation just after I arrived at Little Vegas from Alcatraz. Some of the prisoners had been suspicious of Dat, who had been in isolation for many years. They thought he was a plant. But John McCain messaged me in Little Vegas to recommend that Dat be trusted and allowed into the organization. I had agreed.

Now he occupied the cell next to Risner in Building Zero. A few weeks after he slipped into my cell to shake Stockdale's and my hands, he messaged Risner and asked that the two Thais he was living with be brought into the organization. The Thais, Chai Charn Harrnavee and Chem Barn Rung Uom, had been used as servants for years by the North Vietnamese, and I had seen them carrying food to the buildings at the Zoo long ago. Chai had been shot down in Laos flying with Air America, and then had lived in a bamboo cage in the jungle with an American before being brought to Hanoi. Chem had been in a C47 that had been shot down in South Vietnam. Neither of the Thais spoke English or knew how to tap, but Dat said they could he trusted and would be useful. Right now, they felt left out of things. "If you trust me," Dat said, "you should trust them."

Risner passed this to Flynn, who asked some of us for a recommendation, which was positive. The three men became invaluable, good-natured, and faithful allies. Dat was a genius. He had a quick mind and spoke English, French, and Spanish well. Because his grandfather had been a mandarin under the French, Dat had received an excellent education. He could translate the conversations of the guards and became a sort of secret weapon in our running battle with the camp administration, again a great risk. The North Vietnamese would have been deadly angry had they known that "one of their kind" was cooperating with the Americans. Dat and the Thais had been kept segregated from the Americans until the Son Tay raid, when almost everyone was brought to the Hilton.

Dat and the Thais were brave men and taught us many lessons. There was a broom in each cell, and Dat showed us how to pull bamboo strips from the brooms, tie them together with threads, and make long poles with which to pass notes across the passageway running the length of the cellblock.

Until Dat's intervention, we had been using stolen pieces of lead and burnt matches for notes, but the product was of poor quality. Dat told us how to mix ashes from pieces of burnt bamboo with shavings from our brown soap and produce what amounted to a black crayon. The mixtures had to be in exact amounts, and Dat provided a perfect formula. He also stole a long metal bar about three-eighths of an inch in diameter which he passed to us. We used it to bore holes in the wall through which we could pass notes. This innovation turned Building Zero into a communications headquarters.

Robbie Risner, who was in the cell next to Dat, tells a marvelous story about the introduction of the rod.

One day Risner heard a sound in the wall from Dat's side. After two or three minutes a bit of plaster fell off, and through the hole came the end of a metal rod. Risner peeped through the hole and saw an eyeball. He heard a voice say, "Can you hear me, Kornel? I have just put hole through wall so we can talk. Isn't this buch better?"

"How long did it take you?"

"Oh, three or four minutes."

Risner thought Dat was lying. He and his roommate, Swede Larson, had been trying for days to get through the other wall. Dat shoved the rod through the hole and said, "Here, I will give it to you. Would you like to make one through the other wall?"

Risner was amazed. "Did you get through with this?"

"Yes, Kornel."

Risner took the rod and with Larson's help tried to go through the other wall with it, without success. The wall simply defied the brains and power of two senior military officers. Later, Dat called through the hole and said, "Kornel, did you ever get through to Kornel Kirk?" Risner had to admit that he had not, and furthermore, his hands were blistered from trying.

In a few minutes there was a knock on the wall and Risner pulled out the bread plug which concealed the hole. Through the hole came a piece of paper with a diagram of the wall showing the layers of bricks; where individual bricks were placed, and how Risner could go between them. In five minutes, Risner and Larson were through to Kirk.

Dat improved our communications system enormously, and that was good and bad. The command structure had become an administrative night-mare now that we could easily pass paper through the walls; we were putting out way too much instruction on all sorts of things, including health, athletic, and education programs. The sophisticated command structure was run on a flood of to-from-subject memos, which sometimes included numbered paragraphs and subparagraphs as the instructions and policies grew more complicated. I had nine staff men working for me alone as we developed a hierarchy, and I became swamped with paperwork. Actually, we were all used to command and were sharks cruising for responsibility. Flynn, a judicious leader and excellent administrator, recognized this and tried to spread the responsibility evenly.

The complex dealings with the North Vietnamese continued. They would not recognize the command structure and tried to control the prisoners in their own devious ways. After Flynn wrote a letter in mid-1971 to the camp commander asking to be recognized as senior officer, he and the other three colonels were taken away. We didn't know it at the time, but Flynn received no punishment and was kept in Building Eight, later called Blue because of its Air Force residents with Wynn and Gaddis. Blue was only two buildings from Zero, but the colonels were effectively isolated, and Risner took command again. Stockdale became the deputy of operations, and I assisted him.

In October of 1971 the North Vietnamese shuffled the senior officers again. Stockdale, Jenkins, Mulligan, Rutledge, Jim Hughes, and I were moved to Blue, where we discovered Flynn, Gaddis, and Wynn. The six of us were put in a section at an angle to the cell occupied by the colonels and separated from it by a small room which we used as a dining room. A high wall separated our courtyard in one corner of Camp Unity from the rest of the camp.

The North Vietnamese thought they had us isolated because there were several buildings between ours and Building Zero, our closest neighbor, but Rutledge, as communications officer, and Jenkins overcame the obstacles. We would pound on the back wall so hard that the sound would carry to Building Zero. Also, our captors made the mistake of housing Dat and the two Thais in a cell next to our latrine. We bored a hole through the wall and passed notes which they would then deliver to other buildings as they went about their cleaning chores in the main courtyard.

Stockdale and I were now alternating as deputy for operations. We composed new initiatives and programs, which Flynn would consult on with Wynn and Gaddis before making final judgment. A new Pentagon Southeast Asia had been established.

For a while, the communications system worked, but after a series of mishaps our link with Zero was broken. Stockdale thought of a solution. There was a pipe through the roof of the latrine which acted as a vent. We tied a piece of white cloth to the end of a stick, and by raising and lowering it we could send messages to the other buildings. To prepare the others for the use of this Rube Goldberg contraption, a piece of bread was wadded up around a note and thrown to the next building to tell its occupants they should look up on the roof at noon the next day.

At the appointed hour Rutledge climbed up on Jenkins' shoulders and began moving the stick up and down in code. This worked well for a week or so. Then, one day in the middle of operations there was a tug from above which nearly pulled the stick from Rutledge's hands. He yanked back. The other end let go and Rutledge tumbled to the floor. A guard had spotted the moving flag. We didn't have time to make up a proper story and we were all quizzed and threatened. Later, Rutledge got caught redhanded with a note and was segregated for awhile.

Rutledge was running in bad luck at the time anyway. Most of his teeth had rotted away in prison, and one of his truly prized possessions was a tooth capped with gold. It was one of the few places in his mouth where he could get enough purchase to chew his food, and he was very fond of his gold cap. Occasionally he would spit it out by accident, and the rest of us would spend hours on the floor searching for it. Sadly, one day Rutledge was in the latrine when he sneezed, and the gold cap flew into the huge, concrete latrine. He was crushed and came back to the cell and sulked, sitting in a corner, head down, looking up only occasionally with mournful eyes. Jenkins was especially upset and determined to find the cap despite Rutledge's protestations that the search would be hopeless.

Nonetheless, Jenkins went into the latrine day after day, mining through the latrine hole for Rutledge's lost cap. Each day he would come back empty-handed and smelling awful. He never did find it.

CHAPTER TWENTY

As the dreary days marched on into 1972, even some of the hard-line veterans were losing heart. Despite our best efforts, morale was shaky and arguments frequent. I even heard one prisoner whom I respected say, "After one more year of this my attitude will be the hell with it, I'll go out on any terms."

Colonel Flynn concocted a scheme to gain freedom for one of our hard-liners with the idea that he would go home and tell the whole story. We chose George McKnight because of his impeccable reputation, and put the proposition to him, but he messaged back, "I'll go over the wall with you, or I'll go when everyone else goes, but I won't go out like that." The matter was dropped.

In January I predicted the war would be over on October 24, 1972, reasoning that President Nixon would be on a peace drive to coordinate with his election campaign, while the North Vietnamese would want to settle before Mr. Nixon got another four-year mandate. On January 13, Nixon announced the withdrawal of another 70,000 U.S. troops from Vietnam, which would bring our troop strength there down to 69,000, the lowest in seven years. On January 25, he revealed secret talks between Kissinger and the North Vietnamese in Paris, but on March 25, he announced the talks had been broken off because the enemy would not negotiate seriously.

We got only bits and pieces of this, but we could put enough together to know something was going on, and our hopes rose and fell regularly as we watched, listened and waited, and continued to fight our lonely battles against the North Vietnamese. On March 30, North Vietnam began a giant offensive in the South, using Russian tanks and artillery. It demonstrated plainly the amount of war material the Russians and Chinese were giving to the North, as well as the North's clear determination to subjugate South Vietnam. I believe this represented a betrayal to President Nixon.

He called off the peace talks indefinitely and in May 1972 ordered the mining of Haiphong Harbor. By the middle of the summer, all U.S. combat ground forces had been withdrawn, leaving U.S. participation to the 10,000 or more Navy and Air Force men flying from carriers, and from bases in Thailand and Guam.

My assessment was that the Communist heavy-handedness might give the President more public support for his military moves and increase the chances for a successful conclusion to the war.

In July of 1972 the United States introduced a significant new element into the air war over North Vietnam. Air raids on Hanoi had resumed during that year, and we had a grandstand seat as the F4's, A7's, and A6's roared through the sky. But they were using a new technique that mystified us. The Vietnamese had grouped many of their antiaircraft guns and missile sites near the Hanoi Hilton, and the planes, instead of diving on the emplacement, now circled lazily high in the sky. We were puzzled, and we watched as day after day the planes would come over in ones and twos, circle for a while, make an occasional run, and then fly off. The U.S. had introduced the "smart bomb," a television-guided bomb which was directed to the target by the pilot. It was an amazingly accurate and effective weapon and had a devastating effect on the ring of antiaircraft defense.

As October of 1972 began, Kissinger was in a furious round of negotiations with North and South Vietnam over a nine-point peace proposal by the North, and as President Nixon confirmed to me personally years later, the camp radio was telling the truth for a change when it said that an agreement between North Vietnam and the United States had actually been initialed by both parties. On October 27, Kissinger made his now famous statement, "We believe that peace is at hand. We believe that an agreement is within sight." When I heard that over the camp radio, I knew that we had blown it. Now that North Vietnam had us on record, its leadership would make it impossible for a settlement before the election. They would want to make Nixon and Kissinger out to be liars in the hope that it would help Senator George McGovern win the election.

I consider Kissinger a great Secretary of State, but I think Nixon perceived the dangers of negotiation with North Vietnam better than Kissinger did, and in a preelection speech in November he was far less optimistic than Kissinger on imminent settlement.

Meanwhile the North Vietnamese were playing all sorts of games with the prisoners of war. Two hundred men from Camp Unity were moved by rail to Dong Khe, a town eight miles from the Chinese border, from where they were to be released through Hong Kong when the time came. Apparently the North expected to hold the rest of us, mostly senior officers, as hostages. President Nixon later confirmed that this move was one of the reasons he wouldn't settle in October in 1972.

During the evening of December 18, I heard a distant roar and felt the ground shaking. Plaster began to fall. "I think those are B52's," I said and went to the window. We were supposed to get under bunks, but hardly anyone did. We stood at the window and cheered and clapped as the thunder of the bombs moved closer and the antiaircraft defense rings opened up. We could see missiles going up in groups of two and three after the planes, and occasionally the sky would light up as a B52 was hit. The B52's laid multiple strings of 500- and 750-pound bombs on the railyards and bridges as tactical aircraft moved in to suppress the most extensive and sophisticated air defense system in the world.

Our captors were stunned by the tremendous bombardment and as the B52's continued the assault nightly, leading up to Christmas, the camp hierarchy began to lie low and play strictly by the rules with us. They began to defer to our senior officers and appeared badly frightened.

The bombing stopped on Christmas Eve, and I prayed that the antiwar people would not deter Nixon from resuming the bombing after Christmas. I believe it was the decisive moment of the war.

The bombing resumed on December 26, and the guards changed even more. They began adopting a "remember me, I'm a good guy" attitude.

There was the feeling that our days in Hanoi were winding down.

The waves of B52 bombers had done their job and could fly almost without fear of loss. President Nixon had sat silently in the White House while a hurricane of criticism raged in the country and throughout the world. In a few days, the planes had methodically smashed Hanoi's air defenses. Something that could have been done ten years previously was now successful. The North Vietnamese leadership caved in. The bombing was halted on December 30. Negotiations were resumed in Paris on January 8, 1973.

On January 23, President Nixon announced the end of America's longest war, with the cease-fire to go into effect on the twenty-seventh.

Images of my family running across an airstrip, arms outstretched, swirled through my mind as we plodded through the last days of imprisonment.

Now the North Vietnamese wanted an end to it. They announced terms of the peace agreement over the camp radio and then delivered mimeographed copies of the agreement and protocols of the release to every prisoner, as provided for in the peace agreement. The seniors from Building Zero and Blue returned to the community.

On February 3, when we rejoined the others, the barricades had been torn down and half the camp was allowed in the courtyard at one time for games. I wept in joyful reunion with Bill Tschudy, a face out of the distant past, and Ed Davis, a voice out of the distant past. I remembered as though it were only yesterday the soft, deep voice singing, "Fly Me to the Moon," and the single word "Agony!" being tapped out on the wall. The word expressed perfectly the events of seven and a half years. I attached pale faces to whispering voices: Ray Merritt, Ralph Gaither, Bob Purcell, Phil Butler....

And Red McDaniel came up to me, hand outstretched, and said that many of his friends had seen me on television, in the interview in 1966 with the Japanese reporter, before McDaniel had been shot down.

"That was remarkable, Jerry," he said. I was much relieved. Through all the years of imprisonment, I had worried about the image the North Vietnamese had managed to project of us to the world. Now I understood that our efforts had not been in vain.

Camp discipline was gone, suddenly. The guards still carried their guns, but there were no restrictions on us. No more note drops, covert communications, policy decisions. When they offered us new clothing we thought at first to refuse it and go out the way we had lived for years, in tattered pajamas. But then we said, "Oh, hell," and everyone lined up for the leather shoes, the socks, khaki pants, shirt, and windbreaker that were provided.

To the end there was the quiz, but no more "Shut mouth!" Now the sandal was on the other foot as Risner, Stockdale, and I went in one at a time to be questioned by Mickey Mouse, two other officers, and a civilian.

Mickey Mouse asked what I would say when I got home.

"I haven't answered your questions this long. Why should I answer you now?" I asked. "Why do you care what I say anyhow? There are hundreds of men who will speak when they get home."

"You have credibility, Denton."

"What do you expect? Don't you know I'll tell about the torture?"

"Yes. We expect that."

"Why do you want me to tell you what I will say?"

Mickey Mouse sucked in his breath, paused for a moment, and then said, "We afraid when you get home and make speech, Mr. Nixon will not give us aid he promised. Public would not allow." I was struck by the "mister." They had changed.

"I will say that through 1969 you treated me and the others worse than animals."

I expected a denial, but instead he leaned forward and said, "Yes, but is that all?"

"No. That is not all. Late in 1969 you came off the torture. After that, to my knowledge, you did not resort to extreme punishment. You then acted within your conscience, such as it is."

"That's the truth," Mickey Mouse said, "but others may not tell truth."

"If there is any exaggeration, the senior officers will take care of that," I replied.

The North Vietnamese were at that time obsessed with the idea of American aid. They had no idea that from the depths of defeat they would be permitted, even encouraged, to seize the millions of South Vietnamese people and their resource-rich land through a series of events which I believe will go down in history as the most incredible, and perhaps most dangerous, string of miscalculations and blunders in our history.

But now it was almost over for us. As the thirteenth pilot to be shot down, I would go out with the first group as senior officer. The sick and injured would be in the front ranks and then the others in the order of shootdown.

Our captors agreed to allow us to march out under our own leaders. We would go through the gate in Heartbreak Hotel that I had entered blindfolded and bound so many years ago.

We needed no bands or billowing banners as the men, the lame and the halt in front, formed up. And then it began; heads up, chests out, some men staggering a bit, we marched in cadence to the buses, then were driven, subdued in the solemnity of our thoughts, almost hypnotized, through streets lined with throngs of silent people to Gia Lam airport, three miles from Hanoi. Much of the rest is a blur.

Guards with sidearms...Fox in a sidecar directing the operation through a walkie-talkie...Rat...Flea...the first sighting of the airport and a long, loud cheer from the prisoners. A Red Cross tent.

But no American planes. There had been a delay, and I prayed there hadn't been a last-minute hitch. Rat, who had introduced me to my cell at Alcatraz ("How do you like your new home?"), now gave us good food, beer, and fudge. "We would like this to be a pleasant memory," he said.

He offered us souvenirs of Hanoi. We already had quite a few, I said, and declined for all of my group.

Shortly after noon we heard a low deep droning, and in moments a beautiful sight appeared in the clear sky: the high tail and swept wings of an American C141. Another cheer, then back on the buses; a short drive to the release point; a long table; some foreign guys in uniform; Rabbit at a microphone; and on the other side of the table the handsome men and women in the blue uniforms of the U.S. Air Force, with Frank Sieverts of the State Department and Roger Shields of the Department of Defense. We kept looking toward the waiting C141, its huge ramp opened wide in welcome.

Dazedly, we walked one by one up to Rabbit and gave him our names; he repeated them in a flat voice and we walked to the plane. In moments it was lifting us into the sky on its way to Clark Field in the Philippines.

We were leaving it all behind. Heartbreak, New Guy Village, the Mint, Little Vegas, the Gate, Zoo, Alcatraz.

And Ron Storz, Atterberry, and others buried somewhere in North Vietnam.

Once we were in the air, I was told that the senior officer was invited to make a statement upon arrival. I borrowed a piece of paper from a nurse and scratched out a few words, then tried to memorize them as we flew along. The words mixed in with my random thoughts.

"We are honored..."

I thought about the 50,000 American fighting men who had given their lives in a cause at last won.

"...to have had the opportunity."

I heard a thump as the wheels were lowered. The men began to stir. We had covered the distance between capitivity and freedom quickly.

"...to serve our country...under difficult circumstances."

The plane taxied to a stop. I was shaky, and stumbled on the steps. There was a large crowd waiting.

"We are profoundly grateful to our commander-in-chief and to our nation for this day."

I felt strangely unfulfilled. I hadn't said quite all that was in my heart. Final, unrehearsed words slipped from me: "God bless America!"

Land that I love.

EPILOGUE

My reentry into freedom after more than seven and a half years as a prisoner in North Vietnam has been a mixed experience.

I reported back for duty to Admiral Noel Gayler, Commander in Chief, Pacific. But my happiness on landing at Clark Field in the Philippines was tinged with sadness when I learned that my father had died, but that letter was one of many I had not received.

Then there was the overwhelming joy of reunion with my family shortly after midnight of February 15, 1973, at the Norfolk Naval Air Station. Jane, on the apron of the runway; five handsome sons; two beautiful daughters; and two people I had not met before, daughters-in-law Winship and Branwen. Since then a third daughter-in-law, Marilyn, has joined the family.

Of all the emotions that I have experienced, nothing yet compares with my feeling of pride at the strength of character shown by my family while I was away and during my recovery period. Jane especially cannot get enough credit.

From the moment of release, the prisoners received an excess of warm, loving care from their countrymen. Operation Homecoming was planned and executed to the last detail to provide for our needs, and the doctors, nurses, government people, pilots, and hundreds of citizens who greeted us at the airport all have our everlasting thanks. I received a disproportionate share of the attention by the happenstance of being the first prisoner off the first plane, and still feel somewhat self-conscious, knowing that I was no more than a symbol for a group of men for whom millions had prayed, worn POW-MIA bracelets, and otherwise expressed their sympathy.

Soon after my arrival I was reunited with my dear mother, my brother, Dr. Peyton Denton, and his wife, Renee, and with Jane's mother, Mrs. James Maury.

During my recuperation and through the long period of debriefing, Portsmouth Naval Hospital personnel, from their leader, Admiral Willard P. Arentzen, to the corpsmen and civilian workers and an excellent chef named McNamara, surrounded me with love, kindness, and care. From my window high over the Elizabeth River I could see a sight long denied me. Navy and merchants ships passing, the bustle of life in the busy Hampton Roads port, an American flag, a church steeple.

Slowly, the new America unfolded to me. It appeared cleaner and better groomed. There was obviously a greater sense of commonality of purpose and respect among members of different religions, and more respect between black and white people.

I went to my hometown of Mobile, Alabama, where the citizens put on a roaring Jerry Denton Day, which I was happy to share with my mother, Jane's mother, brother Leo and his wife Mignon, Jane's sister, Madeleine, and her husband Manning McPhillips. This special day was one of the many honors the people of Mobile bestowed upon me.

In the first weeks, unhappily, I began to note some dark corners in America. I saw the evidence of the new permissiveness, group sex, massage parlors, X-rated movies, the drug culture, that represented to me an alien element. I also noted a mood of national political disunity which has damaged the foundations of the most powerful but compassionate nation on earth.

I thought at one point that the title of this book should be *Under God, Indivisible,* because that was my view of the performance of most of the prisoners in North Vietnam. It was difficult to achieve because imprisonment tends to breed resentment, suspicion, jealousy, hatred, and disunity, and in Hanoi our captors fostered these emotions. But most of the prisoners, finding themselves in desperate circumstances, quickly rediscovered God and became indivisible in their resistance, and with the understanding that our way of life, with all its imperfections, is incomparably greater than anything offered by Communism. We can add our testimony to that of great heroes like Solzhenitsyn and Sakharov, who have vividly related what Communism is really like.

Sadly, I believe that apathy and disunity at home led to the betrayal of millions of Southeast Asians. The war that was won by the heavy bombing of North Vietnam in December of 1972 was lost in the following months by a mood of disunity and by a weakness in the national character.

In a democracy, the leadership can't just do what it wants to do. Essentially, it is governed by the mood and morality of the people and what the people will permit. I believe we should have some consideration for the leader who tries to run the country amidst tremendous complexity and ever-ready criticism. For many years now this country had operated without a bipartisan foreign policy, and one result has been a flood of one-sided criticism of the leadership.

In our failure to pass the test of Vietnam, we ignored the nature of the worldwide Communist threat and also lost our credibility. Others will be swayed by the forfeiture of South Vietnam, Cambodia, Laos, and Angola. And they will note that since 1960, our national defense budget has fallen from 51.6 percent of the total budget to 27.8 percent in 1976. In contrast, Communist expenditure for arms has risen steadily. Those nations still undecided may choose to accept Communism as the easiest and safest course.

Arms, of course, are just part of the answer; we must be morally and spiritually strong as well, and believe in our mission. And we must remember that peace is not simply the absence of war. Those in slavery have no peace, as Sotzhenitsyn tells us.

Our laws and customs were constructed to reflect the Ten Commandments, not only to provide for a good life after death, but for a good life on
earth. Christians believe Christ's order to "Love thy God with thy whole
heart, thy whole soul, thy whole mind and with all thy strength, and love thy
neighbor as thyself." We try to live by that Golden Rule in our public and
private life. Unfortunately, the Commandments and the Golden Rule are
being forgotten by our society: to achieve our rebirth, we must recall them.
Only then can we expect to survive.

As William Penn said, "Men must choose to be governed by God or condemn themselves to be governed by tyrants." The tyrants are waiting as we
continue to bleed from self-inflicted wounds.

This nation is carrying the hopes of hundreds of millions of people
throughout the world, both in Communist and in Communist-dominated
countries. Indeed, we must vow to love our neighbor. We must do what we
can to spread among the deprived of the world the fruits of our labor, as any
good neighbor would, and share with them our own spiritual light.

Shall we survive? I don't know. But I think it is possible, so we must try.

Our coin bears the inscription: "In God We Trust."

And our Bible reassures us: "The Lord is just and merciful."

With the Lord thence our protector, whom or what shall we fear?

To My Fellow Americans:

Thank you for taking the time to read this book. Your interest shows a
concern for the basic values that made this country great. The seven and a
half years I spent as a prisoner of the North Vietnamese convinced me that
America's strength depends on the values of morality and patriotism that
come from her families.

When I returned from Vietnam, I was shocked at the deterioration in our
society. It quickly became obvious that the basic problem was a deteriora-

tion in our national attitude towards the family and family life. The personal values of spousehood and parenthood stand too far down the hierarchy of society's values relating to individual responsibilities, accomplishments, and vocations.

The consequences are manifest in our inability to respond effectively to all the major challenges of our society, our economy, and even our national defense. Fortunately, something can be done; we in Congress are doing some things, as we seek to restore voluntary prayer to the public schools.

More can be done by private institutions. That is why I have become Chairman of the Board of United Families of America, one of the fastest-growing, most effective voices for the traditional family in America.

If you would like to know more about UFA, and receive a free copy of the *National Family Reporter*, our monthly publication, just fill out the coupon at the bottom of the page, and mail it to me at the address indicated. I will be happy to send it to you.

I hope you will join us in our efforts to restore America's greatness.

NEW UPDATED EPILOGUE

As related in the closing pages of *When Hell Was in Session*, I suffered a dual sense of shock upon my return to the United States from prisons in Hanoi. This epilogue will summarize a partial list of what I have done after experiencing those shocks. This book will not contain all of what I have been doing, nor all of the thoughts I have on the worsening culture and security situations. I intend to devote the rest of my life to continuing to work and comment on those two increasingly critical situations. And now to the update of the original epilogue.

Perhaps the reader can understand the unusual degree of my shock, which was a stronger reaction than that of those good citizens who were confronted gradually through those years with those adverse changes. I was rather like a frog that had been removed from a pot being heated while the water was still relatively cool, and then was dumped in it later when the water had commenced boiling.

There were two aspects to the shock I experienced in 1973 upon my return.

First, there was the shock at the difference between 1965 and 1973 in terms of cultural standards. I saw the appearance of X-rated movies, adult magazines, massage parlors, the proliferation of drugs, promiscuity, pre-marital sex, and unwed mothers. These resulted in an increase in dysfunctional families, bitter divorces, the neglect, abandonment, and abuse of children, and an increase in sexually transmitted diseases.

At the Naval Hospital in Portsmouth, Virginia, we were shown a film that illustrated what had happened since the POWs were away, and when the film depicted the Peace/Love Carnival at Woodstock, showing hippies fornicating publicly, high on drugs, etc., I threw up, and said I was not watching the rest of the movie review series.

To me, it was a nightmare. This nation, firmly founded as One Nation under God, was in the process of becoming a pagan nation with a shocking degeneration of national integrity.

Second, there were the tumultuous post-war Vietnam political events, starting with Congress forfeiting our military victory, thus betraying our victorious American and allied servicemen and women, who had won the war at great cost of blood and sacrifice.

As you will later read, events since 1975 caused my sense of shock to grow more severe. These events and my reaction and thoughts about them from 1975 up to the date of this book's publication date are what this updated Epilogue is all about.

My Life After 1975

As I addressed the question of what to do with the rest of my life, my mindset had shifted from having an exclusive goal of serving as well as I could as a U.S. naval officer to a mindset focused on the deplorable shifts in U.S. culture and in our national security status.

Were the counter-cultural movement and the steady weakening of our national security going to continue its advance, causing our nation to decay further?

OVER MY DEAD BODY!

I quickly came to realize that if I followed my intention of fighting the counterculture, I could not pursue it while I was still wearing my Navy uniform. I should try to pursue it as a civilian, perhaps through a private non-profit. So I resigned from the Navy upon concluding a highly gratifying tour of duty as Commandant of the Armed Forces Staff College (since renamed the Joint Forces Staff College), and formed a non-profit organization called the Coalition for Decency (CFD). Its objective was to restore the indispensable requirement for the well-being of any nation: a sound institution of the family. I devoted years to that effort, and found many Americans who realized the importance of that objective and supported CFD with their participation in meetings and the organization and execution of various relevant activist programs. I am proud to say that CFD made progress in this field, especially by playing a notably effective role in diminishing pornography, winning an award from the Citizens for Decency through Law.

But before long I came to realize that, important as was the issue of the deterioration of the family, it deserved second place in priority because the developing problems with our national security could destroy our country even faster than could cultural decay.

Ipso facto, I realized that CFD was not a broad enough platform from which to address those security problems. But what suitable platform was it possible for me to achieve?

Then I recalled that for several years various prominent Republicans, including President Ford, had been asking me to run for the Senate. The Senate would be a good platform, but all my life I had refused getting into politics. However, there were now new circumstances, and I began to consider it. When I saw Ronald Reagan coming along as a presidential candidate, I thought he was what the country desperately needed. He was my kind of man. His early work against Communism in Hollywood impressed me. Everything Reagan said was with humility but firmness, and an incomparable sense of humor. He understood the Communists, and he believed in the concept of One Nation under God. I wanted to help him lead the country his way.

I knew I had to make a decision, so I immediately consulted my precious wife Jane, who I knew naturally now wanted me to spend more time with her and our children from whom I had so long been separated.

Jane and I, after praying together almost all of one night, decided I had to say yes, and run for the Senate. It was not an easy decision for us to make because a Senate tour would not only mean another interruption in my family life, but also I believed I was not likely to be elected. Jane gallantly disagreed and suggested that the Senate might be the best place for me to pursue my objectives. The decision was made. We would devote six years to the task and then catch up on family matters.

With wonderful people helping me, in 1980 I was elected to the Senate from Alabama, and found myself again in a position to serve my country as I did with so many gallant comrades in Vietnam.

As soon as I became a senator, I changed the name of my non-profit from CFD to the National Forum Foundation (NFF), and broadened its objectives to include the following: 1. Strengthening national security, 2. Restoring the health of the institution of the family, 3. Restoring this nation as One Nation under God, and 4. To undertake reform of our welfare system. (The name NFF has recently been changed to the Denton Foundation, and can be found on the Web at dentonfoundation.org. A few years later I included the goal of increasing humanitarian aid, especially by finding cheaper means of transporting the aid to distant destinations.

I intended to use NFF as a medium to assist in any senatorial initiatives. NFF would provide exposure and possibly support to my initiatives in the Senate.

NFF got started with a wonderful board of directors whose members strongly supported us with the financial means to pursue our objectives. The Heritage Foundation and other major institutions provided NFF office space. I appointed my son Jim as its executive director. NFF became an active member of the influential Council for National Policy. During my Senate years, the NFF sponsored many press conferences, TV appearances, etc. Their content was widely publicized, and this gained support for my initiatives.

In the Senate, as in Hanoi, I found myself again among some fine Americans, senators who tried to do great things for our country. But sadly, I also found many in Congress who served their own personal political interests more than the nation's interests, and that on a per capita basis, military servicemen and women were far more patriotic and willing to work and sacrifice for their country than many members of Congress.

I was aware that I was joining a Congress that had voted to sell out the freedom-loving people of South Vietnam, a Congress that voted, in spite of our military victory, to abandon Southeast Asia to the Communists.   .

I was not optimistic at first about accomplishing much in such a Congress, but I realized that the members of my staff were just my type, and were extremely intelligent, patriotic, God-fearing, young and middle-aged, and liked and respected me as I liked and respected them.

Then an amazing lift to my morale and hopes took place when President Reagan took me aside and told me he greatly respected me, and asked me to call on him personally if I ever had a thought that I believed he needed to hear. It was the most appreciated compliment I ever received, and ultimately I finally did take him up on that offer, and consequently was enabled to play a leading role in bringing about a major improvement to our national security.

There soon occurred a series of other unexpected developments which buoyed my optimism regarding how well I could help further our national recovery in cultural and security terms.

President Reagan mentioned me prominently in his State of the Union address.

I was appointed to an unusually large number of committee assignments: Armed Services, Judiciary, Labor and Human Resources, and Veteran's Affairs. Among other subcommittee chairmanships, I was chairman of the Security and Terrorism Subcommittee of Judiciary, with jurisdiction over the Federal Bureau of Investigation (FBI) and the Drug Enforcement Agency (DEA).

I had been granted an opportunity to help regain national security and to help defeat the counter-cultural movement. It was up to me to use it. .

At the outset of my senatorial term a number one priority was to arrest the growing list of Latin American countries that had fallen into Communist hands. The rate of Communist expansion was ominous, and the newest example of this was the then-pending Nicaragua-El Salvador issue, with newly Communist Nicaragua trying to add El Salvador and other free nations to the countries already communized.

It was this issue in which I was enabled to make my unusual contribution, which has never been made public until this book. The story of this contribution has become known as The Single Poker Hand Story, which is narrated below.

The Single Poker Hand

The key event which gave birth to the Story of the Poker Hand was my being appointed to a team of freshmen senators picked to oversee free elections in El Salvador. My memory tells me the team included Senators Pete Wilson of California, Mitch McConnell of Kentucky, and Paula Hawkins of Florida. All of these talented friends did great things in the Senate and were supportive of the efforts of my National Forum Foundation, which held frequent press conferences and public meetings on many issues, including the issue of fighting Communism, especially Communism in South and Central America.

Things were not going well in El Salvador or in Washington for the prospects of a free election. It looked as if Communism was going to succeed in taking over El Salvador and take over other Latin American nations. Daniel Ortega was the Communist boss in Nicaragua and his Sandinistas were campaigning to force El Salvador to fly the Red Flag.

The leader of the opposition to Communism in El Salvador was a man named Major Roberto d'Aubuisson. He was portrayed by the American press and regarded by former President Carter and some in Congress to be on the extreme right wing, a man who committed atrocities against Communists for entertainment. And that was an exaggeration promulgated by the mainstream media and an anti-war crowd intent on repeating their dishonorable role during the Vietnam era. This was the technique of the Nazi propaganda minister, Joseph Goebbels, who said: "Tell a lie big enough and keep repeating it, people will eventually believe it."

Major d'Aubuisson was indeed rough-cut, but fought fire with fire to preserve the independence of his country at great risk of losing his life. But saving El Salvador was not going to be easy.

I was making the most trips to El Salvador of any on the Senate team because of my many relevant committee responsibilities. I frequently visited villages, often after they had been raided by Sandinista guerrillas, who pillaged and raped their women. I visited their pitiful dispensaries and hospitals, and gave encouraging talks to them. Hopeful crowds began to follow me everywhere as they observed my chagrin at their treatment and compassion for their suffering that stemmed from the Sandinista attacks, the wretched and deepening poverty, the lack of basic sanitation, and the need for good drinking water.

Our capable ambassador to Mexico, Jack Gavin, sent President Reagan a message praising my work. (Ironically, some years later, on January 7, 2008, Ambassador Gavin wrote me a kind letter of condolence regarding the death of my beloved wife, Jane. His stepson, a highly skilled heart surgeon, had done his best to save Jane's life.)

The more I saw of the terrible problems that afflicted the people of El Salvador, the more determined I became to do something about them. In the Senate I authored the Denton Program in 1985 to permit aid supplies given by charitable organizations to be flown by our military aircraft on a "space available" basis to Latin America at no expense to the charitable donor. This eliminated the biggest barrier to private humanitarian aid, the cost of transportation of the goods.

The bill passed unanimously in the Judiciary Committee and over-whelmingly on the floor. At Senator Ted Kennedy's suggestion, I success-fully amended the Denton Program the next year to expand it from Latin America to be applicable worldwide. It has helped establish more resistance to Communism as well as helping the needy countries get on their feet. The Denton Program has since increased its output.

I learned from the Costa Ricans and Hondurans that the future of their nations' freedom was being threatened by the United States' lack of support for efforts opposing Communist aggression in El Salvador.

While all this was going on, I sponsored and nursed through passage a Posse Comitatus Bill which permitted our armed forces to participate in our DEA/Customs drug-smuggling interdiction effort against Cuban smuggling by sea and air. The Cubans used profits from these drug-arms swaps to aid the Sandinistas.

Meanwhile, my trips south intensified. The Central American upper crust invited me to their homes and offices to give me the whole picture. One college president, who as I recall had been Costa Rica's ambassador to either or both of the U.N. and the U.S., impressed me with his savvy on interna-tional affairs. I lost his name, along with two of his beautifully hand-carved, framed scenes of Costa Rica's landscapes, in the flooding of my home during Hurricane Katrina, August 29, 2005.

That ambassador took me to his home and told me, "Senator, it is not just El Salvador that is at stake here. The whole of Latin America is at stake, par-ticularly Central America. When the Communists consummate their con-quest of El Salvador, they intend to take us over, too. They intend to spread out from there. We in Costa Rica and Honduras are being intimidated by threats against our families and property, and their probability of success in this area has us planning to shift our votes in the U.N. in favor of the Communists."

He said, "I am still fighting them. But current trends say we are going to be taken by them, so we officials may be forced to become Communist supporters in the U.N. because we want to live, we want our families to live. We will have no choice. We will have to buckle under to them unless things start to change fast."

I was beginning to feel more determined to help El Salvador to be treated more honorably than we treated South Vietnam, and I resolved to do what I could to get in a position to do something substantial to make this happen.

Soon, a key event took place that afforded me with an opportunity to begin my successful effort, which is the main subject of the following:

Daniel Ortega, the president of Nicaragua, riding a crest of favorable publicity in American television and the print media, as well as by many in Congress, made a visit to New York to explain to the United States how "democratic" Nicaragua was, how they [the Sandinistas] were not what President Reagan was painting them to be. Ortega claimed that in Nicaragua there was equality of opportunity and freedom of speech.

Ortega, accompanied by admiring media, and welcomed by fawning professors, was in New York about to speak at Columbia University, followed by engagements at Yale and Harvard universities. (This was similar to Harvard inviting Castro to speak in 1959 and Columbia University inviting Mahmood Ahmadinejad to speak on September 24, 2007.) Oretga's professed aim was to give the students, the faculty and the media the "truth" from the perspective of a major leader in Latin America. But he also happened to be the same man who led an effort to spread Communism throughout continental America. President Reagan got fed up with this ploy and publicly forbade Ortega to speak to audiences in the U.S., declaring him to be an enemy of our country and a military aggressor.

Ortega, with U.S. media support, protested. He went so far as to boast: "In Nicaragua we would not forbid anybody to speak in our colleges. Anybody can come there and say anything they want. Reagan, in not permitting me to speak here, proves he is not fit to be the leader of a democracy." This was, of course, the opposite of the truth. But the mainstream media, the vast majority of elite academe, and most of the Democratic Party enthusiastically applauded him. Reagan nonetheless stopped him from speaking in our colleges.

The next morning, while I was in an Air Force plane about to take off from Andrews Air Force Base headed to El Salvador, I reacted strongly as I read the morning newspapers' breaking news of this fiasco.
Immediately after reading the newspaper, I had "the big idea," and the first bet of the poker game was played by me.

On the airplane radio, I got in touch with the State Department. I said, "I request permission to change the destination of my flight from El Salvador to Managua, Nicaragua. I would like to visit Nicaragua and test and disprove Ortega's boasts about freedom of speech and other freedoms in Nicaragua. I could do this by asking to visit Pedro Chamorro, publisher of the defiant *La Prensa* (a famed Managua newspaper), and by asking to visit Archbishop Miguel Obando y Bravo, a high-ranking cleric of the Catholic Church in Managua, later promoted to Cardinal, and who consistently criticized the Communist regime.

"If they permit that visit I will try to get Pedro or the Archbishop to come to Washington and tell the real truth to some Democrat senators whom I respect. Then, hopefully, we can get the votes to shift our aid program from Nicaragua to El Salvador.

"If they do not permit my visit, it will prove what a liar Ortega is about freedom of speech in Communist Nicaragua. If you agree, I would request you to inform the Nicaraguans of my request." The State Department approved my idea and notified the Nicaraguan government of my visit and of my requests.

Meanwhile, in Managua, running things in Ortega's absence was Tomas Borge, the Minister of the Interior [of Nicaragua]. We knew that in reality Ortega was the mouth; Borge was the brains. Borge was educated in Moscow for decades. He was a typical Communist Party apparatchik, giving the Red Party line to Ortega, the puppet politician.

We refueled in Key West, and as we were approaching Managua Airport, the pilot relayed to me that Minister Borge had approved a schedule to match my request. I would have lunch with Bravo and Chamorro at the latter's villa, then meet with Borge at his headquarters.

After we landed, a military car drove to my plane, picked me up, and took me to Pedro Chamorro's door. We had lunch, and he, the Archbishop, and I had a useful conversation. After an hour of intense discussion, I popped the question: I asked if they would come to Washington for a meeting with a few senators.

I got their commitment that one or both of them would come to Washington on a date that I would try to work out with the Papal Nuncio, Pio Laghi, later to be designated the Pope's ambassador to the U.S. The meeting would be in the Nuncio's quarters in Washington and would be attended by some Democratic senators whom I would invite. The object would be to enlighten the senators with truth and cause a shift in U.S. aid from Nicaragua to El Salvador.

From there I went to the headquarters of the Minister of Interior, Tomas Borge. The scene there was not unfamiliar. Borge had a setup there similar to what "Cat" had in Hanoi prisons during our numerous hostile discussions.[1] He was a little squirt sitting at a huge desk propped up on several platforms

---

1 See Jeremiah Denton (with Ed Brandt), When Hell Was in Session (reprint, Lake Wylie, South Carolina: Robert E. Hopper and Associates, 1982), 68. "Cat" was the nickname of the North Vietnamese officer who was in charge of the torture program used on American POWs.

looking down at me sitting on a little chair in front of him. I was perfectly comfortable.

He said, "I hope you are pleased with the arrangements we made for you to meet with the gentlemen you requested. And of course, as a bonus, you and I will have a serious discussion. I will relate to you an important message for you to take back to your president and to Congress. I ask you to pay close attention to my message. After I give you this message you will be taken to the airport where you will have a press conference you probably doubted we would offer you down at the airfield auditorium. There will be many people there from all over the Americas and some from overseas. You can divulge to them the essence of my message."

Wow! So I would host an international press conference in their fabulous auditorium at the airport, which was outfitted with simultaneous translation earphones for the audience. It was a propaganda palace. They had simultaneous translation mikes and earphones. It was comparable to what the U.N. headquarters in New York looked like.

Borge had called my bet and raised me.

To say the least, I was elated at this juncture, and not at all nervous about the rest of the poker game. I knew Borge was calling my bluff and had some kind of game plan to make me look like a fool. But I was ready to play the game with him.

I was confident that he could not win this poker game with me because I had dealt with people just like him on similar issues for almost eight years in Vietnam, sometimes for fairly high stakes. I had had years of formal schooling in international affairs, and plenty of practical experience with the Cold War, including having been commander of the Guantanamo Air Defense Force in the latter stages of the Cuban Missile Crisis. Whatever Tomas Borge said or did, it would not be surprising. It would be the same old Party line for me to contend with as the one I had dealt with for so many years. I did believe that God had dealt me a lifetime of experience that had prepared me as much as anyone in the world to play this game successfully all the way.

Having called his bet of inviting me into his office, I expressed my gratitude for permission to talk with Bravo and Chamorro.

After a pause, he donned a rather sneering expression, and said, "Senator, I want to give you a very important message to take back to your president. It will give him convincing evidence that it would be extremely unwise for the U.S. to oppose us in El Salvador, abandoning the previous prudent policy of President Carter."

He paused again for about ten seconds, then turned his swivel chair to the left and pointed to a large window on my right, and barked in a suddenly harsh voice, "Look out that window." We were close to a large window looking out on a major street; I saw a number of workmen digging holes in the sidewalk and in the street, a familiar sight.

He said, "Do you see those men out there digging holes?" I said, "Yes, I do." He said, "Do you know what those holes are?" I said, "Yes, those are Ho Chi Minh shelters." (Holes in the ground used to protect their personnel from air attacks, large enough to accommodate one or two persons.) He continued, speaking slowly and distinctly to emphasize the importance of his words.

"Well, my message for you to bring to your president is the following: if the United States—still suffering from its inevitable surrender to Vietnam—thinks it had a hard time with North Vietnam, which outlasted and defeated them, I want you to know that if he opposes us, we will be the mother of all 'North Vietnams' to your country. No matter what you do to us, no matter how much power you employ against us, we are going to persevere. We are absolutely committed to succeed in liberating El Salvador.

"I want you to tell your president that we will use the same methods the North Vietnamese did, informing your people through the media (we have

WHEN HELL WAS IN SESSION

many friends there) of the justice of our cause, which our president is starting to do on his present trip. Then with your people on our side we will convert the people of El Salvador to join our glorious cause. If he doesn't relax his pressures against us and resorts to something military, it is going to start the biggest nightmare any of your presidents ever had.

"Do you understand the message, Senator Denton?"

Calmly I said, "Yes, I understand."

He then resumed spinning the usual party line ranting which ran on for a half hour more. When the tirade ceased, he sat back in his chair and indicated with his eyes that it was finally my turn to talk.

After a pause, I cleared my throat and quietly asked, "Mister Minister, how many Ho Chi Minh shelters did you say you planned to build out there?" He said, "Three hundred thousand." I said, "Hmm, isn't the population of Managua upwards of over a million souls?" He said, "Yes. Why do you ask such a question?"

I responded quietly, looking him right in the eye, "Well, having heard your plans, I will respond by offering some personal suggestions to you.... I suggest to you that you build at least three million shelters because some civilians might find themselves in the wrong place to get into the few shelters that you have built. And you better build some spare spaces because we would hope you would be able to get all your civilians into it. We don't like to kill civilians.

"If you continue your aggression against El Salvador, which we know is a predecessor for other aggressions you are planning, I assure you that you are going to find a reaction from the United States under President Reagan different from what you found under President Johnson in North Vietnam. First, President Reagan is going to stop your president from spreading propaganda in our country because you are threatening peace and the free people of Central America.

"Then, if you continue on your present path, if necessary to stop you, we are going to blast you and your military-industrial complex off the face of the earth. We are going to do to you what we did to North Vietnam during the last few days of the war with massive bombings and a blockade by which we won the war militarily. Yes, your propaganda and our media succeeded in swaying our Congress into forfeiting that victory. That will not be repeated. This time it is not going to be like that because President Reagan is a wise, strong, and determined leader, neutralizing your fellow travelers among our media by having earned overwhelming support from among the people, and the Congress is going to have to sense and to react to that popular support. I suggest that very soon Congress will be shifting its support from you to El Salvador and the democracies."

He looked quite startled and at the moment not sure of what to say. I went on:

"We learned a lesson in Vietnam and we will not deal with you like we dealt with our enemy in Vietnam, attempting to withhold our might and win the war gradually, employing a wrong strategy, fighting the war on the enemy's terms, man against man in the jungle where they hid in tunnels. We are not again going to try to be like guerrillas ourselves. If you do not desist, we will soon blockade your ports. Within a week after hostilities begin, we will bring our full military might to bear, and we will utterly destroy your military industrial complex. We would prefer not to kill any civilians, but some may die in spite of our intentions, so I advise you to build them more shelters."

By then, his expressions had gone through several transitions. His face changed. It became almost purple, and then gradually turned a ghastly pale. Recovering his voice, he abruptly ended the conference, dismissed me with a wave of his hand, and as I was proceeding toward the door with his guard, he got on the phone before I got to the door. I knew that on the phone he was cancelling the news conference.

I also knew that there would be planted questioners at the conference who would try to spin the Q and A period in a manner that would make it impossible for me to make a case for our side.

As the car approached the airport, I could see from a distance that there were maybe a thousand people, including scores of newsmen, walking out of the doors of the building because they had been told it was canceled. When they saw the car approaching with me, the newsmen halted the car. An indignant American correspondent said loudly, "Senator, they just canceled your news conference and hundreds of us have been waiting inside for hours." I said, "What did you expect? Did you think they would permit me to speak freely to their people?"

He hesitated and after a moment seemed to have an inspiration and said, "Why don't we hold it now, right where we are? They won't dare stop a conference they had scheduled, they would make fools of themselves. Come on, Senator, this is a wide street and wide sidewalk."

"Fine," I said. So he shouted out in Spanish and in English to the people, and they lined up about ten deep on the sidewalk, spreading out in a line maybe a hundred yards long with me facing them from about twenty yards from their center. Their backs were to the big hangar-auditorium. They set me up with cameras in the middle of the street facing the hangar. There must have been more than twenty TV cameras, and many microphones. An interpreter stood beside me.

The first question was from a Latin-American newsman, obviously an apparatchik for the Reds. He said, "Senator Denton, is it not true that you have racial prejudice in United States and that the black people are discriminated against?"

I responded, "Our laws are against discrimination, but some small percentage of our people, as in any country, feel or show prejudice.

"The ones who exercise discrimination of any form are arrested and punished. We regret that we were the last major country to eliminate slavery. But after much national division and heated debate over the issue since our nation was founded, the first decisive step to resolve that issue was taken during a Civil War, which cost us more Americans killed than all our other wars put together.

"And in subsequent years the United States freed all slaves, and outlawed racial discrimination. Our government, our people, our nation, puts those people who discriminate in jail. That's the way it is now. Yes, some may choose to discriminate, but there are law-breaking people in every nation, and some who discriminate in each country in the world. Indeed "slavery" has other names, such as the oppressed peoples under Communist or other kinds of totalitarian government. There is no question that slavery is immoral. And the U.S. paid a heavy penalty for failing to enforce that reality into its law.

"The overall truth is that the United States of America has proved to the world's people that there is more individual freedom and happiness in the U.S. than anywhere else. More people, including people of all races, immigrate to the U.S. than to any other country, and more people *wish* they could immigrate there than to anywhere else. Our country is still not perfect, but it is the best there is."

The questions became more polite and seemed motivated by curiosity and genuine interest. I said, "You know, I am glad to have a news conference here, because Mr. Ortega is saying to the people of America that freedom of speech is a fact down here, that there is equality of economic and political opportunity regardless of color, creed, or political belief.

"Mr. Ortega is saying that President Reagan is not permitting free speech in our democracy, that Communism is better for people than our form of government. That is one of the big lies of Communist imperialists.. We can disprove that lie simply by pointing out a few hard facts.

"May I now ask *you* some questions?" The newsmen assented by their silence.

Then I asked something like the following: "Regarding what your president is saying, is it true there is complete freedom of speech here in Nicaragua?

"Is there any discrimination by the [Sandinista] Party against those who disagree with it? I saw a lot of that among the people of Vietnam. How about jobs? Does it help if you are a party member?"

After a few more questions like this, the crowd went dead silent; not even the planted communist agents would dare deny what the entire crowd knew, but dared not complain about in that police state.

The conference ended. Of course I assume the government prohibited any of the video or audio tapes to leave Managua. But I did not consider that the hand played at the news conference won Borge any chips.

I knew my next bet would be the critical wager of the whole game. I was going to try to arrange to have the interview at the Papal Nuncio's office which would then result in Congress shifting our aid to El Salvador, which would give President Reagan the green light to follow the rest of my plan which I hoped he would choose to do. If all of that happened we would have won the whole pot in the poker game regarding El Salvador and the progress of Communism in Latin America.

I went back to the States and went to see Pio Laghi. I outlined my request for the meeting. He agreed, and we got word that it would be Obando y Bravo who met with us. I then called on [U.S. Senator] Sam Nunn of Georgia. I went to see [Senator] Bill Bradley of New Jersey and about five other Democratic senators that I considered to be good Americans, honest, and though not in my party, were in Congress to serve the national interest, not primarily their party or themselves. They all accepted my invitation to the meeting with Obando y Bravo.

I had all the people lined up except President Reagan. I had never taken him up on his offer to call him on anything I thought he should know about.

I knew the time had come. I asked his office if it would be convenient for him to see me. The answer was yes.

It was quite a meeting. Here is my best memory about how it went.

He and I had small talk for about five minutes before the fireplace. Then Vice President George H.W. Bush came in. I believe the next man in was Richard Allen, the National Security Advisor, then maybe next was Bill Casey (CIA). Others, my memory tells me, included the Secretary of State, Chairman of the Joint Chiefs of Staff, and a few others.

President Reagan said, "You all know Jerry Denton. I have invited him to air some thoughts he has about how we should plan to act in case the Nicaragua thing approaches the point of requiring a military solution."[2]

"Gentlemen," I said, " the main point I'm going to make is I don't think we should handle it in the way that we handled Vietnam. As you have all probably realized, we didn't do that very well and dragged the war out. If you accept my plan, I don't think that we are going to have to fight a war with Nicaragua. I am going to suggest some moves that I recommend we make within a few weeks, moves which will show them the handwriting on the wall, the writing that says if they persist on their present course regarding El Salvador, they are going to be defeated.

"I would suggest you begin by making public announcements or letting it leak that you are sending a number of wings of B-52s with some defensive fighters into Honduras. Send no large number of ground combat troops. Then after a pause of a week or so, send two naval task forces, one consisting of a carrier task force with our two battleships (whose recent reactivation they knew I had successfully debated for), four carriers, four cruisers, and a lot of destroyers off one of their coasts, implying heavy shore bombardment.

"And send another task force with as many carriers and protective destroyers as we can afford off their other coast, potentially to augment the Honduras-based B-52s." I went on and outlined some other thoughts on a sample

---

2   Ronald Reagan, The Reagan Diaries (New York: HarperCollins Publishers, 2007), 158. President Reagan noted in his diaries: "Thursday, July 14, 1983, Sen. Denton came by with a plan or idea of getting a combine of Latin American countries to help stem the spread of Communism there…"

deployment which would demonstrate our readiness and capability to initiate action that could blockade Nicaragua totally or incrementally, and/or could bomb or bombard their military-industrial complex away in a couple of days.

"The greatest handicap we are going to have to overcome is the temptation to fear that the Russians will react in such a way that will make an unfavorable difference. For example, we cannot worry that exposing our ships in this manner will subject them to Cuban submarines sinking them. I feel certain that the Russians would restrain them from that. Here is why:

"Please look at it like a poker game. With blue chips worth ten dollars and white chips worth one dollar, saving El Salvador represents some five hundred blue chips to us. To the Soviets, considering the overall Cold War, this issue represents about ten white chips. If we demonstrate our willingness to risk opposing them militarily on this issue, they are going to prove that they know when to call, when to raise, and when to walk away.

"If we use this approach, I predict that the situation will cool down very suddenly without either side firing a shot. And I have arranged a meeting between Archbishop Obando y Bravo and some good Democrats which I am confident will result in Congress shifting our aid to El Salvador. That will permit the President to use his extraordinary executive mandate to order militant maneuvers in the interest of preserving our national security."

I concluded my pitch and looked at the President, who smiled, did not ask for comments or questions, and thanked me for coming.

By the grace of God, everything I had proposed came to pass. The strategy and tactics I recommended were carried out to the letter. The meeting at the Papal Nuncio's quarters took place with the desired effect. The vote on our aid was changed. The movement of our ships to threaten Nicaragua was made.

The Communist movement against El Salvador stopped and elections took place successfully. Publisher Pedro Chamorro's mother, Senora Chamorro, was elected president of Nicaragua some years later.

Then, after I successfully recommended the establishment of some Gulf Coast naval bases from which we could more rapidly reach Central and South America with combat ships, Communism started subsiding all over the Southern Hemisphere, and soon the previously growing number of existing Communist governments in Central and South America was reduced to zero. Only the lonely island of Cuba flew the Red Flag. The Russians folded their cards and walked away, ending the story of the Poker Hand.

In the security field, there was a spell in which national security began improving. With Ronald Reagan as president, and with a Republican majority, national security improved immensely in the 1980s, and I feel honored that I was able to help in several ways.

During that improvement phase, many of my patriotic Senate colleagues and I fought hard to win one close vote after another, many absolutely vital to national security. The loss of any one of these votes would have been most unfortunate for our country and for the cause of freedom globally. The Berlin Wall would not have come down. The media did not report the significance of such votes.

Since Reagan's time, things have not gone as well. One malady continues to worsen: the on-going influence exerted by the misinformation campaign waged by the liberal media/academic community continues to confuse the citizenry. This is resulting in politicians being elected who find it unwise to support efforts by leaders like George H.W. Bush and George Bush to stem the progress of fanatic terrorism, to deal with the various threats in the Mideast, to provide confidence that we have adequate security involving among others Russia, China, Korea, etc.

The United States is in more danger than ever before. Communism is again at new heights in our Southern Hemisphere, along with a dangerous loss of our degree of credibility to assure ourselves or anyone else that the

Cold War will not be resumed by the Russians. Our borders are porous to the smuggling in of weapons of mass destruction. China has the greatest number of military and maritime ships in world history. One wonders what it plans to do with that force, while our ownership of commercial shipping is among the lowest in the world, and we are going all-out to handle the Iraq situation satisfactorily with our already over-stretched armed forces.

We seem not to recognize that our vast stockpile of weapons of mass destruction (WMD) can no longer to be logically regarded as assuring us that we can adequately defend our vital national interests. Let me further explain that assertion.

When our enemies snip away at our interests by incremental steps, which are not considered as justifying the risks taken if we resort to the use of WMD, we find ourselves in an untenable situation.

We have a situation which requires us to have a sufficient arsenal of conventional forces which are adequate to use conventional weapons in various trouble spots around the world. We used to have that capability during the Cold War period in the years from 1941 until the end of the century. Now we have neither the level of military manpower nor weaponry required, and if we did, we would still be without the transport and the logistics capacity to retain that capability, so we are unable to use conventional forces to quell incremental incidents threatening our interests. Note that we would not choose to resort to WMD if an aggressor took one nation at a time, gradually, without using WMD himself. Conventional deterrence is the only answer in those cases, and we do not currently hold the cards for that. National security is an absolute necessity and cannot be subjugated budget-wise to social programs or to any other programs.

The Russians and Chinese and others know that we are vulnerable in the above sense. The existing situation is simply untenable and must be corrected.

With new global threats against us, we need to increase our national security forces in terms of conventional power and adequate logistical capability to be able to employ that power in remote areas as the need arises. Movement of conventional forces in this manner is enabled only when you have sufficient maritime resources: naval and commercial shipping. Presently we lack that sufficiency.

There are also fatal weaknesses in the cultural area.

In the academic/media influence area, there is more than the unfavorable effect on our culture. There is also a detrimental effect on our national security capabilities.

There are two historically proven elements indispensable to preserving the survival of any nation. Adequate national security is but one; the other is maintaining a sufficient degree of social well-being (especially the health of the institution of the family). These are both crumbling at a startling pace in the United States and Europe.

The "liberal" media/academic influence on our security has already been briefly discussed above. Let us now turn to the effect on the institution of the family.

The most disastrous trend affecting our national survival is the trend to dismiss God as the fundamental source in determining what is right and what is wrong. There is substantial progress already made by this trend toward materialistic atheism. The trend is fed in large measure by the academe/media "liberal" bloc. Although at least 84 percent of our people have not yet been brainwashed enough to regard this trend as a favorable one, the "liberal" bloc has succeeded in creating a feverishly active minority of our citizenry who are trying to arrive at winnng a total victory in the fight over whether this is still One Nation under God.

Their progress so far has been sufficiently advanced to cause most of our public schools and many private schools at all levels of education to eliminate the mention of God, not only from the curricula, but in their administration's attitude toward student extracurricular activities and out-of-schoolroom behavior.

There are some good educational institutions, and the evidence is that more parents are moving their children into them. The balance in the media has changed somewhat favorably. Media and educational institutions must continue to improve.

On social issues that are deteriorating, a small minority of God-fearing Americans have finally passed their threshold of outrage at where our society is failing and why. They are beginning to think of useful tools such as boycotts against sponsors of entertainment, products, and education, etc. who sell sin and/or false ideals or even treason.

And liberals in government continue to propose flawed policies like advocacy of a nuclear freeze, which had heavy support from the above-mentioned elite of media, publishers and academics. I alone stopped this by the rarely used tactic of placing a senatorial hold on taking up the bill on the day it reached Majority Leader Howard Baker. For doing so, I was flayed by an all day and night session consisting of the Democratic senators taking the floor and condemning me for my act. The mainstream media flocked to shout agreement with the condemnation. But the Nuclear Freeze demonstration was successfully blocked.

Had this latter effort succeeded during my Senate term, uniformed Russians would be walking in our streets today. Reagan would never have been able to adopt the goal, much less achieve the goal of winning the Cold War, assisted by the Vatican and the reasonableness of [Soviet leader Mikhail] Gorbachev. The elite never admit the stupidity of their sanctimonious advocacy of the nuclear freeze, or the false premises upon which they demanded a time schedule for withdrawal from Iraq. And the public never learns the truth. The most important misconception of the people is about what really happened in the Vietnam War and what the lessons of it are.

The truth about Vietnam is that in pursuit of a just cause, the U.S. used tragically flawed tactics and strategy under the Johnson-McNamara leadership. Finally under President Nixon, correct strategy for Vietnam evolved, and our ground forces along with the critically important Linebacker II operations and the effective blockade of NVN ports in 1972 were a knockout blow, finally achieving a total military victory for the United States.

I can swear, with the use of truth serum, how the North Vietnamese leadership just prior to my release acknowledged to me, explicitly enough to convince anyone, that they had no will for further fighting, and were satisfied to settle on the terms of settlement before the outrageous cave-in by Congress in 1972, when it cut off funds to the South Vietnamese. In February of 1973, all our captors were concerned about was being tried for war crimes for illegally mistreating us. There is some specific testimony from me on that subject in *American Admiralship: The Moral Imperative of Naval Command* (Annapolis, Maryland: Naval Institute Press, 2005), by Edgar F. Puryear Jr. For good reason, I could not relate that testimony in the time frame in which *When Hell Was in Session* was written.

The dishonest part played by the influential liberal elite bears the major burden of responsibility for Congress' abominable decision to stop all further appropriations for continued military operations in Vietnam. And North Vietnam, along with the USSR and Red China, having known and accepted the fact that they were totally defeated, began to come to the realization that the U.S. Congress was annulling the military victory. The Russians and Chinese then realized they had only to rebuild with no opposition the military power of North Vietnam and walk into the vacuum of military power of South Vietnam.

Assuming the U.S. survives the growing peril it is now in, it will be because a new, honest set of history books, media outlets, and schools will ultimately refute the leftist lies which prevailed during and after the Vietnam War and into the early part of the second millenium.

A sound national consensus can gradually be formed. And the nation can be America again. Our national concensus will realize the falsity of the myths that resulted in the the abandonment and betrayal of our military victory, our South Vietnamese, Laotian, Cambodian, and other allies whose independence we had sworn to safeguard.

Similarly in this story about Nicaragua, the media, using lies, convinced the likes of large numbers of Maryknoll nuns, Jesuit priests, most of Congress, and much of the American public into believing that somehow it was preferable to support Ortega's Communist regime, rather than supporting democracy in El Salvador and the rest of Central America. The media did not seem to grasp the importance of stopping Communism in our own backyard. The liberation of Grenada was another case of Reagan being right and the so-called elite being wrong. In the overall Cold War, Reagan's much derided threat to implement "Star Wars" was the straw that broke the camel's back in Russia.

Now, in the Middle East and elsewhere in the world, we have an enormously greater stake than in any of the previously mentioned security crises except the Cold War. And the same information elite (and the same political party) which established the wrong public perspectives are again selectively and erroneously reporting "facts" in such a manner as to create conditions which make it difficult for the electorate to perceive the truth, and for the commander-in-chief to carry out his Constitutional mandate to lead our country in times of national security crises.

My winning the poker hand of this story could not have been done without having good cards. We had a great president. We had a Republican majority in the Senate and House, which we now do not have. We had enough good Democrats who bore the country's national interests at heart, rather than what we have now. We also had a public consensus closer to sanity.

In having watched truth being replaced by left-wing myths toward the end and after the Vietnam War, I don't like the cards now held by those who try to initiate sound policies for ensuring our national security and well-being. I am gravely concerned that we will continue this streak of ignoring the essentials of our national survival interests. I see our public consensus as becoming increasingly misled and malformed by the influential sectors of our society: mainline media, most of our educational institutions from grade school to postgraduate, the bias of publishers, and too many in government offices, all of them contributing to a flow of false information.

For the right cards to be held for planning and executing successful national policy for our country, we the people need to install and support truly patriotic, honest and qualified public opinion-formers and political leaders. Party and personal motivations must be subordinated to national interests, or the greatest nation on earth will be destroyed. And this security threat is not the only pending threat to our survival.

We should note that many democracies throughout history, after having attained major material success, have commonly lost their vitality in an average of about two hundred years, committing suicide caused by the inability to cope with success, earned by adherence to sufficiently valid fundamental principles, and failure being caused by abandonment of those principles.

We are ignoring good advice such as given by Secretary of State Daniel Webster, who warned: "If we abide by the principles taught in the Bible, our country will go on prospering...But if we and our posterity neglect religious instruction and authority; violate the rules of eternal justice, trifle with the injunctions of morality, and recklessly destroy the political constitution which holds us together, no man can tell how sudden a catastrophe may overwhelm us and bury all our glory in profound obscurity."

The founding of the United States of America was an explosion in the cosmos of political science, as recognized by our Founding Fathers, and by authorities of other nations. The great English prime minister, William Gladstone, not too long after the War of 1812 ended, acknowledged that, "The

United States has established the best form of government ever conceived by the minds of men."

The great French historian, Alexis de Tocqueville, perceived from his study and visits in the United States that we Americans were great for one identifiable reason: because our great number of devout churchgoing citizens were generally obedient to the laws of God, and America was great because America was good, and as long as America continued to be good, we would continue to be great.

The wisest of our Founding Fathers acknowledged that this nation began as a conscious experiment in granting that an unprecedented degree of unfettered freedom to the citizenry would certainly fail if our people's personal faith and allegiance to God would fail. The restoration of good conscience of a devout citizenry is essential. Those consciences can be shown to have made it possible for this nation to adhere to the high and valid principles laid down as the foundation of our revolutionary form of government.

Ronald Reagan said it best on August 23, 1984, at an Ecumenical Prayer Breakfast at the Reunion Arena in Dallas, Texas: "Without God, democracy will not and cannot long endure....America needs God more than God needs America. If we ever forget that we are One Nation under God, then we will be a nation gone under." (My favorite current authority writing on the above subject and in proving the real meaning of the First Amendment is William J. Federer, whose books I commend to all Americans.)

The courageous work of World Net Daily is a leading example of the newly born media effort to refresh with truth the current liberal torrent existing among the media. Joseph Farah's recent book is an example of the same favorable new trend in the publishing of books. I believe that such new examples of well-justified outbursts of long suppressed public indigation require the support of all good americans. With that support we can win the survival struggle.

It cannot be overstated today that our Founders' principal thrust was that the major role of government is to ensure that our people could have access to their God-given rights ("rights endowed by their Creator"). In contrast, previous democracies had professed to believe in God and his laws, but reserved to government the right to interpret and often alter those laws as they saw fit ("they" being chieftains, emperors, kings with/or without parliamentary participation or presidents).

The democratic governments before ours simply did not intend, as our Founding Fathers did, to really actualize the belief that all men are endowed BY THEIR CREATOR with certain inalienable rights: LIFE, LIBERTY, AND THE PURSUIT OF HAPPINESS. Life, liberty, and pursuing happiness were sincerely to be exercised according to God's Laws as He wrote them, not as Henry VIII, for example, decided to interpret them. Our government for some two hundred years (with the exception of being the last major Western nation to abandon slavery in gross contradiction to its number one stated principle that all men are created equal) has adhered to the basic religious beliefs upon which we were founded. But lately our government has begun to depart from God's Laws, deeming permissible the murdering of unborn children, and the marriage of persons of the same sex. Euthanasia is gradually increasing in accordance with the ongoing governmental propensity to adopt the counterculture no matter what the majority of citizens think.

Religions of all kinds are permissible within our system. But behavior of all citizens has always until lately been restricted to the inalienable rights granted under Judeo-Christian principles, and all Americans regardless of their personal religious beliefs, had to behave in accordance with our laws, which are based on the Ten Commandments, tempered by the Christian principle of "Love your neighbor as you love yourself."

Now in recent decades has come the genre of modern "progressive" democracies, which ours is becoming. These all have, in differing but significant degrees, effectively and sometimes formally discarded God and inserted utterly secular government (with its predilection to heed modern political correctness rather than Judeo-Christian principles) with the prerogative to define human rights.

Sufficient historical evidence exists that our Founding Fathers were from the beginning aware and even skeptical that too much freedom afforded to our citizenry could result in chaos. The fulcrum was the likelihood that the citizenry would succeed or fail based on their ability to use their own consciences in the absence of a government police force. Many called it an "experiment" in that conscience was not certain to fill the gap left by such a government so generous in granting freedoms to the citizenry. But in our founding days, hardship, not satiety, abounded, and in that situation so did prayer, faith, and moral dispositions. It worked for over two centuries.

On October 11, 1798, President John Adams wrote to the officers of the First Brigade of the Third Division of the Militia of Massachusetts: "We have no government armed with power capable of contending with human passions unbridled by morality and religion. Avarice, ambition, revenge, or gallantry, would break the strongest cords of our Constitution as a whale goes through a net. Our Constitution was made only for a moral and religious people. It is wholly inadequate to the government of any other."

Now, we as a people are acquiescing in the dismissal of the principles constituting the great American Revolution in governmental theory. For more than two hundred years those features remained the reliable source of the continuing success of this nation's attainment of unprecedented power: political, military, social, economic, and psychological power.

Down through the many years after our Founding Fathers, our presidents have reiterated their founding principles.

Franklin D. Roosevelt acknowledged on the four-hundredth anniversary of the printing of the English Bible, October 6, 1935: "We cannot read the history of our rise and development as a nation, without reckoning with the place the Bible has occupied in shaping the advances of the Republic...Where we have been the truest and most consistent in obeying its precepts, we have attained the greatest measure of contentment and prosperity."

President Harry S Truman remarked at the Attorney General's Conference on Law Enforcement, February 15, 1950: "The fundamental basis of this nation's laws was given to Moses on the Mount. The fundamental basis of our Bill of Rights comes from the teachings we get from Exodus and St. Matthew, from Isaiah and St. Paul. I don't think we emphasize that enough these days."

President Calvin Coolidge addressed that question at the 150th anniversary of the Declaration of Independence in Philadelphia, July 5, 1926: "The Declaration of Independence is a great spiritual document. It is a declaration not of material but of spiritual conceptions. Equality, liberty, popular sovereignty, the rights of man, these are not elements which we can see and touch... They have their source and their roots in the religious convictions... Unless the faith of the American in these religious convictions is to endure, the principles of our Declaration will perish. We cannot continue to enjoy the result if we neglect and abandon the cause."

In laying the cornerstone of the Jewish Community Center in Washington, D.C., May 3, 1925, President Calvin Coolidge stated: "It is a lesson which our country, and every country based on the principle of popular government, must learn and apply, generation by generation... The patriots who laid the foundation of this Republic drew their faith from the Bible...We cannot escape the conclusion that if American democracy is to remain the greatest hope of humanity, it must continue abundantly in the faith of the Bible."

But by now, what our Founders had feared has begun to grow visibly. Selfish materialism, immoral social behavior, and secularism all have grown, with a significant diminution of national faith in and conformance to the will of God in every sector of America. Concurrently, there have been great pressures from the elite—including the ACLU, academia, and the entertainment sector—who are persuading the government itself to take its own part in a new belief that faith in and obedience to God have no part in the principles, morals, and legal standards imposed by our Founders and their followers for two centuries, standards set forth in the Declaration of Independence and the true intent of the Constitution. For example, the ACLU has totally reversed the original meaning of the First Amendment of the Constitution of the United States.

On February 25, 1984, President Reagan said: "Sometimes I can't help but feel the First Amendment is being turned on its head....the pendulum has swung to intolerance against religious freedom...The First Amendment of the Constitution was not written to protect the people from religion; that Amendment was written to protect religion from government tyranny."

Humanity's greatest temptation and most capital sin is pride, with its attendant evils such as placing self-interest and immoral personal gratifications far above regard for neighbor, for spouse, for duty to one's country, with each person being his or her own god. This situation of decay is as old as Adam and Eve, fatal to government, and to peace among and within nations.

Only benign religious beliefs, held strongly enough, have been proven by history to influence a citizenry of any era to co-exist with the degree of order, discipline, and cohesion required for persevering in national well-being and security. There has never been a good culture without a good cult. Our particular Founders chose to base our government and culture on Judeo-Christianity.

And a case can be made that since about the year A.D. 400, Judeo-Christian nations, individually and in various degrees of political union, clearly hold the record for their relative pace in establishing and maintaining long periods of political, economic, social, and military success and sustainability. Their failures or periods of weakness occur when they, in apathy or self-indulgence, sufficiently depart in behavior from their Judeo-Christian principles. Are we in the Western World today trying to imitate what happened to Germany when Hitler and Fascism abandoned their traditional Judeo-Christian foundation, or imitate what happened to Russia after the Communist revolution in 1917, or to the French after their barbaric period during and immediately following their revolution?

Noah Webster wrote in his History of the United States, 1832: "The religion which has introduced civil liberty is the religion of Christ and His apostles, which enjoins humility, piety, and benevolence; which acknowledges in every person a brother, or a sister, and a citizen with equal rights....All the miseries and evils which men suffer from vice, crime, ambition, injustice, oppression, slavery, and war, proceed from their despising or neglecting the precepts contained in the Bible."

The Obama Administration and the Democratic majority in Congress appear not to believe in one of the most important biblical mandates: Render unto Caesar what is Caesar's and unto God what is God's.

It is not Caesar who can pronounce that killing a child in its mother's womb is right.

The murder of sixty-one million babies because a government mandated that monstrous crime, and the mandating of mixed-gender marriages, is not the prerogative of any government, it is among the behavioral rules of which only God rules upon.

We are truly in an advanced stage of degeneration. But we cannot and need not despair because we know that good and bad cycles have happened to nations throughout history. Individuals and peoples can change from bad to good.

France and Germany once recovered from drastic declines, though now they, along with most of Europe, appear to have begun another downhill cycle even further along than ours.

Former anti-war, countercultural fanatics, such as Peter Collier and David Horowitz, converted along with many other former pro-Communist intellectuals, who after seeing the post-war events in Vietnam and Southeast Asia, became convinced that their anti-war activities had been based on misconceptions. And they have become zealous workers for truth and reformation. Our foundation formed a group like Collier and Horowitz, known as The Second Thoughts Movement. It fought a good fight against the ultra-liberal, or things would be even worse today.

I am not a partisan politician who believes that the Democrats have always been bad, and the Republicans good. Parties change over time.

As a Democrat-turned-Republican following the Kennedy assassination, I can believe that the best instincts in the Democratic Party can eventually sort things out as they face the reality of urgent danger to our nation. I believe they can lead their party to regain the realism and courage of the days of Franklin D. Roosevelt, Harry S. Truman, and John F. Kennedy. All of us have sinned and most of us have repented and improved.

The most important reason for being optimistic about beating back the countercultural movement is the realization that we are following God's will by conducting that effort. And history has proved that God has frequently helped those who are acting as we are even when they face apparently impossible odds.

For our task of improving our culture and our security to succeed, several things must happen.

The vast majority of our citizenry must come to realize that we the people of today are now deciding the fate of our Founders' noble experiment. The nature of our enemy is the same as humanity has faced since the time of Adam and Eve. We must resist slavery to selfishness and materialism. We must fight the many material and sensual temptations besetting us while we are weak with the intoxication of excess and freedom from want. We must shake that tendency and act to preserve what Lord Gladstone of Great Britain called "the greatest form of government ever conceived by the minds of men." The magnificent principles of that nation were established with the blood, sweat, and tears of our forerunners.

Not only is ungodliness ruinous of nations—civilization itself cannot exist without religion or without the solidarity of the institution of the family.

Ungodliness leads to loss of security. Too many Americans are falling prey, after so many years of apathy, to forgetting how we got where we are.

In our apathy we are taking security for granted. In 1975, in Washington, D.C., Alexander Solzhenitsyn warned: "I...call upon America to be more careful...because they are trying to weaken you...to disarm your strong and magnificent country in the face of this fearful threat—one that has never been seen before in the history of the world."

To be anti-war is fine, but in doing so we must realize not only that war is hell, but that there are worse conditions even than war, and that there are times when military means must be used in the cause of preserving peace, justice, and national survival.

When we commit ourselves to war in a just and necessary cause, we must be untempted by those advocating fixed, self-defeating timetables for withdrawal, and refuse to establish deadlines urged by Congress and anti-war groups, and instead must promote appropriately timely and adequate mobilization with a firm will to win with perseverance in justified sacrifices. Pulling troops out of harm's way is a constant motivation but it must be tempered by what alternative harm would befall us if we pull our troops out early and suffer the loss and harm resulting from losing the cause we were committed to win.

We must stop the utter folly of tipping the enemy off that they can outlast us in any military struggle. It wastes lives of gallant warriors, and is fatal to the health of our security.

WHEN HELL WAS IN SESSION

Americans now in government must begin to honestly face themselves in the mirror, and try to sense the many threats to our country from within and without which demand a degree of bi-partisanship to overcome.

National interest must replace party and self-interest. Love of God and neighbor must replace pagan self-indulgence! If we do not effect these replacements, we will deserve the horrible fate we shall reap. It may be stylish today to laugh at "family values," but when that type of liberal progressive theme prevails, national suicide is the inevitable result.

I swore to defend this country "against all enemies, foreign AND DOMESTIC." I am trying to fulfill that oath.

All is not yet lost, but our position is extremely perilous. In conclusion, I must say that if I had known when I stepped off that plane to freedom at Clark Air Force Base in February 1973 what I know now, I would not have said, "God bless America," I would have said, as I say now, "God Save America!"

Let us pray that He shall, and let us help Him in any way we can.